The Rise of a
GAY and **LESBIAN**
Movement

D0556346

SOCIAL MOVEMENTS PAST AND PRESENT

Irwin T. Sanders, Editor

The Rise of a
GAY and LESBIAN
Movement

Barry D Adam

Twayne Publishers·Boston
A Division of G.K. Hall & Co.

The Rise of a Gay and Lesbian Movement

Barry D Adam

Copyright © 1987 by G.K. Hall & Co.
All Rights Reserved
Published by Twayne Publishers
A Division of G.K. Hall & Co.
70 Lincoln Street, Boston, Massachusetts 02111

Copyediting supervised by Lewis DeSimone
Designed and produced by Marne Sultz
Typeset by Compset, Inc. of Beverly, Massachusetts

Printed on permanent/durable acid-free paper
and bound in the United States of America

Library of Congress Cataloging-in-Publication Data

Adam, Barry D.
The rise of a gay and lesbian movement.

(Social movements past & present)
Bibliography: p. 194
Includes index.
1. Gay liberation movement—History.   2. Homosexuality
—History.   I. Title.   II. Series: Social movements past and present.
HQ76.5.A33   1987   306.7′66′09   86-29549
ISBN 0-8057-9714-9 (alk. paper)
ISBN 0-8057-9715-7 (pbk. : alk. paper)

Contents

About the Author   *vii*
Preface   *ix*

Chapter One
Origins of a Homosexual People   **1**
     The Medieval World
     The Molly Houses
     Capitalism and Romantic Love
     The Stage Is Set
     Prelude to a Political Movement

Chapter Two
Early Movements and Aspirations   **17**
     Germany
     France
     England
     United States

Chapter Three
The Holocaust   **45**
     New Sources for Old Fears
     Stalinism
     Nazism

Chapter Four
The Homophiles Start Over   56
    The McCarthy Terror
    Homophiles under Siege
    The Rise of the New Left

Chapter Five
Gay Liberation and Lesbian Feminism   75
    From the Stonewall Rebellion . . .
    . . . to a World Movement
    Lesbian Feminism
    The Movement and the Grass Roots

Chapter Six
The New Right Reacts   102
    Anita Bryant on the Loose
    The Rise of a New Right
    Under Attack in the United Kingdom, Canada, and Australia

Chapter Seven
The Movement in the 1980s   121
    Civil Rights and Electoral Politics
    Coming Out Everywhere
    The Sex Debates
    The AIDS Crisis

Chapter Eight
Conclusion   161

Notes   167
References   174
Selected Bibliography   194
Index   197

About the Author

Barry D Adam is a sociologist at the University of Windsor (Ontario, Canada) and a graduate of Simon Fraser University and the University of Toronto. His 1978 book, *The Survival of Domination* (Greenwood Press), compared coping strategies employed by Jewish, black, and gay people in the face of inferiorization. Subsequent research on social mobility in the legal profession has appeared in the *Canadian Bar Review* and the *Canadian Review of Sociology and Anthropology.* Anthropological and historical reflections on the social organization of homosexuality have been published in the *Journal of Homosexuality* and *Comparative Studies in Society and History.* Active in Canadian, American, and International sociological associations, Professor Adam has served on the Committee on the Status of Homosexuals in Sociology of the American Sociological Association. His current research interests are in comparative analyses of the social organization of sexuality and in neighborhood democracy in Nicaragua.

Preface

This book, delineating the formation of gay and lesbian movements as a world phenomenon, would have been inconceivable a decade ago. It is only through the impact of the movements themselves on the larger society that gay and lesbian history has come to be a "fit" subject to write about and a "legitimate" topic for research. And it is only through the pioneering investigations of scholars such as Jonathan Katz, Jeffrey Weeks, Lillian Faderman, James Steakley, Ilse Kokula, Hans-Georg Stümke, Rudi Finkler, Jacques Girard, Marie-Jo Bonnet, and countless others who have written for the gay press that the story of homosexual people is coming into view.

The study of social history is itself part of a historical context; the present work is no exception. It suffers from certain limitations owing to the state of the literature on and by the movement—and certainly owing to personal limitations of the author. Almost nothing has been written from the perspective of the gay and lesbian movement as a transnational event, nor has an international flow of information been well developed. Like other communications systems, knowledge of the movement follows a "center-periphery" pattern. The movement in New York City is the best known and the United States movement in general is much better documented than movements elsewhere. Though Italians know about the Stonewall Rebellion in Greenwich Village and mark it with a gay pride day, few Americans know about Bologna's city-sponsored gay community center. Most movement documents have appeared in English, French, German, and (some) Spanish, and these references are reflected here. Very significant movements have developed in Scandinavia, the Netherlands, Italy, Brazil, and Indonesia, but almost all accounts of them remain in their national languages. My coverage is once removed from these movements, since I have had to rely on characterizations of them in the first four languages. Thus I have not fully remedied the information economy. New research, however, will no doubt allow a future fleshing out of the overall picture.

This study is, as well, a sociological treatment of the rise of the gay and lesbian movement; it shows its roots in what Theda Skocpol (1984) calls "comparative-historical sociology" or what Doug McAdam (1982), referring specifically to social movement analysis, calls the "political process model." The sociologist cannot be content with tracing the development of any social formation as the simple unfolding of unanchored ideas, the creature of charismatic leaders, or an unexplained sequence of events. Alain Touraine views "society as a cultural field torn apart by the conflict between those who take over historicity for themselves and those who are subjected to their domination and are struggling for the collective reappropriation of this historicity." He defines a social movement as "collective organized action through which a class actor battles for the social control of historicity in a given and identifiable historical context" (1981, 62, 32-33). The course of social movements depends on a sometimes hidden context of political economy and social conflict. Larger social structures and historical changes allow for the possibility of a movement and inevitably shape its agenda. Its transformation partakes of shifts in the total social system as much as in outcomes of internal decisions and strategies. The terms of debate shaped by competing social coalitions can give way, intensify, or shift to new ground according to conflicts apparently far removed from the social movement at hand.

Following his review of social movement theory, McAdam identifies a set of critical issues to be addressed for understanding the rise of a movement:

- Latent political leverage available to most segments of the population
- Subjective transformation of consciousness
- Level of organization within the aggrieved population
- Collective assessment of the prospects for successful insurgency
- Alignment of groups within the larger political environment (1982, 36–38)

And Jean Cohen (1985, 690) cautions that in studying the "new social movements," we must find them on the terrain they now occupy as "contemporary collective actors consciously struggle over the power to socially construct new identities, to create democratic spaces for autonomous social action, and to reinterpret norms and reshape institutions."

With these recommendations in mind, this book aims to take a step toward revealing the underpinnings of antihomosexual practices and their collective alleviation. Thus where my earlier work, *The Survival of Domination,* focused upon the effects of domination upon the actions of largely unorganized individuals, this book looks at the other half of the story: how a movement develops to challenge domination.

The task at hand is, first, to fulfill the mandate of this series on social movements by getting the story right for those with little acquaintance with the gay and lesbian movement (many of the events detailed here will already be familiar to those who know the movement well) and then to set these events in their sociological contexts to offer a sense of how and why they happen.

I am fortunate to have been able to benefit from the comments of a number of readers drawn from several countries, from both inside and outside the movement itself, and from several academic disciplines. To those who read the entire manuscript or large portions of it, I owe a particular debt: Beth Schneider, Thomas Ford Hoult, Meredith Gould, Stephen Murray, Jim Monk, Irwin Sanders (the series editor at Twayne), and Henry Minton. Many others offered advice and assistance on specific topics: Henning Bech and Fredrik Silverstolpe on Scandinavia, Rob Tielman and Judith Schuyf on the Netherlands, Isabel Hull and James Steakley on Germany, Carlos Luis on Latin America, Robert French, David Hilliard, and Craig Johnston on Australia, as well as John Dufour, Peter Nardi, Rovan Wernsdorfer, and Edward Sebesta. Of course, none of these people can be held responsible for interpretations and any errors I may have made.

Finally, my gratitude to John Dufour for his perseverance in the face of the inherently unsociable act of writing. Parts of the manuscript in progress were aired with the assistance of Jim Monk and Kevin Bishop on radio station CJAM in Windsor and a portion of it was presented to the 1985 Sex and the State conference in Toronto.

Chapter One

Origins of a Homosexual People

The first social movement to advance the civil rights of gay people was founded in Germany in 1897. To understand where this early gay movement came from and where today's movement is going, it is necessary to look at the social conditions that made the movements possible. Before any social movement comes into existence, a set of prerequisites must be in place. An identifiable social group with considerable political awareness must be presumed before a movement is conceivable; those conditions came about relatively recently on the historical stage for same-sex relationships. Homosexuality has not always been organized as a separate "people." The evidence from non-Western cultures shows clearly that relationships we call "homosexual" were organized in quite different ways, making the development of a group identity and movement highly unlikely.

A glance through historical and anthropological research reveals a great variety of ways of being homosexual. In societies as far-flung as Melanesia, Amazonia, central Africa, and western Egypt, it has been common for many (sometimes all) males to have homosexual relations, at least for a period of their lives (Adam 1985a, 19; Herdt 1984; Lévi-Strauss 1969, 446; Evans-Pritchard 1970, 1430; 'Abd Allah 1917, 7). In these societies, sexual relations between older and younger males are thought to be part of parenting and growing up. Indeed, without this sexual socialization, some Melanesian societies believe that their sons would fail to grow into worthy and robust men.

Where sexuality between men is both obligatory and common to all, the idea of homosexual "persons" makes little sense. K. J. Dover (1978) offers another example. The classical Greek and Roman literature, the foundation of much of Western thought, leaves no doubt as to the general acceptability of same-sex bonding in those societies (see also Foucault 1984b). In ancient Greece, adolescence was a time when young men left their biological families to become the lovers of adult men. Sexuality was but one element of an affectional and educational relationship in which youths learned the ways of manhood. Though less is known about similar relationships that may have existed among women, the writings of Sappho from this same era gave the name of the island of Lesbos to love between women.

Anthropology records as well the existence of gender-mixed persons among many of the native peoples of North and South America, Polynesia, Indonesia, and eastern Siberia. The gender-mixed North American *berdache* and the Polynesian *mahu* cannot be equated with the modern notion of the homosexual (Collender and Kochems 1983; Blackwood 1984; Levy 1971). Still, it is known that female berdaches sometimes married women, and male berdaches, men. Sexual relationships between conventional men and male berdaches appear usually to have met public acceptance if not approval. Even these examples of socially recognized homosexual relations do not cover all the forms of same-sex intimacy expressed in these and in homophobic societies. The creative anarchy of human experience is never fully contained by the social institutions of societies, and the varieties of homosexual experience have always exceeded their publicly recognized forms.

Sexual relations between women and between men, known in a great many cultures and in the history of our own, were rarely separated out to create persons known as "homosexuals." The task in this chapter on the origins of a homosexual people is to find out how women-loving women and men-loving men became thought of as "homosexuals." From this it will become possible to understand how a sexual preference became a people and how lesbians and gay men became a minority. Once homosexuality is transformed into a people, the idea of a gay movement finds its place.

The Medieval World

Historically, domestic arrangements have varied, as have other spheres of life. Just how the erotic and affective spheres fit together with economic, political, social, ideological, and aesthetic aspects of life is the subject of a good deal of thought among present-day scholars. Certainly new strides in empirical and theoretical research will further sharpen our understanding of how gender, production, and reproduction influence our emotions and attractions. Suffice it to say that shifts in fundamental social arrangements of producing and distributing the goods of society have influenced such unexpected areas as sexuality and love. In the development of modern capitalist societies, family, gender, and sexuality took on new meanings, and homosexuality eventually re-formed into the lesbian and gay worlds of today. From the fifteenth through the nineteenth centuries, Western societies were transformed from agrarian to urban industrial systems. People who once produced what they ate and what they wore, as well as the places where they lived, gradually became wage earners who sold their labor in a commodity market. People who were once limited to village and agrarian life became mobile city dwellers. People who were once guaranteed a livelihood in farming lost the land base that provided self-sufficiency.

Though the effect of all these changes on family, gender, and sexuality was both complex and indirect, personal, private, and intimate relationships changed during this period at least partly as a result of the rise of capitalism. For workers in urban labor markets, the meanings of mateship underwent subtle but profound alterations. The authority of parents over new generations declined, and the constraints and responsibilities of family ties began to give way to personal freedoms and an individualistic ethic. The decline of the old order brought new freedoms, and in the new milieu a gay world emerged.

In the feudal period, the importance of family can scarcely be overestimated. Families held the key to one's future well-being. Personal happiness and success depended on cooperation with family members, as it was their labor and goodwill that determined how well one ate, how one survived sickness, and how one resisted injustices committed by others. Individual prosperity hinged largely upon inheritance, and marriage was necessarily a practical arena wherein family ambitions could be played out. The fates of individuals often rested on advantageous alliances with appropriate partners. With the future prosperity of both marital partners and their families at stake, marriage could not be merely a matter of personal choice. In the words of the family historian Lawrence Stone:

Among the upper and the middling ranks, it [marriage] was primarily a means of tying together two kinship groups, of obtaining collective economic advantages, and securing useful political alliances. Among peasants, artisans, and laborers it was an economic necessity for partnerships and division of labor in the shop or in the fields. (1977, 5)

In this context, the personal preferences of marital partners could figure as only one factor among many in the selection of mates. Romantic love, in fact, posed dangers if taken too seriously. Stone continues, "Romantic love and lust were strongly condemned as ephemeral and irrational grounds for marriage" (85). Love was thought to be a base and unbecoming motive for mateship when the practical questions of survival and the material quality of life were at risk (Flandrin 1979, 164), and theologians and moralists remained resolute in their condemnation of it. Emotional attachments ideally grew up between husband and wife after marriage out of duty and mutual dependence. Failing that, affectional and emotional interests would have to be pursued outside marriage (Adam 1982, 50; cf. Stone 1977, 102). Such social arrangements left little room for any publicly organized gay existence.

We are now accustomed to thinking of homosexual relationships as alternatives to the nuclear family system as lesbians and gay men are able, much more than before, to form exclusive, long-term relationships in the midst of a supportive subculture. But in the feudal period, same-sex mateships were more likely to come about between neighbors, friends, and household members or arise in same-sex institutions like seminaries, colleges, or armies (Bray 1982, 43; Sylvestre 1983). Several of these relationships in the historical records occurred between well-known literary men and their manservants. Sixteenth-century sodomy trials often involved servants, apprentices sharing common beds, or noblemen and household members. The trial of the earl of Castlehaven in 1631 is among the most notorious (Bingham 1971, 448). King James I of England and Sir Francis Bacon are other well-known examples. Records of the early American colonies confirm that intimate relations typically arose in already existing social networks among those who knew each other well (Katz 1983, 75). The household and the community, then, were the matrix for almost all affectional ties, and same-sex friendships were no exception.

Romantic friendships among women flourished as long as women fulfilled their roles as wives and mothers. Because to the traditional mind sexuality was a male preserve, women's relationships were usually thought not to be sexual by definition. In Lillian Faderman's words, "because love without a penis was an impossibility to sixteenth century England, women were allowed to demonstrate the most sensual behavior toward one another without suffering the stigma associated with such behavior in more recent times" (1981, 32). So pervasive was this social definition that even those few women who were able to form lifelong exclusive relationships escaped the suspicion of sexuality.

Perhaps the best-known case in point is that of the ladies of Llangollen. As upper-class Irish women, they were among the few who could support themselves, thus avoiding dependence upon men. Their 1778 elopement

> was considered not only socially permissible but even desirable. . . . Women envied them because they seemed not to have to be bothered with what many eighteenth century females considered the duty and burden of sex. Romantic men admired them because they seemed to keep by choice "the crown of their virtue"; they lived together because they were too spiritually pure to be sullied by the "physical." (122)

Not having to risk symbolic masculinization through entry into the male-controlled labor market, they were able to pay homage to the trappings of femininity and preserve a distinctly prefeminist consciousness. As Faderman notes, "at the start of the French Revolution they feared only for the safety of the nobility" (123) at the same time as the revolution was spawning the first serious feminist challenges to feudal patriarchy. Even in the nineteenth century, older definitions survived to remove female intimacy from the category of things sexual, so that there was little reason for such relationships to be called sexual or homosexual and no warrant for women to identify themselves in terms of a sexual orientation.

In 1811 when the mother of a schoolgirl accused Marianne Woods and Jane Pirie, mistresses of a boarding school for daughters of the wealthy, of "improper and criminal conduct" with each other, the British courts debated whether a sexual relationship between women was even possible—this at the same time as an increasing number of men were going to the gallows convicted of sodomy. Should one partner dare to break out of her gender by passing as a man and assume male privileges, however, punishment could be harsh (Faderman 1981, 51, 147; Crompton 1981, 11; Bonnet 1981, 51-57; see also Faderman 1983). As long as women married, fulfilling their roles through dowry, domestic labor, and the production of heirs, their relationships with each other escaped attention, whether punitive or supportive.

There can be no doubt that the feudal era was a difficult one for those who would love members of their own sex, especially if they tried to abandon heterosexual strictures in doing so. At the public or official level, sodomy was severely condemned and the church and state were vigilant in their suppression of it. Since the great moral crusades of the twelfth and thirteenth centuries that hounded sodomites, heretics, Jews, and rebellious women to their deaths (Boswell 1980), sodomy had been a capital crime. Much of the record of the ensuing centuries is a sorry tale of cruel persecution and death at the hands of priests and judges (Crompton 1976, 277; Oaks 1978, 268; Monter 1981, 41; Katz 1983, part 1; Ruggiero 1985). Homosexual relationships were forced underground; their exposure was almost always due to misfortune. Indeed, much of the history of same-sex friendships is lost to us because of their careful concealment. What is known today of this period is seen through the prying eyes of their enemies, and it is early persecutory campaigns that make us aware today of the origins of the gay world.

The Molly Houses

What distinguishes the modern lesbian and gay worlds from anthropological and historical examples of homosexuality is the development of social networks founded on the homosexual interests of their members. In precapitalist societies, homosexuality was enclosed by already existing social relationships. It emerged within the household, the larger family, and local groups. In the modern period, people who may have had no previous contact with each other discovered each other through mutual attraction. First a gay male and then a lesbian world grew up in new territory. Same-sex friends and lovers began to carve out social spaces, progressively freeing themselves from the encumbrances of their antihomosexual environs. From these beginnings came the lesbian and gay worlds that we recognize today:

1. Homosexual relations have been able to escape the strictures of the dominant heterosexual kinship system.
2. Exclusive homosexuality, now possible for both partners, has become an alternative path to conventional family forms.
3. Same-sex bonds have developed new forms without being structured around particular age or gender categories.
4. People have come to discover each other and form large-scale social networks not only because of already existing social relationships but also because of their homosexual interests.
5. Homosexuality has come to be a social formation unto itself characterized by self-awareness and group identity.

These criteria distinguish the gay and lesbian worlds from anthropological and historical forms of homosexuality, and it is on this foundation that the gay and lesbian civil rights movements have been built.

Some scholars claim that a continuous homosexual subculture has existed since as early as the twelfth century (Monter 1981, 42; Trumbach 1977, 9), and Guido Ruggiero's (1985) work on fifteenth-century Venice, then the imperial power of its day, offers intriguing possibilities. While the ruling mercantile elite largely presumed that sodomy followed the classical model of older with younger men, it also turned up the beginnings of public homosexual networks centered around apothecaries, pastry shops, and church porticoes, suggesting an embryonic gay system. But the best evidence for a gay male world (with the characteristics described above) comes from the early eighteenth century. Once again, the ruling elites of that era bequeathed us the documents that describe what happened. Gay people, rarely allowed to speak for themselves on the historical record, became known to us through the writings of those who aimed to condemn, punish, and annihilate them.[1] Alan Bray notes that moral crusaders turned up a fairly well developed gay male world in London in a series of raids launched in 1699, 1707, and 1726 (1982, 86-87). In the prosecution of Mother Clap's Molly House in 1726,

a police constable gave evidence that he had visited the house on a Sunday evening and found between forty and fifty men "making love to one another, as they called it." Some, he reported, sat on another man's lap, kissing them, and using "their hands indecently." Others would dance, curtsy, and mimic the voices of women. After settling on a partner for the evening, they would go to another room on the same floor "to be married as they called it." (Bullough 1976, 480-81)

By the early 1700s, a network of gay meeting places was frequented by men from all walks of life. One trial docket listed defendants drawn from the food trades and the ranks of cabinetmakers, upholsterers, printers, lawyers, clerks, footmen, servants, watermen, and soldiers, all of whom were among those scooped up in a molly house raid (Trumbach 1977, 19). Jeffrey Weeks notes,

Edward Ward in *The Secret History of London Clubs* (1709) records the existence of "the Molly's Club" where a "curious band of fellows" met in a tavern in the city and held parties and regular gatherings. A writer in 1729 described in more detail "their walks and appointments to meet and pick up one another and their particular Houses of Resort to go to. . . ." About twenty such places were known, most of them in the Covent Garden/Lincoln's Inn area (1977, 36)

In France, too, police authorities were becoming alarmed by what they perceived to be an increase in sodomy. A wave of arrests swept up men from public parks and *sociétés d'amour* in the early 1700s. D. A. Coward notes that in Paris, "the Tuileries was the traditional temple of male love" (1980, 243). One writer noted in 1724 a need to control the growing audacity of sodomites lest "these kinds of persons lift their masks believing everything is permitted to them, to form influential leagues and societies by putting respected people at their heads" (Rey 1982, 116; my translation). Paris police records from the same year include a confession from one man that another had proposed "that he wanted very much to get to know me, and that we would live together, that he would pay for half of the room, that we would live together like two brothers, that we would drink and eat together" (Rey 1985, 180).

And in the Netherlands, there is a reference as early as 1689 to buildings frequented by sodomites. Amsterdam, too, endured its first major exposé of homosexual networks in 1730–31, resulting in three hundred prosecutions and seventy executions. Several more prosecutorial waves followed through 1798 (van der Meer, 1985).

These early attempts by gay men to claim a few spaces for themselves drew the battle lines still being fought over to the present day. Governments and their police, moral reformers, and reactionaries seem still to begrudge lesbians and gay men the freedom they have created and defended for themselves. One 1725 raid on a molly house in Covent Garden met "with determined and violent resistance" (Bray 1982, 97). One man, William Brown, entrapped in 1726 at Moorfields, retorted upon his arrest, "there is no crime in making what use I please of my own body" (114). But despite the modern efforts of feminists and gay liberationists, this right has yet to be fully recognized in the Western world.

Capitalism and Romantic Love

In brief, the developing capitalist economy provided new options for people confined to agrarian families. Wage labor opened new possibilities for people once dependent upon access to land for their livelihood. Expelled from its traditional land base over a period of several centuries, the Western European peasantry eventually found itself in a market where survival depended on the ability to sell one's labor. With this new source of income, the meaning of family and marriage changed considerably. Marriage no longer determined the entire economic life of its (male) members, nor implicated a lineage, and decisions about whom to marry fell increasingly into the hands of the marital partners themselves. The emotional functions of family life loomed larger, as productive economic life split off into the public realm.[2]

These changes had very different effects upon men and women. Men became much more able to select mates on the basis of personal considerations. For women, however, whose access to the wage labor market was more limited, marriage retained much of its practical economic meaning. A young women's future well-being was bound up in making a correct marriage. For men, whose advancement had less to do with their family lives, simple personal preference could be a major factor—and men who preferred men could more easily discover each other in the expanding urban milieus: in pubs and coffeehouses, public parks and railway stations, particular walkways and streets.

The public sphere remained a male preserve. Women could be far less mobile, and female bonding continued much in the feudal mode into the nineteenth century.[3]

As men developed clandestine meeting places out of the sites of public encounters, women's romantic friendships formed through existing social networks. The traditional patriarchal denigration of women's activities as trivial and inconsequential has made their historical rediscovery that much more difficult. It also, ironically, provided a level of freedom that was pushed back only later. Just as the molly houses flourished between raids, public inattention to women's relationships allowed for an "entire female world of love and ritual" (Smith-Rosenberg 1975, 1; Lengerke 1984). A vast network of women's friendships grew up among neighbors and kin and, in the nineteenth century, in colleges. An 1882 American letter details college women

falling violently in love with each other and suffering all of the pangs of unrequited attachment, desperate jealousy, εc εc. . . . And they write each other the wildest love letters and send presents, confectionery, all sorts of things like a real courting of the Shakespearean style. If the "smash" is mutual, they monopolize each other and "spoon" continually, and sleep together, and lie awake all night talking instead of going to sleep. (Sahli 1979, 22)

A few enterprising nineteenth-century women did move into the public sphere, making the difficult leap out of the constraints of Victorian femininity by passing as men. Jonathan Katz reports on Mary Anderson/Murray Hall, a New York politician who married (women) twice and successfully maintained a male identity until her death (1976, 232ff.). Few women, however, could risk independence from husbands and fathers without being perceived as "fallen women," and, indeed, the history of prostitutes may yet reveal an arena where women asserted their own sexual and emotional interests with other women, as well as with men.

But for almost all "kindred spirits," a life together could be nothing more than a utopian fantasy (Taylor and Lasch 1963, 23). It was not until the end of the nineteenth century that some romantic friends became lesbians in the modern sense. As women began to enter wage labor and acquire some financial independence, they were better able to realize their personal preferences and some chose women as life companions. Lesbians began to turn up in the public gay world. An 1889 Parisian *Guide des plaisirs* refers to a lesbian restaurant in Montmartre (Altman 1982, 7; see also Jay 1983, 18). Lesbians appeared in New York's gay world in the 1890s (Katz 1983, 218), and as they slipped away from male control they began to share the opprobrium of homosexual men.

The Stage Is Set

With material reality so fundamentally altered, traditional ideas could survive no longer. The French Revolution, which swept away a monarchy and symbolically marked the end of the feudal era, brought with it reforms improving the lot of peoples oppressed by the traditional order. Jews and national minorities acquired the rights of citizenship, and sodomy was dropped from the new Napoleonic Code. Sexuality joined religion—at least ideally—as a private confession outside the legitimate interests of government. The liberal ideals of the bourgeois era proclaimed the equality of all. For the purposes of the capitalist labor market, competence at one's job and the ability to produce a profit were the first principles. Accidents of birth and personal characteristics declined in importance now that ambition, hard work, and inventiveness were to constitute the road to success. Liberals foresaw an age when inherited and private traits would fade from the public economy, and a new system of opportunity and liberal ideals would set the agenda for traditionally disenfranchised minorities. Women and ethnic groups, religious and sexual minorities, took to heart the promise of equal opportunity and wondered why they should be denied full participation in civil society.

Two centuries ago, then, the stage was set, the actors assembled, and much of the script worked out for the dramas of the modern era. The liberal promise of equal rights for all became the rallying cry for the victims of the old system. Still, sharp breaks are rare in history, and these changes remained hedged about by many traditional structures. The capitalist revolution proved not to be so far-reaching as liberals and socialists anticipated. Traditional disabilities woven into the fabric of the emerging society, were not so easily expunged. The dominant classes resisted any compromise of their powers, and egalitarian trends ran up against serious obstacles and reverses. The agrarian morality, developed through centuries of accumulated human experience in response to an earlier reality, was still embedded in the foundations of Western cultures and preserved in religion and tradition. In feudal societies, founded on production relations organized by patriarchal assumptions, neither homosexuality nor the independence of women had a place; they made "no sense." And as capitalist societies emerged, traditional distinctions could be enlisted to fulfill new functions: families could be reshaped to complement the needs of capital, and subordinated peoples could be recruited into the reserve army of labor. Political elites, of course, fearful of all challenges to their preeminence, struck at those who were associated with the rising social order. As the French Revolution swept forward, the British elite, for example, reacted with a general crackdown against dissident elements and directed a wave of executions against sodomites in the first decades of the nineteenth century (Gilbert 1977, 98)[4]. Gay bars came under renewed attack, the 1810 attack on the White Swan on Vere Street being the best known.

Despite these formidable odds, however, a male homosexual underground was well established by the nineteenth century and the first signs appeared of a gay intelligentsia and public existence. By the end of the nineteenth century, astonished outsiders were describing the extensiveness of the gay world. Lydston, writing in the United States in 1889, remarked:

There is in every community of any size a colony of male sexual perverts; they are usually known to each other, and are likely to congregate together. At times they operate in accordance with some definite and concerted plan in quest of subjects wherewith to gratify their abnormal sexual impulses. (Burnham 1973, 41)

And Francis Anthony, in a paper read before the Massachusetts Medical Society in 1898, stated:

I have been told—and I am informed that the fact is true of nearly every centre of importance—a band of urnings, men of perverted tendencies, men known to each other as such, bound by ties of secrecy and fear and held together by mutual attraction. This band . . . embraces, not as you might think, the low and vile outcasts of the slums, but men of education and refinement, men gifted in music, in art and in literature, men of professional life and men of business and affairs. (Katz 1983, 293)

The German Social Democrat W. Herzen wrote in 1898:

The homosexuals of Berlin, Hamburg, London are certainly not less numerous than those of Paris or Brussels. There are places here where homosexuals hold their gatherings, baths they frequent, premises where they hold their dances, streets in which male prostitutes offer themselves to homosexuals. Homosexuals have their *Café National* in Berlin. (1977, 37)

Havelock Ellis, too, remarked on "homosexual baths, pensions, and hotels" in Berlin and on baths in Sydney, Australia (1942, 4:133-34). The 1899 Mazet committee in New York City found a series of gay clubs in the Bowery and the Tenderloin district (Katz 1976, 44ff.; Katz 1983). And a few of these nineteenth-century accounts spoke of lesbians involved in the bar culture.

Karl Marx believed that men thrown together in the industrial workplace would develop a new solidarity expressed as working-class consciousness. It is an irony of social theory that industrialization did produce the conditions in which arose a new form of male and later female bonding. In this entirely unexpected way, the "alienation of man from man," which Marx believed to be an inevitable consequence of workers competing against one another for jobs in a capitalist society, led to a vast range of responses and solutions, both personal and collective. Modern gay and lesbian worlds, born of the changes wrought by capitalism, have been among the solutions, offering oases of refuge and intimacy in a depersonalized atomized world. And, along with feminist visions of the nurturant women's culture at the margins of capitalist production, they have developed ambivalent relations with societies that would contain or suppress them.

Prelude to a Political Movement

During this era a new generation of poets and writers sought to articulate a modern vision of homosexual experience. In the nations of Europe and North America, a new people came to consciousness of itself in the mid-1800s. Still these first voices raised in defense of gay rights in the nineteenth century were marked by the pervasive heterosexism of the day. Those who first sought to give public expression to the gay experience had to grope for a language in which to embody a new reality. There were no ready channels to give shape to homosexual lives, and early writings drew on a range of discursive resources to present a public face for same-sex love. The weight of antihomosexual prejudice complicated the task, leading often to indirect morally acceptable characterizations of gay life. This development of a self-understanding was a critical step toward locating oneself in the world and arranging social and political priorities that would crystallize into a movement.

British writers often drew on the classical education they received as schoolboys to make sense of their affections for boys and men. John Addington Symonds's 1868 ode from his *Tales of Ancient Greece* tells of the courtship of Eudiades and Melanthius and their subsequent love affair:

> But day by day living with him he learned
> New sweetness, and the fire divine that burned
> In the man's heart was mirrored in the boy's,
> So that he thirsted for the self same joys,
> And knew what passion was, nor could abide
> To be one moment severed from the side
> Of him in whom whatever maketh sweet
> The life of man was centred and complete.
> (Reade 1970, 122-23)

In the United States, Walt Whitman envisioned male love in optimistic and democratic terms as an extended egalitarian network of "adhesive comrades" (see Martin 1979; Katz 1976, 337-65). The North American landscape formed an ever-present backdrop to Whitman's celebration of the sensual body and his very modern synthesis of democratic values, equality for women, and "manly friendship." The *Calamus* poems retain a freshness and immediacy that continue to attract adherents today. Whitman's homoeroticism reflected contemporary America with its belief in the possible, its pioneering optimism, and its sense of comradeship among peers. Yet Whitman's vision retained a critical—even utopian— thrust. In a society that was beginning to betray its own ideals, Whitman posed an almost subversive alternative. As ideals of liberty and equality were transformed into the liberty of business tycoons and the reality of class privilege, Whitman expressed a concrete sense of the rallying cry of the French Revolution, including its third element: "Liberty, equality, *fraternity.*" Whitman's affirmation of nature, the common man and wom- an, and comradeship implicitly rejected the machine and urban alienation. And his instructions to posterity could not be clearer:

Recorders ages hence,
Come, I will take you down underneath this impassive exterior, I will tell you
  what to say of me,

Publish my name and hang up my picture as that of the tenderest lover,
. . . . .
Whose happiest days were far away through fields, in woods, on hills, he and
another wandering hand in hand, they twain apart from other men,
Who oft as he saunter'd the streets curv'd with his arm the shoulder of his
friend, while the arm of his friend rested upon him also.
(1955, 118-19)

On the other hand, Whitman's contemporary Herman Melville looked away from America to Polynesia for a more hospitable climate in which to set his homoerotic romances (Austen 1977; Katz 1976, 467). And from the intense and tempestuous relationship of Paul Verlaine and Arthur Rimbaud came the poetry of renegades with its contempt for all things conventional and its leap into the radical possibilities of love without rules:

> Lovers who would be friends—
> Without vows, always true,
> Free-hearted, without promises—
> Such are we and our virtue.
> (1979; see Schmidt 1979)

Karl Ulrichs, a Hannover lawyer, opened the debate on homosexual rights in the political and legal arenas in the first book of his twelve-volume work published in 1864. His timing was critical: Napoleon had brought an enlightened legal code born of the French Revolution to much of Europe. As the German states became unified under Prussian auspices, the new German Empire was adopting the Prussian legal model, which recriminalized homosexuality. Ulrichs, imprisoned in 1866 by Prussian authorities for protesting their takeover of Hannover, took his plea for equal treatment of homosexuals to an 1867 Congress of German Jurists, only to be shouted down from the podium (Steakley 1975, chap. 1; Kennedy 1978a, 23; Kennedy 1978b, 24; Baumgardt 1984a). In 1869, K. M. Kertbeny, a Hungarian physician, joined the fray with a lengthy open letter to the Prussian minister of justice (in which he coined the word *homosexual*) to plea for the omission of love between men from criminal law (Lauritsen and Thorstad 1974, 6-8). Despite Ulrichs's and Kertbeny's efforts, Paragraph 175 was reinserted into German law in 1871, subjecting gay men once again to legal prosecution throughout unified Germany.

Ulrichs's lifework showed its origins in the popular scientific currents of the day. Caught up in the evolutionist rhetoric that framed most Victorian social theorizing, Ulrichs formulated homosexuality as a congenital anomaly (*Naturspiel*) like left-handedness or a cleft palate. This transitional work squeezed same-sex relationships into heterosexual molds by inscribing male-female sexuality into the homosexual psyche. The homosexual male (called "Urning," from the Greek classic, *The Symposium*) was presented as "a feminine soul confined to a masculine body" (Kennedy 1981, 106; Ulrichs 1975, my translation). Lesbians ("Dioning") were thought to be males encased in women's bodies and thus, being men, were "naturally" attracted to women. Gay people became nothing more than mistaken heterosexuals in this quaint formulation; consequently "homosexual individuals were seldom attracted to one another" but only to "normal" members of their own sex. (The attraction of "normals" to cross-gender people was something of a mystery in this theory.) At the same time, these biological foundations allowed Ulrichs to argue that homosexuality was as "healthy as fish in water" and that criminal penalties could never be more than needlessly cruel and useless punishments. But even Ulrichs found it necessary to add a labyrinth of new categories to his theory to accommodate the many homosexual people who showed no disjuncture between "soul" and "body."

At the same time, his third-sex theory did express how much homosexual men had come to believe themselves to be a people apart. An intolerant society, refusing same-sex bonds a place, separated homosexually inclined people in attempts to suppress and control them. Homosexually interested people were taking on the traits of ethnicity: separate social ties and subcultures, collective identity, and a folklore about how to cope with a malicious outside world.

The gay world was also attracting unsympathetic attention from self-appointed guardians of moral order and respectability. In the late nineteenth century, a few gay people began to fall into the hands of physicians and psychiatrists who reported on them in medical journals. Case studies of the 1880s and 1890s started to outline a "homosexual personality type" concocted out of Victorian morality, phrenology, and personal apprehensions. This is the era when the medical profession was consolidating itself as an expert monopoly over a series of "disorders." Physicians were transforming masturbation into a disease and busying themselves with new machines, constraints, and surgical operations to bring it under control (Parsons 1977, 55). Medical scrutiny moved on to cultivate a set of "feminine disorders," and the profession campaigned to suppress abortions throughout the United States. Homosexuality too fell under the disapproving gaze of the medical profession, and some physicians did not hesitate to remove ovaries from women and castrate men in their war against "perversion" (Katz 1976, chap. 2; Katz 1983, part 2). Ulrichs's third-sex theory, shorn of its claim for civil rights, reappeared as a medical syndrome subject to the reformative technocracy of the experts. Medicine thereby became another weapon among the armaments arrayed against same-sex love, opening a century of experimentation, drugging, electroshocking, mutilation, and psychological manipulation (Adam 1978, chap. 2). Medical ideologies were to find their way into new legislation to confine lesbians and gay men to prisons and mental hospitals and block them from professional and governmental employment, immigration, and the simple right to live unmolested.

In 1891, John Addington Symonds printed fifty copies of *A Problem in Modern Ethics,* a systematic review of the existing scholarly literature on homosexuality. There he sought to refute such vulgar errors as the confusion of male homosexuality with effeminacy and the belief that homosexuals "prey" upon youth. He set cross-cultural variation in attitudes about homosexuality against the tortuous reasonings of the medical ideologues who would turn homosexuality into a disease and argued for decriminalization in a set of fourteen propositions at the book's conclusion. What interested Symonds most, whether he treated classical sources in *A Problem of Greek Ethics* or Ulrichs's third-sex theory in *A Problem of Modern Ethics,* was the simple valorization of male love. In the end, he remained most deeply impressed by Whitman's "intense, jealous, throbbing, sensitive, expectant love of man for man . . . a love that finds honest delight in hand-touch, meeting lips, hours of privacy, close personal contact . . . a daily fact in the present, but also a saving and ennobling inspiration" (123).

This swirl of conflicting ideas, then, closed the nineteenth century and led to the birth of the first homosexual social movements. It was a period of creative ferment; a series of disparate discourses emerged out of distinct national and theoretical foundations. This generation took the first steps toward dialogue among those who embarked on lifelong quests for the classical and contemporary traces of a sexuality actively suppressed for centuries. But more important were the urban subcultures creating folklores about surviving, succeeding, and enjoying gay and lesbian lives.

It is against this backdrop that the first gay civil rights movement was founded.

Chapter Two

Early Movements and Aspirations

The founding of the Scientific-Humanitarian Committee (Wissenschaft-lich-Humanitäres Komitee) on 15 May 1897 in a Berlin apartment inaugurated the first of several gay organizations that sprang up in Germany over the next thirty-five years. Founded by Magnus Hirschfeld, a physician, Max Spohr, a publisher, and Erich Oberg, a civil servant, the committee became the leading voice for equal rights for homosexual men and women until its suppression by the Nazis in 1933.[1] It had a profound impact outside Germany as well as within, with adherents such as the Dutch lawyer Dr. Jacob Schorer setting up a Netherlands committee in 1911 and the Swedish steelworker Eric Thorsell taking its message to Sweden in the 1930s (Rogier 1969; Tielman 1982).[2] In other countries of Europe and North America, where gay organizations remained much more limited, the German movement offered a lifeline for isolated but aware lesbians and gay men, influencing their thinking and helping lay the groundwork for movements that emerged after World War II.

The development of gay and lesbian subcultures has varied considerably from nation to nation, and this chapter surveys those countries where gay political writing and organization arose before the Holocaust.

Germany

The liberation of homosexuals can only be the work of homosexuals themselves.

—1921 United Front Action Committee appeal

Germany of the 1890s was an unstable mix of feudal and modern elements; the early homosexual movement was but one of many liberal, middle-class, and workers' movements that developed at this time. With the German states united in 1871 under the auspices of the Prussian monarchy, Germany entered the twentieth century with a state system still largely in the hands of a conservative coalition composed of the old landed aristocracy (*Junkers*) and a growing capitalist class, which together held its army, bureaucracy, and established church. The Prussian monarch continued to exercise real power, representing the interests of a traditional patriarchal order that looked with suspicion upon the reform, and sometimes revolutionary, movements taking root among the urban masses and new middle classes. The late 1800s was an era of considerable social rethinking and experimentation. The cautious women's movement, standing for motherhood and moral purity, began to develop a left wing with the publication of the journal *The Women's Movement (Die Frauenbewegung)* in 1895 (Evans 1976). A series of "life-reform movements" (*Lebensreformbewegung*) were emerging: a youth movement (*Wandervogelbewegung*), a health movement (*Naturheilbewegung*), nutrition reform (*Ernährungsreform*), clothes reform (*Kleiderreform*), and nudism (*Freikörperkultur*) (Steakley 1975, chap. 2).

The appearance in 1896 of the first homosexual journal, *Der Eigene*, under the editorship of Adolf Brand,[3] and of Magnus Hirschfeld's book, *Sappho und Sokrates*, presaged the founding of the Scientific-Humanitarian Committee itself. In his book Hirschfeld set out the mandate for homosexual advancement. Deriving his ideas directly from Ulrichs's evolutionary theory, he wrote that homosexuality shows itself as a "deep, inner-constituted natural instinct" and as a gender stage between the extremes of masculinity and femininity (1975; my translation). Each of the antihomosexual theories is refuted in turn. The sickness theory: its conclusions, based on samples drawn from psychiatric clinics, are biased. The criminal theory: countries where homosexuality is legal (France, Italy, Holland, Belgium, Luxemburg, Bavaria, Württenberg) do not experience unusual problems. The degeneracy theory: consider the "robust" but prohomosexual Albanians, Scythians, Dalmatians, and Celts— and the "great" homosexuals of history. Indeed Hirschfeld rebukes science for its failure to stand for justice.

At the beginning, the Scientific-Humanitarian Committee resolved upon a petition and publicity campaign to garner support for the abolition of Paragraph 175, which subjected homosexuality to legal penalties, and to educate Germans about "uranian" men and women. As early as 1898, the petition received support from the leader of the Social Democratic party, August Bebel, who stood up in the German parliament *(Reichstag)* to urge other parliamentarians to sign it (Lauritsen and Thorstad 1974, 13). (Bebel was a noted supporter of women's rights and had published a book on women and socialism in 1878.) By the following year, Spohr's printing house had published twenty-three titles on homosexuality and the committee had issued a scholarly journal, *The Yearbook for the Intermediate Sex (Jahrbuch für sexuelle Zwischenstufen),* which continued to be published until the inflationary crisis of 1923 (Steakley 1975, 24). Publicity intended to educate the elite was sent out to newspapers, administrators, mayors, and courts, and a pamphlet called, *What the People Should Know about the Third Sex,* was produced in 1903, seeking to inform Germans about the "uranian" fact. This opening text was deeply influenced by the progressive thought of the day, taking Ulrichs's essentially congenital theory to argue against persecution. It demonstrates the ubiquity of homosexuality through anthropological references and insists that homosexuals are among the benefactors of humanity, concluding, "every uranian owes a duty to himself [*sic*]: self-realization is his right, of that which has come to him by birth he must make the best" (Brit. Society 1975, 10).

In addition, the committee in 1903 sent out 6,611 questionnaires to Berlin students and factory workers in the first sex survey of its kind. From it Hirschfeld concluded that 2.2 percent of the general population was homosexual. (Hirschfeld was fined 200 DM for his trouble, after six of the students charged him with "obscenity") (Steakley 1975, 33; Baumgardt 1984, 20). In the same year, the petition reached six thousand signatories including such luminaries as writers Hermann Hesse, Thomas Mann, Rainer Maria Rilke, Stefan Zweig, and Lou Andreas-Salomé; the philosopher Karl Jaspers; artists and musicians George Grosz, Carl Maria Weber, and Engelbert Humperdinck; socialist politicians Rudolf Hilferding, Karl Kautsky, and Eduard Bernstein; sociologists Max Scheler and Franz Oppenheimer; the sexologist Richard von Krafft-Ebing; the theologian Martin Buber; and the physicist Albert Einstein (Lauritsen and Thorstad 1974, 14; Stümke and Finkler 1981, 422).

In 1905, reform of Paragraph 175 came up again in the Reichstag when Adolf Thiele and Bebel argued for its abolition. The liberal and conservative parties expressed outrage at the idea and the law remained on the books.

Whatever the Scientific-Humanitarian Committee's merits, not all agreed upon its medical-scientist orientation or its endorsement of the gender-mix conceptions of Ulrichs. In 1902, those around *Der Eigene,* Adolf Brand along with Benedict Friedländer and Wilhelm Jansen, organized the Community of the Special (Gemeinschaft der Eigenen) centered on a more purely ancient Greek understanding of intermale relations (Steakley 1975, 43; Stümke and Finkler 1981, 27; Baumgardt 1984c, 27). As set forth in Friedländer's 1904 *Renaissance des Eros Uranios,* homosexuality was idealized as the relationship between an adult bisexual male and a youth in a strictly masculine context, a concept that found resonance in the literary circle around the poet Stefan George. As such, the Eigene offered nothing to women and ruled themselves out of the increasingly friendly alignment of the committee with the Social Democrats, retreating instead to the extreme individualist philosophy of Max Stirner. By 1907, the Eigene completed the split from the Scientific-Humanitarian Committee and the group successfully maintained its journal until 1931.

Hirschfeld attempted to engage more women in the committee's work, and by 1901, the *Yearbook* was publishing confessional statements by women. As E. Krause declared in an article titled "The Truth about Me," "I am proud of my exceptional state. . . . What I demand is humanity, an impartiality, equal rights for all" (Faderman and Eriksson 1980, 23, 30).

At the same time, the mainstream women's movement *(Bund Deutsches Frauenverein)* was preoccupied, as were its Victorian counterparts elsewhere, with women's rights articulated within traditional conceptions of femininity—motherhood, purity, and morality—rather than women's gender role. In the 1890s, it campaigned with evangelical Christians and the anti-Semitic right to stiffen penalties against prostitution, "obscenity," and "immorality." Helene Stöcker's questioning of gender ideology in the early 1900s attracted supporters who gathered together in a New Morality movement which challenged the old guard. Stöcker, arguing against the mainstream, declared that many of the attributes of femininity were the result of socialization and not women's inherent nature. She believed that marriage was often constricting and that "individual women should be allowed to dispose over her own body without interference from the state" (Evans 1976, 138). Her break with the Bund came in 1904 when she pressed for support and protection of unmarried mothers, a group considered immoral and a threat to the family by the contemporary women's movement. This led to the founding of the Association for the Protection of Mothers and Sexual Reform (Bund für Mutterschutz und Sexualreform), which initiated sharp debates within the Bund and extended the logic of its position toward support for divorce law reform, contraception, and abortion. It was this opening in feminist theorizing that eventually led Stöcker to join the directorship of the Scientific-Humanitarian Committee and begin a dialogue between the two movements.

In 1904, Anna Rüling addressed the committee's annual conference with the question "What interest does the women's movement have in the homosexual question?" pointing out to the largely male gay movement (as lesbians have had to do so many times since), "In order to obtain for homosexuals and all women generally the opportunity to live according to their natures, it is necessary to actively aid the women's movement's efforts to expand educational opportunities and new professions for women" (Faderman and Eriksson 1980, 86). Adopting the third-sex framework, Rüling decried middle-class opposition to "uranian liberation" and castigated the women's movement's silence on lesbian issues, looking toward the New Morality movement and the Scientific-Humanitarian Committee for help in freeing "uranian women" from having to marry.

By 1910, the Bund succeeded in purging its radicals in order to reestablish its earlier precepts, a mix of *völkisch* nationalism and the cult of motherhood, fidelity, and spirituality opposed to male carnality and abortion (Evans 1976, 156). Mutterschutz went on to rally against a 1911 Reichstag committee proposal to extend Paragraph 175 to women (Lauritsen and Thorstad 1974, 15; Pieper 1984), but became a much weaker political force owing to internal dissension and its exclusion from the federation of women's organizations.

In 1907, the Scientific-Humanitarian Committee was canvassing political parties for their positions on law reform as Reichstag elections approached. A public debate on Paragraph 175 sponsored by the committee attracted more than two thousand (Lauritsen and Thorstad 1974, 15). But 1907 also brought the first major crisis to afflict the fledgling gay movement in the form of the Eulenburg scandal. The affair began when an independent Berlin newspaper launched a series of increasingly direct articles implicating the highest echelons of the imperial administration—perhaps even the kaiser himself—in homosexual practices (Steakley 1983, 22). In one sense the Eulenburg affair was not about homosexuality at all; the charges were simply convenient weapons to disrupt and embarrass the conservative coalition. The scandal was fueled, then, by deeper divisions in German society and directed at discrediting the ruling aristocracy. The issues posed particularly acute problems for the two gay organizations. The imperial government represented a deadweight they had little interest in maintaining, but the homosexual weapon posed other dangers, for the gay movement could scarcely go along with the unfolding logic of the scandal, which presumed that homosexuality constituted a disqualification from public office. The general format for the scandal had been set five years earlier when the Italian government had expelled the German industrialist Alfred Krupp for his dalliances with Italian boys on the elite resort island of Capri. A subsequent exposé in the Social Democratic newspaper *Vorwärts* had resulted in Krupp's suicide (Manchester 1968, 229-34).

In the ensuing courtroom maneuvers, Magnus Hirschfeld appeared as an expert witness in the trial of General Kuno Count von Moltke, military commandant of Berlin; he stated that "Moltke's 'unconscious orientation' could 'objectively' be labeled 'homosexual,' even if he had never violated Paragraph 175" (Steakley 1983, 71-72). Adolf Brand, who had added the German chancellor, Bernhard Prince von Bulow, to the list of high-placed homosexuals, was brought to trial on libel charges and sent to prison for eighteen months. The trial of Philipp Prince zu Eulenburg-Hertefeld, the kaiser's close friend and adviser, was suspended for "health reasons" as the evidence accumulated of his sexual friendship with a Bavarian farmer. It seems that both Hirschfeld and Brand hoped to expose the hypocrisy of a government that included homosexually interested men in its ranks while penalizing homosexual acts. Their testimony, however, was assimilated instead into a more traditional moral grid, resulting not in law reform but in a hardening of the battle lines. The trials ultimately sharpened the homosexual-heterosexual cleavage and overwhelmed more traditional conceptions of intermale sexuality, feeding into eugenic and militarist ideologies of the day that typified homosexuals as a conspiratorial threat to the nation's "manhood" and birthrate.[4] These were conceptions shared by the mainstream women's movement and bourgeois political parties along with more reactionary elements of German society.

The immediate effect upon the gay movement was a serious flight of support among those frightened that the movement might be willing to betray even them to the authorities by violating the most common defensive strategy employed by gay people—self-concealment. Any significant gains to be made by the life-reform and socialist movements would have to await more fundamental changes in the structure of German society.

New hope arose in the closing days of World War I when the imperial order was forced to give way in the face of military defeat. In the autumn of 1918, war-weary soldiers and workers deserted their commanders and bosses to form popular democratic councils of their own, and the kaiser fled to the Netherlands. This German revolution swept throughout the nation in less than a week in November of 1918, and Magnus Hirschfeld was among the speakers to welcome the masses who surged, red flags aloft, into the square in front of the Reichstag at the height of the insurrection. There, he declared:

Together with a true people's state with a genuinely democratic structure, we want a social republic. Socialism means solidarity, community, reciprocity, the further development of society into a unified body of people. . . . Long live the free German Republic! (Steakley 1975, 71-72).

But the tragedy of the German revolution was its failure to dissolve the traditional power bases of the old ruling elites: no land reform ensued to dispossess the Junkers nor did industrial democracy overturn capitalism. Though displaced from government, the conservative coalition (with collaborationist Social Democratic politicians) rallied its forces and dissolved the workers' and soldiers' councils to reconstitute itself as a major force in German society—now increasingly resentful of the abrogation of its traditional privileges. The tragedy of the ensuing Weimar Republic of 1918 to 1933 was its failure to resolve this volatile mix of reactionary and emancipatory forces.

Still there were causes for optimism in the 1920s: the Social Democrats came to power in Parliament, the right to vote was granted to women, and gay society experienced an unprecedented flourishing. In 1919, Hirschfeld founded the Institute for Sex Research (Institut für Sexualwissenschaft), which became an internationally respected center for the documentation of sexuality, "offering marriage and career counseling, venereal disease testing and treatment, family planning and sex education programs, and psychiatric and physical therapy," as well as a library and museum of "biological, sociological, and ethnological materials" (Steakley 1975, 91). A movie, *Anders als die Andern*, appeared in the same year, featuring the injustice of blackmail and a lecture by Hirschfeld. It was a popular success despite disruptions in the audiences and police closures in several cities. It was suppressed by the censors in 1920 (Theis 1984).

In the same year, a united front *(Aktionsausschuss)* of gay groups was organized by Kurt Hiller, a pacifist, socialist, and committee director. Hiller brought together the Scientific-Humanitarian Committee, the Eigene, and the new German Friendship Association (Deutscher Freundschaftsverband) to issue this appeal for its second congress:

We must demonstrate that we have learned to win our human rights ourselves and have created an organization which demands respect. We no longer want only a few scientists struggling for our cause; we want to demonstrate our strength ourselves. . . . No homosexual should be absent—rich or poor, worker or scholar, diplomat or businessman. . . . we must show whether we have developed into a fighting organization or just a social club. He who does not march with us marches against us. (Steakley, 1975, 77)

In 1921, Hirschfeld set up a World League for Sexual Reform, which gained 130,000 members worldwide through the 1920s. The appointment of a Social Democratic minister of justice, who was himself a petition signer, prompted the Scientific-Humanitarian Committee to submit its petition to the Reichstag in 1922 (Lauritsen and Thorstad 1974, 16, 30).

And yet, as James Steakley remarks,

it appears that the almost legendary flowering of the homosexual subculture during the heyday of the "Golden Twenties" worked to the detriment of the emancipation movement; a contradiction between personal and collective liberation emerged, for it was far easier to luxuriate in the concrete utopia of the urban subculture than to struggle for an emancipation which was apparently only formal and legalistic. (1975, 78, 81)

As early as 1905, Hirschfeld had documented a Berlin gay world of "more than twenty bars" catering to a variety of social classes and tastes, plus "restaurants, hotels, *pensions,* baths" as well as dance clubs, party circuits, and drag balls. He noted lesbian cafes *(Konditoreien)* (including one preferred by Jews) and costume balls. Personal advertisements for special friends placed by women and men were common in the newspapers (1975a, my translation; see also Rich 1981, 16). A glimpse of the same community eighteen years later comes from a remarkable article in *Mercure de France* in 1923 where Ambroise Got, a French diplomat in Berlin, described the German gay world through the eyes of the shocked bourgeois, characterizing it as "a mad whirl of pleasure . . . a wild rush to enjoyment" (655, my translation). In a visit to the Kleist-Casino (still in existence in the 1980s), Got found a largely white-collar clientele and "a tiny orchestra consisting of a piano and a violin, playing soothingly sentimental and langorous airs. . . . some chat, hand in hand, of inconsequential things; others touch, caress and look longingly at each other. There are men of all ages" (673). Got then goes to the Eros Theatre (first opened in 1921) to see an adaptation of Marlowe's *Edward II* and a play by Sudermann called *Friend (Freundin)* about a woman who leaves home and child for another woman. Got is astonished by the diversity of cabarets, restaurants, and branches of the Friendship Association scattered throughout Germany, many with clubhouses sponsoring dances and other social activities. By the mid-1920s, more than thirty journals had come out, one of which, *Die Insel,* reached a circulation of 150,000 in 1930.

Some fourteen bars and clubs for lesbians flourished in Berlin during the 1920s. With the mainstream women's movement firmly entrenched in naturalist and essentialist doctrines about femininity, no opportunity arose for the theorization of lesbianism as a general women's issue and none of the alliances of lesbian liberation with feminism that emerged in the 1970s became possible in the 1920s. Lesbian organizations remained closely aligned with gay male forms throughout the Weimar Republic with social clubs typically meeting in the same clubhouses and journals printed on the same presses as their male counterparts (Kokula 1984).

At the close of the 1920s, the movement's long struggle for law reform seemed ready to bear fruit. Kurt Hiller drew together the Scientific-Humanitarian Committee, the Institute for Sex Research, the Bund für Menschenrecht, Mutterschutz, and three other nongay sex reform groups into a Coalition for Reform of the Sexual Crimes Code (Kartell für Reform des Sexualstrafrechts), which called for equality for women, liberalization of marriage laws, distribution of contraceptives, abortion reform, and abolition of illegitimacy. It also sought to overturn Paragraph 175, and in 1929, in a close vote, a Reichstag committee approved a penal reform bill that would at last drop the infamous paragraph from German law (Kokula 1984, 83, 85; Baumgardt 1984b). But, in fact, the work of the early gay movement was soon to be so thoroughly obliterated that few would remember that it had existed at all. Gay people were to suffer a systematic campaign of intimidation, harassment, and ultimately genocide. For consideration of this era, we must turn to an account of the Holocaust—but first, let us look at contemporary developments elsewhere.

France

Love alone matters and not the sex to which it is dedicated.

—Natalie Barney, "L'amour défendu," in *Traits et portraits*

Love is to be reinvented.

—Jean Cocteau, *Le livre blanc*

Though Germany was unique in its development of a sustained gay political movement before World War II, France merits attention for the artists and writers who reflected upon the meanings of their homosexuality during the same period. In the words of Gilles Barbedette and Michel Carassou:

Unlike the German homosexual movement created by "men of science," it is undeniable that homosexuals in France felt their first hours of freedom when men and women of letters set out to write on the subject, thereby partly thwarting the psychiatric trap which sought to contain homosexuality. (1981, 102; my translation)

Between the Commune and World War II, Paris was a cultural mecca for both native and expatriate artists, becoming a crucible for such creative trends as impressionist and surrealist art, the ballet, and the shaping of the modern novel. Homosexuality is relevant to this cultural florescence in two ways: (1) among the creative circles were social networks formed and held together by their participants' shared fate as homosexuals, and (2) as homosexuality became an element in bringing about particular combinations of personalities, these circles, in turn, began to reflect upon their experiences of being homosexual. These thoughts on homosexual experience in repressive societies set forth conceptions that still influence modern understandings.

If we step back to compare the political economies of Germany and France in this era, it is clear that French culture emerged from a very different set of social forces. Unlike the German experience, the 1789 French Revolution had swept away (in Karl Marx's words) "all manner of medieval rubbish," thereby incapacitating the feudal classes that in Germany exercised power for so long. The nineteenth-century partial restoration of empire in France suffered further defeats in the Franco-Prussian War of 1870 when the reigning prince fled with his supporters, leaving Paris in the hands of its workers. In their hour of freedom, the workers declared the short-lived Commune. The Dreyfus case at the turn of the century further marked a symbolic victory for republicans and liberals over the church and aristocracy.

By the first decades of the twentieth century, then, France was at the forefront of European nations in the fragmentation of traditional coalitions and, thus, in many respects was among the most "modern." The result of this was a "weak" state, decried by some historians, but good news for the grass roots who took advantage of the new freedoms to invent and imagine. As Gertrude Stein remarked, in her inimitable style, of French tolerance:

> It is not civilised to want other people to believe what you believe because the essence of being civilised is to possess yourself as you are, and if you possess yourself as you are you of course cannot possess any one else, it is not your business. It is because of this element of civilisation that Paris has always been the home of all foreign artists, they are friendly, the French, they surround you with a civilised atmosphere and they leave you inside of you completely to yourself. (1940, 56-57)

Everyone had their enclaves and balls: students, underworld gangs, Arabs and blacks, sailors and servants (Brassai 1976). Gay people were no exception with a world of "disreputable bars, high-society bars, dance halls, drag balls, night clubs, and music hall promenades" (Barbedette and Carassou 1981, 15). Best known of these was the famed Magic City transvestite ball, a glamorous and outrageous celebration akin to Mardi Gras. Lesbian nightclubs and restaurants are reported at least as early as 1881 (Altman 1982, 7) and three were well established in the 1920s, among them, Le Monocle which, like Magic City, specialized in the transvestite style. Says André du Dognon, "it was the epoque of 'sacred monsters.'. . . We were sort of princesses condemned to the sidewalk" (Barbedette and Carassou 1981, 60).[5]

Parisian life attracted such refugees as Oscar Wilde, following his release from prison, and Sergei Diaghilev, dismissed from the Imperial Theatre of Russia owing to artistic rivalries and gossip campaigns around his homosexuality. It was on French soil—free of the absolutist Russian state—that Diaghilev organized the Russian Ballet with the assistance of French artists and musicians. Though analysis of the complexities of the financial and artistic creation of the Ballets Russes falls outside the scope of this book, suffice it to note the existence of a homosexual "strand" in the process of cultural production. Igor Stravinsky's characterization of "Diaghilev's entourage—[as] a kind of homosexual Swiss Guard" cannot be ignored when considering the relation of the ballet to its Parisian milieu, nor can the fact that the major dancers and choreographers, who shaped much of the Ballets Russes repertoire, themselves matured artistically as Diaghilev's lovers."[6]

Much of French artistic life was as gregarious as Paris street life with its literary salons and cafés. Though much history is typified as the actions of handfuls of great individuals, cultural production is not simply the work of lone geniuses but the outcome of fruitful collaborations, whether explicit or implicit, that are nurtured by a complex of favorable conditions.

Most remarkable of the salons was that of Natalie Barney, a charismatic American heiress who so inspired a generation of artists that she appears as a character in many books and was the object of published love poetry and epigrams and a subject for portraitists. Most of Paris's literary elite passed through Barney's salon and some, as her friends and lovers, generated early reflections on the new lesbian. Barney's circle, composed largely of independent creative women, moved beyond the "romantic friendship" model of the nineteenth century toward explicitly "lesbian" definitions of women's relationships. Out of Barney's early affair with Liane de Pougy came a volume of love poems, *Quelques Portraits—Sonnets de Femmes,* in 1900, and Pougy published *Idylle saphique* in 1907 (Wickes 1976, 40ff.). Her ten-year intermittent love affair with Renée Vivien included pilgrimages to the Greek island of Lesbos, and her weekly soirées (with a Greek *Temple à l'amitié* amidst the garden) paid homage to Sappho in poetry readings and impromptu dramas.

Lillian Faderman takes exception to the lesbian discourse produced by the Barney circle (1981, 268). Notions of the "sapphic" or "lesbian" were in circulation as early as the period leading up to the French Revolution, and they were revived in the late nineteenth century by such male authors as Balzac and Baudelaire.[7] The influence of this so-called aesthetic-decadent tradition is clear in the writing of many of the texts of Barney and her friends. It is a sensibility not far removed from Catholic orthodoxy in its use of lesbianism as a sign of morbidity and exoticism. Certainly Renée Vivien's domestic arrangements could have been lifted from the pages of Baudelaire with their "odor of incense, of flowers, of overripe apples." Colette remarked, "nothing could dispel the uneasiness engendered by the strangeness of the place, bound to astonish a guest, the semi-darkness, the exotic foods on plates of jade, vermeil, or Chinese porcelain, foods that had come from countries too far away." Barney's gifts to her of "jades, enamels, lacquers, fabrics. . . . ancient Persian gold coins . . . glass cabinets of exotic butterflies . . . a colossal Buddha" show similar inspiration (Wickes 1975, 91-93). The literary connections with the decadents are direct enough with Pierre Louys, author of *Les Chansons de Bilitis,* often featured at Barney's gatherings.

Still, the revaluation of these inherited symbols cannot be ignored. Though Faderman excoriates Baudelaire's Victorian "childish wallowing in the deliciousness of 'sin'" (1981, 269), the thrust of the aesthetic initiative is decidedly two-edged. Whether it was Oscar Wilde and Aubrey Beardsley or Renée Vivien and Djuna Barnes, the writers of this era reconstituted the symbols of lesbian and gay worlds provided to them by luxuriating in and affirming their specialness. In delighting, with Aleister Crowley, in "evil," this romance with things "wicked" ultimately negated the received dogma that labeled them "sinful" in the first place—an insight not lost on readers of the period.

Despite the liberalism of French society, lesbian writing was nevertheless accomplished against a number of more conservative trends of the published word. The French medical profession, like its counterparts in Germany and the United States, occupied itself with "the homosexual" as it might with a peculiar insect, "scientifically" classifying and dissecting him or her for public inspection. Medical textbooks appeared with "just-so" stories about "pederasts" designed to intimidate the unwary with depictions of "perverts" heading toward a bad end (Hahn 1979; Bonnet 1981, 90)—a tradition not much changed in modern academic texts (Adam 1978, 32; Adam 1986; Norton and Crew 1974, 274). Popular novels of the day consigned homosexual characters to the obligatory "final solution" of suicide or some other untimely death (Barbedette and Carassou 1981, 107; Adam 1978, 30-34). This feudal ideology dressed up as medicine or biography had its practical counterpart in harassment by police, who would seize gay men cruising in the Tuileries or dancing at the Bal de la Montagne Sainte-Geneviève (Hahn 1979; Brassai 1976). It is against this backdrop that we must understand the pioneering efforts of those like Natalie Barney, who published her *Pensées d'une Amazone* in 1920, consolidating her reputation as the "matron saint of Lesbos" (Wickes 1976, 171). *Pensées* is a volume that reflects the issues of the day with its references to Whitman, Ulrichs, and Symonds and its defense of Oscar Wilde. Natalie Barney was the model for Valerie Seymour in Radclyffe Hall's 1928 *The Well of Loneliness*. She is described as follows:

Valerie, placid and self-assured, created an atmosphere of courage: everyone felt very normal and brave when they gathered together at Valerie Seymour's. There she was, this charming and cultured woman, a kind of lighthouse in a storm-swept ocean. (Wickes 1976, 177)

Marcel Proust's *Sodome et Gomorrhe* appeared in 1921, the fourth volume of his monumental *A la recherche du temps perdu*. Proust's work is most notable in its presentation of a topic generally shielded from public view. As one unsympathetic observer of the Parisian scene remarked, "the publication of the first part of *Sodome et Gomorrhe* was like the staking out of new ground by an adventurous colonist" (Huddleston 1928, 273). Still *Sodome et Gomorrhe* was deeply marked by the medical ideologies and Germanic theories of its time. Proust's portrayal of the gay world shows profound ambivalence in its willingness to embrace "illness" metaphors, its reliance on the third-sex theory, and its assumption of a number of stereotypes linking homosexuality with conspiracy, neurosis, and effeminacy (Rivers 1983). Much of Proust's view was colored by his experiences at the salon of the Count Robert de Montesquiou, "a great dandy and aesthete who entertained on a lavish scale, organizing elaborate parties in his Pavilion of the Muses, presenting dances from the Ballet Russe, the music of Debussy, or the poetry of Mallarmé and Verlaine read by the stars of the Comédie-Française." (Wickes 1976, 106). This, with Proust's juggling of his character's genders, provoked disdain in Natalie Barney (112), and André Gide found the book a "dissimulation, a desire to protect himself, a camouflage of the cleverest sort" (Rivers 1983, 155). What is modern in Proust is his depiction of homosexuality not as a few isolated individuals but as a social world. The gender-inscribed discourse of the third-sex idea ruptures in the face of these first descriptions of everyday gay encounters. Homosexuals become "a race accursed, persecuted like Israel, and finally, like Israel, under a mass opprobrium of undeserved abhorrence, taking on mass characteristics, the physiognomy of a nation" (Proust 1963, 276). "They form in every land an Oriental colony" in diaspora from Sodom, which leads Proust in pursuit of his analogy to Israel to imagine (but discount) a new Sodomite nation.

It is no doubt partly in response to *Sodome et Gomorrhe* that André Gide published *Corydon* in 1922. It had been written eleven years earlier, but like so many other gay texts of the day, such as E. M. Forster's *Maurice* or Gertrude Stein's *O.E.D.*, it languished in a drawer to await a more progressive era. Like many other gay people, Gide undertook the personal odyssey of coming out over a number of years, discovering Whitman in the 1890s (Rhodes 1940, 156) and wrestling with a religious upbringing. Unlike the heterosexual script, which equates the discovery of sexuality with loss of innocence, Gide abandoned the torment of asceticism to find innocence through sexual encounters with Arab youths, regretting only "the irretrievable years wasted with sanctity" (Mann 1948, 53). *Corydon,* too, opens with Whitman and a call for "someone who would lead the attack" against "the thick evil of lies, conventions and hypocrisy" surrounding the topic of homosexuality (1950, xiv, 10). With Symonds, Gide dissents from the gender logic of the third-sex idea and, perceiving the enemy to be medical moralism, presents a lengthy set of ethological findings to contradict taken-for-granted notions about the "natural." *Corydon* closes with the noble image of the Theban army of lovers honored in the Greek tradition. When questioned by a reporter following his winning of the Noble Prize for literature, Gide insisted that *Corydon* was his "most important" book, knowing well that the prize had come in spite of it. (xii).

Gide was very much a topic of conversation in 1924 when *Inversions,* the first French gay journal, was issued. It published five numbers before being shut down by the police as an "outrage to good morals." Founded by Gustave-Léon Beyria, an office worker, Gaston Lestrade, a postal worker, and Alfred Zahnd, a Swiss carpet maker, *Inversions* made this appeal in its opening statement: "We wish to cry out to inverts that they are normal, healthy beings, that they have the right to live their lives fully, that they owe nothing to a morality created by heterosexuals" (Barbedette and Carassou 1981, 170, my translation).

Inversions was very much aware of the German movement, printing translations of Ulrichs and Hirschfeld. It addressed the trial of Oscar Wilde, the formulation of the Napoleonic Code, the Greeks, the "great" homosexuals of history, even zoology. After the police raid ended *Inversions,* it was revived as *L'Amitié,* but this too succumbed to state repression. Without the scientific legitimacy of the *Jahrbuch für sexuelle Zwischenstufen* or the cachet of elite literature, this potentially popular magazine aroused the anxiety of French officials who charged that it was a "cynical apology for pederasty, a systematic appeal to homosexual passions and an incessant provocation to the most unhealthy curiosities" (Barbedette and Carassou 1981, 272). With eugenic ideas circulating under the sponsorship of the Catholic right, the prosecution described *L'Amitié* in a closed trial in 1926 as "propaganda liable to compromise the future of the race with its neo-Malthusian tendencies." The outcome was ten months in prison for Beyria and six for Lestrade.

Prewar France, then, offered a unique social milieu for the exploration of cultural identities. Jean Cocteau's motto, "What the public reproaches you for, cultivate! It's you," was adopted by many. And yet a comparison of France and Germany yields several ironies. Despite (or perhaps because of) their authoritarian state, Germans organized a public gay and lesbian movement before 1918, whereas the relatively liberal political climate of France nurtured no equivalent. The comparatively public openness of German gay and lesbian life contrasted with the apparent social conservatism of the French, where gay political thought was displaced into literature. When Cocteau published his erotic confessions in *Le livre blanc* in 1928, it appeared anonymously despite its closing line, "But I'm not willing just to be tolerated. That wounds my love of love and of liberty" (1958, 88). Even in Paris, the expression of same-sex love had to resort to masks and subterfuges in the face of the heterosexist hegemony.

England

Wickedness is a myth invented by good people to account for the curious attractiveness of others.

—Oscar Wilde, *Phrases and Philosophies for the Use of the Young.*

A map of the world that does not include utopia is not worth even glancing at.

—Oscar Wilde, *The Soul of Man under Socialism*

In the fifty years before World War II, gay networks in England as on the Continent developed an increasingly public literature. All of this resulted in a very cautious British Society for the Study of Sex Psychology, a public forum for homosexual issues, but no organized gay or lesbian movement. These tentative initiatives were undoubtedly marked by the 1895 trial of Oscar Wilde, which, as Jeffrey Weeks observes, "created a public image for the homosexual and a terrifying moral tale of the changes that trailed closely behind deviant behavior" (Weeks 1977, 21).[8] The willingness of the British courts to condemn the nation's leading playwright to two years hard labor created a symbolic victory for the "moral purity" forces of the day and chilled the coming-out process of the British gay world. The trial of Oscar Wilde was an act of public labeling so widely publicized that few in the English-language world escaped its effects. It provided the stamp of legitimacy for the suppression of any public mention of same-sex love and served as a warning to its adherents. In the year following the trial, Edward Carpenter's *Love's Coming of Age,* which contained a chapter on "Homogenic love," and Havelock Ellis's volume on "sexual inversion" both lost their publishers. Carpenter's book eventually appeared with the small socialist Labour Press, and Ellis's was published in Germany.

Still, the trial of Oscar Wilde was not an isolated occurrence but the culmination of decades of contending political forces in Victorian England. Although none of the mid-nineteenth-century movements aimed to persecute gay people—indeed few identified homosexuality as an issue at all—an unlikely mix of physicians, middle-class moralists, and established policymakers produced a legislative compromise that caught homosexuals in its net.

As physicians campaigned to make medicine their professional monopoly, they battled midwives, abortionists, and other folk practitioners to extend their professional "expertise" over a new range of unregulated human behaviors. Among these "new found lands" was sexuality, and medical texts spread a veritable hysteria through the 1880s about the "dangers" of masturbation that resulted in fiendish machines to prevent children from indulging in the "evil deed" and surveillance systems in families and hospitals to stamp it out. Soon enough, homosexuality was colonized as yet another widespread phenomenon that could be cultivated as a "disease" requiring medical intervention (Neuman 1975, 1; Gilbert 1975, 217; Parsons 1977, 55).

As well, protests raised by the women's movement against the compulsory testing of suspected prostitutes for venereal disease ultimately contributed to legislation that raised the age of consent for all sexual activities and extended police surveillance over prostitution. Judith Walkowitz remarks:

> Begun as a libertarian struggle against the state sanction of male vice, the repeal campaign helped to spawn a hydra-headed assault against sexual deviation of all kinds. The struggle against state regulation evolved into a movement that used the instruments of state for repressive purposes. (1980, 1; see also Walkowitz 1983)

It was an amendment to this parliamentary bill on prostitution that in 1885 recriminalized male homosexuality (the medieval sodomy law having fallen into disuse).[9]

The "purity" campaign went on to win new laws suppressing the distribution of contraceptive information; then in 1889, the Indecent Advertisements Act banned publicity for VD remedies. An 1898 law prescribed flogging for "soliciting for immoral purposes," a penalty imposed primarily on homosexual propositioning (Bristow 1977, 126, 193, 204).

The roots of antihomosexual repression in England show significant differences from Germany. With its aristocratic classes long since politically neutralized, this legislative wave was no feudal remnant but rather a modern development that required the assent of England's ruling classes, now capitalist. It was only in the nineteenth century, with the growth of state bureaucracies, that governments became able to supervise the masses through the extension of compulsory education, the expansion of the penal system, the development of military conscription, and the implementation of censuses. The creation of population and family policies became possible on this foundation, and with national statistics at their disposal, Malthusian and eugenic ideas came into their own. The intrusion of the capitalist state into the private familial and sexual realms proved functional to a system that needed a high birthrate (though eugenicists at times feared the proliferation of the "wrong kinds" of people). The prohibition of "irregular," nonreproductive sexuality and the promotion of reproduction came about at a time when the rapidly expanding capitalist economy required an immense supply of labor power. Indeed, an oversupply of workers would ensure the lowest possible wage rates. To sustain the socioeconomic configuration most favorable to the capitalist class, the least desirable outcome would have been a scarcity of labor, which would force employers to compete against each other by raising wages.

Through the nineteenth century the demand for reproduction was reflected in increasing state regulation of family life. The Factory Acts of the 1840s moved women out of wage labor; common-law marriages were forced into legal straitjackets; and medical and "helping" professionals developed to supervise family stability. Women increasingly were redefined as mothers and wives incapable of performing wage labor (see esp. Weeks 1981; Donzelot 1979; Harrison and Mort 1980, 84). Humanitarian legislation to protect women and children from the degradations of factory work helped revalue women's *reproduction of* laborers over their *production as* laborers. As employment was withdrawn from women, they necessarily became more dependent upon men and thus possessed fewer options in determining their own lives. Lesbianism as an alternative to the nuclear family (and as opposed to "romantic friendship") became an even more remote possibility, and male homosexuality fell under the baleful eye of the state and its agents.

Though Oscar Wilde is best known today for his apparently frivolous drawing-room comedies, his epigrams and sly observations flow from deeper sources. His mauling of upper-class pretense came from a viewpoint shaped by his mother's Irish nationalism, his own utopian socialism, and his love of young men. His marginality as an Irishman and homosexual no doubt contributed to his aesthetic and socialist protest against bourgeois meanness and vulgarity.

Wilde's 1890 essay, *The Soul of Man under Socialism,* contains this prescient line: "As one reads history . . . one is absolutely sickened, not by the crimes that the wicked have committed, but by the punishments that the good have inflicted" (1973, 1087-88). When sentence was pronounced against him in 1895, Mr. Justice Wills could scarcely contain his righteous indignation, stating "it is the worst case I have ever tried" and naming Wilde as "the centre of a circle of extensive corruption of the most hideous kind among young men" (Hyde 1948, 339). Wills's condemnation of Wilde as a "corruptor of youth" recalls the classical parallel of the trial of Socrates, and Wilde's now famous defense consciously invoked Greek ideals. When asked by the crown prosecutor about the "love that dare not speak its name," a line drawn from a poem written by his lover, Lord Alfred Douglas, Wilde replied:

[It] is such a great affection of an elder for a younger man as there was between David and Jonathan, such as Plato made the very basis of his philosphy, and such as you find in the sonnets of Michelangelo and Shakespeare. It is that deep, spiritual affection that is as pure as it is perfect. . . . It is in this century misunderstood, so much misunderstood that it may be described as the "Love that dare not speak its name," and on account of it I am placed where I am now. It is beautiful, it is fine, it is the noblest form of affection. There is nothing unnatural about it. (Hyde 1948, 236)

But certainly the preeminent English thinker on homosexuality was Edward Carpenter. An active lecturer for socialist causes, Carpenter's work shows the now familiar combination of progressive Victorian ideas on sexual issues: Ulrichs's third-sex theory, Whitman's democratic vistas, and the doctors' busy reprocessing of Christian moralism into scientific dogma. Carpenter was deeply uncomfortable with his Victorian milieu, rejecting its "commercialism, . . . cant in religion, . . . futility in social conventions, . . . denial of the human body, . . . class-division, . . . cruel barring of women from every natural and useful expression of their lives," and sexual hypocrisy (Rowbotham and Weeks 1977, 27). Carpenter delved into the alternatives to his own society in his search for a place for "romantic comradeship," voyaging to the United States in 1877 and 1884 to see Whitman and to India in 1890, and joining English socialist movements to find refuge from bourgeois propriety (Tsuzuki 1980).

A chance meeting in a railway carriage led to a lifelong relationship with George Merrill in 1891, and their rural retreat attracted pilgrimages by reformers, bohemians, lesbians, and gay men inspired as much by the example of their life together as by Carpenter's work.

In *The Intermediate Sex* (1908), Carpenter mapped "homogenic love" onto the terrain of contemporary debates, sorting through distinctions between masculinity/femininity, body/soul, spiritual/sensual, and nature/nurture. German influence was clear in his association of uranians with androgyny, characterizing males as having "gentle, emotional dispositions" and females as "fiery, active, bold and truthful" (27). He discounted Krafft-Ebing's morbidity theories, finding neuroses "the results rather than the causes of the inversion," but allowing for a distinction between congenital "born lovers of their own kind" and situational "confused" or curious inverts (55-62). A denunciation of "self-abuse" and "sensuality" in youth owed much to the medical viewpoint. Carpenter strained to re-contextualize "comrade attachment" as an altruistic and spiritual sentiment and endorsed the Greek ideal of the "continent," "temperate," "even chaste" sublimation in "finer emotions," cautioning against "a too great latitude on the physical side" (34, 69-70). Carpenter envisioned a place for homosexuality in an ordered universe in terms of the heroic friendships of the ancients or the "fervid comradeship, . . . the counterbalance and offset of materialistic and vulgar American Democracy" articulated by Whitman.

This spiritualization of "homogenic love" partook of the same strategy used by the nineteenth-century women's movement, which adopted "passionlessness" as an attribute to emancipate women from the temptress imagery of the Judeo-Christian tradition (Cott 1978, 219). It protested the relentless sexualization of the world finally accomplished in the post-Freudian period; today Carpenter's very rich set of names for same-sex bonding has given way to the triumph of "homo*sexuality*," which reduces lesbians and gay men to the meeting of body parts. Carpenter's work is a final plea for a more whole understanding of same-sex love. His historical and anthropological anthologies revolve around "romantic friendship" and "comrade attachment," not orifice and orgasm (Carpenter 1982; 1975).

Carpenter's work is a proposal for a full-blooded concept of friendship and a protest against the emotionless, "tough" masculinity that was coming to the fore. The booming nineteenth-century capitalist system created a labor market that pitted man against man to exhibit the requisite personality types. Masculinity was reconstituted to reflect the machine to which the worker had to adapt. The industrial economy sought to discipline and regularize workers as steady, reliable, emotionless, hard, and instrumental. Even the fashion system showed the revaluation of male purpose, as the flamboyance of the aristocracy gave way to the "fastidious austerity" of the businessman and sober practicality of the male worker (Ewen and Ewen 1982, 132). Homosexual friendship as a form of male tenderness and avenue to male bonding became disvalued (or disvalued again) by the logic of capitalist competition as a "failure" betraying masculine "virtues" necessary for "success." Any male temptation to sexual exploration would be contained by the monogamous family. A dependent wife and children ensured that men would be "good" workers who would not risk unemployment through industrial rebellion (Horkheimer 1972, 120; Rapp 1978, 286).

At the same time, Carpenter's caginess about sexuality participated in the "denial of the human body" he longed to escape, but his reticence ought to be assessed in light of the conspiracy of silence instituted in the wake of the Wilde trials. Even his own books fell under the ban. In a 1911 visit to the British Museum, Carpenter found that *The Intermediate Sex* was not listed in the library's card catalog. It took two years of pressure to convince the library to acknowledge the book's existence to its borrowers (Weeks 1977, 117-19).

When one of Carpenter's admirers, Laurence Housman, pulled together a small network of gay professional men in the Order of Chaeronea, it made no attempt at public education but met clandestinely (Weeks 1977, 122-27). After Magnus Hirschfeld addressed the International Medical Congress in London in 1913, however, the network became the nucleus for the new British Society for the Study of Sex Psychology. Carpenter became its first president in 1914.

The society sponsored public lectures and produced pamphlets throughout the 1920s, publishing among others Stella Browne's *Sexual Variety and Variability among Women,* Havelock Ellis's *The Erotic Rights of Women,* Edward Westermarck's *The Origin of Sexual Modesty,* Laurence Housman's *The Relation of Fellow-Feeling to Sex,* and Edward Carpenter's *Some Friends of Walt Whitman* (Weeks 1977, 134). The society attracted such distinguished members as George Bernard Shaw and E. M. Forster, the communist publicists Maurice Eden and Cedar Paul, and Oscar Wilde's son, Vyvyan Holland. It also maintained links with Bertrand Russell and Magnus Hirschfeld, as well as the American birth control advocate Margaret Sanger, Soviet feminist Alexandra Kollontai, and writer Radclyffe Hall.

Carpenter looked with hope to the women's movement, seeing it as an advocate of egalitarian marriage ("a true comradeship between man and woman") and a herald of romantic comradeship for same-sex pairs (1982, 39). As women asserted increasing power over their lives through the women's movement, he looked forward to "a marked development of the homogenic passion among the female sex" (1908, 77-78).

The irony of the Victorian mapping of intimacy, which opposed male carnality to female purity, however, was that same-sex bonds took on radically different meanings. It was an attitude expressed in Gertrude Stein's characterization (if Hemingway's account of it is to be believed) of male homosexual acts as "ugly and repugnant," whereas "in women it is the opposite. They do nothing that they are disgusted by and nothing that is repulsive and afterwards they are happy and they can lead happy lives together."[10] This interpretation allowed "romantic friends" to participate in the Victorian women's movement, which occupied itself with "morality" legislation, antiprostitution campaigns, and temperance along with right-to-work and right-to-vote issues. The Labouchere amendment, which recriminalized male homosexuality, by being tacked onto an antiprostitution bill thereby ranged male and female "homosexuality" (to use a too modern word) on opposite ends of a moral spectrum.

Nancy Sahli and Lillian Faderman use the language of a "fall" from "innocence" to contrast the idyllic, prestigmatized ties between Victorian women to the carnalized and perverse lesbian, a transition occurring in the early years of the twentieth century (Sahli 1979, 17; Faderman 1981, 241). Without denying the role of the sexologists and novelists who helped recategorize lesbians with gay men, it is important not to forget the changing political economy of the era. It is only because of the powerlessness of Victorian women that patriarchal authorities could afford to trivialize women's relationships and tolerate them as not very serious. It is when women first began to achieve financial independence in wage labor that romantic friends could divest themselves of the constraints of marriage and heterosexuality (see Ferguson 1981, 11). And it was at this moment, when women threatened to escape male control, that lesbianism crystallized as a suppressed and reviled identity.

First steps toward articulating a lesbian identity are scattered references made by Edith Lees (married to Havelock Ellis) and by Stella Browne, a birth control and abortion law reformer, who implicitly linked lesbian emancipation to the principle of the right to control one's own body. In "Sexual Variety and Variability," Browne remarks that

many women of quite normally directed (heterosexual) inclinations realise in mature life, when they have experienced passion, that the devoted admiration and friendship they felt for certain girl friends had a real, though perfectly unconscious spark of desire in its exaltation and intensity. (1977, 102-3)

Most significant of all was the 1928 publication of Radclyffe Hall's *Well of Loneliness,* a tortured polemic for the "merciful toleration" of the "pitiful plight of inverts" (Faderman 1981, 320, 467). The presentation of lesbianism as a "painful anomaly" (Weeks 1977, 110; see Ruehl 1982) caused Romaine Brooks (Natalie Barney's lover) to remark that it was a "ridiculous book, trite, superficial" (Faderman 1981, 322). Despite its highly ambivalent approach, *The Well of Loneliness* was, in a rerun of British history, abandoned by its publisher and subsequently printed in Paris. When imported to Britain, it was seized by Customs and forced through an obscenity trial where the courts convicted it of not having "stigmatised this relationship as being in any way blameworthy" (Weeks 1977, 109)! This time the British mania for silence subverted itself as an instrument to suppress the book and generated such international publicity that *The Well of Loneliness* became the best-known English-language book with a lesbian theme of its generation. And simply by breaking the silence about lesbianism, it gave hope to thousands by daring to portray an independent relationship between women as viable and right.

United States

We stand in the middle of an uncharted, uninhabited country. That there have been other unions like ours is obvious, but we are unable to draw on their experience. We must create everything for ourselves. And creation is never easy.

—F. O. Matthiessen, in a letter to his lover, Russell Cheney, 1925
(Hyde 1978, 71; Katz 1983, 415)

In the decades before World War II in the United States, medical definitions of homosexuality enjoyed a dominance unparalleled in Europe. Despite the supposed guarantee of freedom of speech in the United States Constitution, state and city governments suppressed the first gay and lesbian voices raised in arts and politics, thereby establishing medicine as the only approved dogma on homosexuality. Only the short-lived Chicago Society for Human Rights dared put forward the question of civil rights for gay people, though abundant evidence points toward a well-developed gay underground in all the major cities. Edward Stevenson's 1908 *The Intersexes,* the first book of its kind by a gay American writer, identified social clubs and baths, cafés and restaurants, bars and music halls in such cities as New York, Boston, Washington, Chicago, New

Orleans, St. Louis, San Francisco, Milwaukee, and Philadelphia (see Mayne 1975; Katz 1983, 326-30).

Jonathan Katz's remarkable documentary collections offer a wealth of insight into turn-of-the-century gay society through the eyes of writers, state commissions, doctors, and correspondents with the German movement. The 1911 report of the Chicago Vice Commission scarcely conceals its astonishment on finding

> whole groups and colonies of these men who are sex perverts, but who do not fall in the hands of the police on account of their practices, and who are now known in their true character to any extent by physicians. . . . It appears that in this community there is a large number of men who are thoroughly gregarious in habit; who mostly affect the carriage, mannerisms, and speech of women; . . . they have a vocabulary and signs of recognition of their own. (Burnham 1973, 47; Katz 1983, 335)

Nor was American gay society the preserve of only men or white people. Though the literary evidence suggests that romantic friendships among women were common until World War I and beyond (Faderman 1981, 298), lesbians too were known in the largely male bar circuits of New York (Katz 1983, 218-19). Racial segregation ironically opened the way for the artistic expression of homosexual experience. While gay topics were being pushed out of white theaters in the 1920s, "race records" (ignored or misunderstood by white authorities) included Ma Rainey's renditions of "Sissy Man Blues," "B[ull] D[yke] Woman's Blues," and "Fairy Blues" (Katz 1983, 443). Bessie Smith's participation in Detroit's "buffet flats" and Claude McKay's observations of "the dark dandies loving up their pansies" in Harlem bars leave little doubt about organized gay life among black Americans (Katz 1976, 80; Katz 1983, 367, 443, 447).

Meanwhile public awareness of lesbians and gay men was limited to occasional lurid newspaper articles linking "sex perverts" to murder and other crimes and to the advice of "experts" warning against masturbation and "darker" evils. Medical journals published case studies of unrelieved misery—sad tales designed to frighten anyone who dared fall in love with a friend. An infrequent report would recognize that the social condemnation of homosexuality was the problem and not homosexuality itself (Katz 1976, 150), but the preponderance of medical attention was devoted to the armory of repression: castration, hypnosis, surgery, electroshock, drugs, and hormones (Katz 1976; Weinberg and Bell 1972).

As in England, the domination of American politics and economy by big business molded legal and moral norms after its own image. As Michel Foucault remarks, a regime of supervision and control was established to protect the means of production while it was in workers' hands through a "formidable layer of moralisation deposited on the nineteenth-century population" (1980, 41; see Foucault 1979). Early industrialists showed no reluctance in examining the "moral lives" of workers and did not hesitate to dismiss those who violated Victorian ideals of sexual propriety.[11] In North America, there were a number of instances of industrial towns founded, built, and governed by a single capitalist family who enforced moral standards. Antonio Gramsci argues:

The new industrialism wants monogamy; it wants the man as worker not to squander his nervous energies in the disorderly and stimulating pursuit of occasional sexual satisfaction. . . . The exaltation of passion cannot be reconciled with the timed movements of production, motions connected with the most perfected automatism. (1971, 302, 304-5; see Poster 1978, 169)

Industrial labor shaped men's experiences and organized a masculine ideology through which men were to understand and direct their lives. The repressive climate "inoculated" most men against homosexual activity and convinced them of its inutility. Competitiveness counteracted male bonding and the "team" absorbed intermale affection. Even the male gestural repertoire for affection needed to be dressed in the language of aggression: intermale touching could occur legitimately only as mock punches, slaps, and jabs.

No subordinated group that is victim of the same practices and information sources as the larger society can entirely escape the malevolent effect of so much indoctrination.[12] But even the most overwhelming propaganda system cannot completely convince people to ignore their own experiences, pleasures, and satisfactions when they seem so "natural, pure, and sound" (Katz 1976, 376).

And there were leaks in the American ideological umbrella, often provoked by European thought. Representatives of the Scientific-Humanitarian Committee lectured in New York in 1906 and 1907, creating links between the German movement and gay Americans (Katz 1976, 381-82). Even more remarkable was Emma Goldman's inclusion of freedom for homosexuals among the anarchist issues for which she campaigned in her 1915 lecture tour across the United States. In an article written for the *Jahrbuch für sexuelle Zwischenstufen* in 1923, Goldman acknowledged the influence of lesbians she met in prison as well as the writings of Hirschfeld, Carpenter, Ellis, and Krafft-Ebing on her awareness of antihomosexual oppression. Edith Lees also defended the sexually "abnormal" in a lecture tour of the United States in 1915, prompting Margaret Anderson to take her to task for understating the pain of those "tortured or crucified everyday for their love" (Katz 1983, 366). Anderson's *Little Review* continued to publish fiction about women-loving women into the 1920s even as the subject was falling under the pall of medical pathology (Faderman 1981, 308). Popular literature continued to reflect an unselfconscious celebration of female romantic friendship at least into the 1910s, but new trends were evident (Faderman 1981; see Simmons 1979). The potential of female relationships as alternatives to heterosexuality was put forward positively in Florence Converse's 1897 novel *Diana Victrix,* but negatively in an 1898 Women's Christian Temperance Union advice book, *What a Young Woman Ought to Know,* which rejected women's friendships as "a sort of perversion, a sex mania" (Faderman 1981, 168; Katz 1976, 295).

For women in North America as in England, the winning of access to paid work and to the vote were necessary prerequisites for self-determination. With the masses of women only beginning to filter into wage labor (and, at first, into subordinate and poorly paid positions), the degree of financial independence needed to found one's own household and escape dependence on men was available to only a few.

The Society for Human Rights was the first formally organized gay movement group in the United States. Founded by an itinerant preacher and laundry, railway, and postal workers, the society was incorporated in Chicago on 10 December 1924. The inspiration for a gay rights group came from Henry Gerber, a German-American who had served with United States occupation forces in Germany from 1920 to 1923 and had been able to participate in the German movement at that time (Katz 1976, 385-89; Katz 1983, 554-61). The Society for Human Rights succeeded in putting out two issues of a (now lost) journal, *Friendship and Freedom,* and quickly contacted its counterparts in Europe. *L'Amitié* noted, "The first page of *Friendship and Freedom* is composed of an article on 'Self-control,'. . . a poem of Walt Whitman, and an essay, 'Green carnations' on Oscar Wilde" (Barbedette and Carassou 1981, 263, my translation). The society came to a sudden end when the wife of one of the directors caught wind of it and called the police. Three directors were dragged through court and the *Chicago Examiner* trumpeted, "Strange sex cult exposed." In Gerber's words, "we were up against a solid wall of ignorance, hypocrisy, meanness and corruption. The wall had won" (Katz 1976, 393).

The fate of the Chicago Society for Human Rights was no isolated incident. American democracy had long been compromised by an authoritarian underside. Governments had been quick to sweep away constitutional guarantees of freedom of speech and assembly when workers sought to organize themselves into unions during the late nineteenth century and when peace advocates questioned the reasons for the entry of the United States into World War I (Goldstein 1978). In 1919, urban riots broke out in Chicago and East St. Louis as black veterans returning from the war found unemployment and racism in the ghettos. Increasingly nervous about the recent Russian Revolution and about domestic political restiveness, the federal government plunged into the Red Scare of 1919–20, arresting thousands suspected of socialist or anarchist sympathies. Emma Goldman was among the deportees. Like British repression following on the heels of the French Revolution, American authorities sought to eliminate all signs of "disorder," including homosexuality. It was also in 1919 that investigation of homosexuality at the Newport (Rhode Island) Naval Training Station resulted in the jailing of sixteen sailors. An official committee, which reviewed the incident, found that a forty-one-man "pervert squad" had sought to entrap navy men and that "these boys not only permitted one [sexual] act to be performed upon them, but returned time after time to the same suspect and allowed a number of acts to be performed. . . . Not one boy declined the assignment" and several had received citations for their "interest and zeal in this work"![13]

It was in this inauspicious climate that the first American gay civil rights group came into existence.

After his dismissal from the post office, Henry Gerber went on to become circulation manager for *Chanticleer,* where he wrote occasional progay articles and critically reviewed the maudlin gay-themed novels of the 1930s. In later correspondence with Manuel Boyfrank, he alternated between disillusionment and fantasies of a restored movement to fight the religious fanatics, blackmailers, psychiatrists, and "imperialist and fascist politicians who want a big population for cannon fodder" (Katz 1983, 558). In his words, "capitalism, loyally supported by the churches, has established a Public Policy that the Sacred Institution of Monogamy must be enforced; and such a fiat is the deathknell to all sexual freedom" (Katz 1976, 394). (Gerber died in 1972 at the age of eighty.)

When homosexual themes turned up in the movies, censors sliced Alla Nazimova's 1923 *Salomé* and Carl Dryer's *Mikael* (released in New York as *Chained, The Story of the Third Sex*) (Russo 1981, 22, 27). The staging of Edouard Bourdet's *The Captive* (which played unmolested in Paris) and Mae West's *The Drag* sparked police raids in 1927 and led to a toughened

New York state censorship law that banned any reference to "sexual perversion" (Katz 1976, 87).

The Well of Loneliness endured another obscenity trial, this time in New York, but was ultimately acquitted by an appeals court. The establishment of the Motion Picture Code in 1930 assured ideological purity through self-censorship, introducing a new period of revisionist history. Thus, when *Mädchen in Uniform* opened in 1932, depictions of romantic friendships among schoolgirls were cut out. The lesbian *Queen Christina* of Sweden was married off to a Spanish ambassador in the 1933 production in violation of history, and the 1936 movie of Lillian Hellman's *Children's Hour* was completely rewritten to heterosexualize it (Russo 1981, 57, 63, 65). It was not until the 1950s that lesbian and gay Americans tried again to break through the "conspiracy of silence."

Chapter Three

The Holocaust

[Gay people] had their golden age a half century ago, a lost continent obliterated by the totalitarian bloodbath.

—Guy Hocquenghem, *Race d'Ep.*

New Sources for Old Fears

The breaking up of feudal society organized around kin and hierarchy created a world with new possibilities, especially for traditionally oppressed classes: peasants and serfs, women, national minorities, and Jews. In this new world, "comrade attachment" between men and between women found new avenues for expression and new voices. But capitalism is no unitary phenomenon and its development through the particular political makeup of different nations resulted in divergent conditions for the emergence of a gay people. Increasingly evident from the historical record is the fact that "homogenic love" faced difficulties that were not merely a question of overcoming older holdovers but hindrances stemming from modern sources (Adam 1985b).

Though the rise of capitalism opened new channels for homosexual expression, it also laid the groundwork for the reorganization and rejuvenation of older doctrines proscribing it. This unstable mix of ambivalent and contradictory trends presented little security to lesbians and gay men whose social niches remained vulnerable to larger events beyond their control. In countries where feudal remnants, still smarting from recent defeats, combined with big business, particularly murderous coalitions came about to crush the gains of traditionally disenfranchised peoples. In countries where the state itself became the sole capitalist, there was no countervailing force to the imposition of particularly virulent forms of the productivist/reproductivist ideology.

To understand the changing prospects of the gay and lesbian movement, we cannot neglect the larger social milieu that provided both the resources for the emergence of a homosexual people and an impetus for other social classes to seek the destruction of the gay world. Nor can the postwar movement ignore the lessons of the Holocaust, where the early gay movement came to such a bitter end.

Stalinism

When the Russian Revolution succeeded in abolishing Europe's last absolute monarchy, all eyes turned toward the new social experiment in the East. In a single blow, an ancient autocracy had apparently given way to a popular democracy of workers' councils and peasant communes accompanied by sweeping reforms in family and sexual life. The new constitution mandated the legal equality of women, voluntary marriage and divorce, legalized contraception and abortion, state-supported day care, employment rights for women, and maternity leave provisions (Millett 1969, 168). Criminal penalties for adultery and homosexuality were dropped in favor of an official policy of withdrawing the state from the private realm. Soviet delegates to the World League for Sexual Reform reiterated the official position throughout the 1920s. In the words of Dr. Baktis's *The Sexual Revolution in Russia:* "As for homosexuality, sodomy, and whatever other forms of sexuality that are considered as moral violations by European legal codes, Soviet law treats them just the same as so-called natural intercourse. All forms of intercourse are private matters." (22, my translation).

This clear-cut policy helped influence the leftward drift of the gay movement in Germany as the German Communist party assured gays in the 1928 election campaign that "there is no need to emphasize that we will continue to wage the most resolute struggle for the repeal of these laws [Paragraph 175] in the future" (Steakley 1975, 85). Wilhelm Reich's Sexpol movement became active within the party in 1930–31 and Communist deputies supported repeal in parliamentary committees at this time.

The dream of a land with the freedom to love recurs frequently in gay writing. Whether in Melville's voyages to Polynesia, the flight of so many American writers to Paris, Isherwood in Berlin, or Gide in Algeria, many sought (and some found) countries where they could escape the anti-sexual suffocation of their homeland. The socialist critique of bourgeois morality promised as well to overcome the contemporary system that claimed liberty and equality for itself but instead appropriated them for the monied classes. That the Soviet Union raised such hopes in the 1920s cannot be surprising, and Gide among others became increasingly involved in the Communist movement (Mann 1948, 151). With high expectations, Gide went to Moscow in 1936 where he found not freedom but a new bureaucratic class upholding the Stalin personality cult and enforcing a rigid ideological conformity in the press, in art and music, and in family and sexual life (see Gide 1937).

What went wrong? The debates over the "betrayal" of the Russian Revolution continue unabated today, though few efforts have been made to explain the dramatic reversals of Soviet policy on the family and sexuality. What we do know is that grass-roots organizations gave way to a new dictatorial state that exerted unprecedented control over all of Russian life. As early as 1921, workers' councils were replaced by a central administration for directing economic production and distribution. By 1929, unions had lost "rights to participate in enterprise management and to bargain over wages and working conditions on behalf of their worker members" (Skocpol 1979, 219, 228); moreover, the nonparty press was choked off (Medvedev 1977, 205). The Communist state under Stalin's leadership embarked on a crash program to industrialize an essentially peasant society and to seize direct control of agricultural production from its peasant holders. The result, in Alvin Gouldner's words, was "a regime of terror aiming at the collectivization of property" conducted by an "urban-centered power elite that had set out to dominate a largely rural society to which they related as an alien colonial power" (1980, 214, 226). This war against the peasantry consolidated a centralized state that suppressed all opposition through a massive police and prison apparatus that knew no bounds in imagining enemies.

From 1933 to 1938 the terror encompassed the Communist party itself. Half of the party membership was arrested, and as Nikita Khrushchev later revealed, 70 percent of the party's Central Committee was "arrested and shot": "Stalin killed and tortured more Communists than any other dictator in the 20th century" (233, 256). Thus, Stalin and the Soviet state bureaucracy succeeded through the 1930s in eliminating most of the original revolutionaries and much of the socialist program. "Persons were jailed, shot or exiled not because of what they had done but because of their supposed readiness to do injury to Soviet society inferred on the basis of their social category: social origin, nationality or group membership" (234). Ironically, Stalin restored many of the characteristics of absolute monarchy in his personal dictatorship and persecution of traditional outgroups of Russian society: Jews, intellectuals, national minorities—and gay people.

John Lauritsen and David Thorstad state:

In January 1934, mass arrests of gays were carried out in Moscow, Leningrad, Kharkov, and Odessa. Among those arrested were a great many actors, musicians, and other artists. They were accused of engaging in "homosexual orgies," and were sentenced to several years of imprisonment or exile in Siberia. (1974, 68; see also Hauer 1984)

Homosexuality was recriminalized in 1934, punishable by a five-year prison sentence, and other social legislation was rolled back: abortion of first pregnancies was outlawed in 1936, and all abortions in 1944. Divorce became subject to fines and common-law marriage lost legal recognition (Millett 1969, 172).

Because the subject of homosexuality remains under ban in the Soviet Union today, little is known about early gay life in the country. Mikhail Kuzmin's 1904 book, *Wings,* suggests the existence of an early gay intelligentsia in Russia similar to that found in the rest of Europe (see Karlinsky 1979). Hirschfeld includes Saint Petersburg among the European centers with a gay life in his 1905 book (1975). Kuzmin's lover was among the victims of the terror and "Kuzmin himself was reportedly on the list of those to be executed when he died in 1936" (Lauritsen and Thorstad 1974, 65).

Herbert Marcuse's analysis of Soviet Marxism suggests one explanation for the reactionary morality of Stalinism (1961). As the Soviet state pressed for rapid industrialization, it installed the productivist/reproductivist ethic favored by Victorian capitalists, which similarly aimed to create an expanding labor supply and disciplined work force. The anti-homosexual laws of the Stalinist period remain on the books to this day, and the state monopoly of the communications media assures an almost unbroken silence on the subject. The full story of the Stalinist terror and gay people has yet to be told (but see Jong 1985).

Nazism

In 1933 the early gay movement came to an abrupt end. With the Nazi party in power, the German state made every effort to wipe away the restive, subordinated groups who agitated for their rightful places in German society. The Nazi machine crushed workers' and women's movements, Communists and socialists, peace activists and dissidents. With a racial ideology glorifying the "Aryan," it developed a network of concentration camps to contain and destroy "inferior" peoples: Jews, Slavs, Gypsies, criminals, the disabled, Jehovah's Witnesses—and gay people. The Nazis wanted to roll back history to an earlier, supposedly more harmonious era of German greatness. To do so required the removal of the "abrasive" groups of the modern period. Ernst Röhm, leader of the Nazi party militia (the *Sturmabteilung*), characterized the ascendance of Nazism in these words: "National Socialism signifies a spiritual rupture with the thinking of the French Revolution of 1789" (Gallo 1972, 36). Not only would the peoples released by the collapse of feudalism be driven out; even the memory of them would be extinguished. And, with the gay movement, they almost succeeded. Even after World War II, the early gay movement shrank to no more than a rumor and a hope for the mass of lesbians and gay men. A new generation grew up isolated from a cultural heritage that had embodied its experiences and possibilities.

Extreme conservative forces had always been forthright in their hatred of gay people. They had assaulted Hirschfeld in 1920, and in 1921 he was so badly beaten that some newspapers printed an obituary. With shifting government coalitions in the 1920s, censorship returned and gay and lesbian journals were banned in 1926 and 1928. Anti-vice crusaders, some with roots in the established Protestant church, called more stridently for the suppression of homosexuality.[1] The Nazi party had been unambiguous in its reply to Adolf Brand's survey of candidates for the 1928 election: "Anyone who even thinks of homosexual love is our enemy. We reject anything which emasculates our people and makes it a plaything for our enemies, for we know that life is a fight and it's madness to think that men will ever embrace fraternally" (Steakley 1975, 84).

Still, it seems that many in the gay movement—like so many others—did not take the Nazi threat seriously in the early days. Was not Ernst Röhm himself homosexual and a member of the Bund für Menschenrecht? Still even the Social Democrats, in a replay of 1907, could not resist baiting the Nazis with the charge of homosexuality in high places, thereby adopting the Nazi's own rhetoric by claiming that the "moral and physical health of German youth stands at risk" because of it (Stümke and Finkler 1981, 124). As the Gestapo closed the gay press in the first months of the Nazi regime, the final issues of gay journals were announcing upcoming dances and meetings, showing few signs of their impending fate.[2] Christopher Isherwood remarked, "Boy bars of every sort were being raided, now, and many were shut down" (1976, 124). (Isherwood subsequently fled Berlin for England.) On 27 February 1933, Max Hodann and Felix Halle of the Institute for Sex Research were arrested, and on 23 March Kurt Hiller, the leading organizer of the sex law reform coalition of the 1920s, was seized and imprisoned in the Oranienburg concentration camp. (Hiller was released after nine months and escaped to Prague and later London with Walter Schultz, a man he met in the Oranienburg camp who was to become his lover of thirty years.)

On the morning of 6 May 1933, a hundred Nazi students from a nearby school for physical education appeared at the doors of the Institute for Sex Research.

They smashed the doors down and rushed into the building. They spent the morning pouring ink over carpets and manuscripts and loading their trucks with books from the Institute's library, including many which had nothing to do with sex: historical works, art journals, etc. . . . A few days after the raid, the seized books and papers were publicly burned along with a bust of Hirschfeld, on the square in front of the Opera House. (Isherwood 1976, 129).

Like the sacking of the ancient library at Alexandria, which blotted out a good deal of ancient culture from human history, the Nazis destroyed twelve thousand books and thirty-five thousand pictures (Steakley 1975, 105), burning much of the heritage of those who dared to love others of their own sex. Hirschfeld was already outside Germany and tried to start again in Paris, but he died in Nice on 15 May 1935. His lover, Kurt Giese, once a secretary at the institute, moved on to Prague, where he committed suicide in 1936 (Isherwood 1976, 129).

Switzerland became a sanctuary for other refugees from Nazism. Helene Stöcker, Anita Augspurg, and Lida Heymann, all veterans of Mutterschutz and the struggle to define a progressive women's movement, fled to Switzerland. Stöcker continued on to the United States. All three died in 1943 (Evans 1976, 264). Stefan George, the homoerotic poet, also took refuge in Switzerland, and *Der Kreis,* a publication founded in

1932, became the only gay journal to survive the war by moving to Zurich (Hocquenghem 1979, 93; Bullough 1976, 664).

Just what elements of German society propelled the Nazi party to power remains a subject of scholarly debate. Most evidence points to a threefold coalition. Among the early adherents of Nazism were followers of the old conservative political parties: the agrarian aristocracy (the Junkers), the military, the bureaucracy, and the church—in short, the old imperial establishment deposed at the end of World War I. The second major bloc of support came from major industrialists, who still remembered the 1918 revolution and saw Nazism as a bulwark against the popularity of socialism among German workers. When the Nazis did come to power, they assured a passive work force for the capitalist elite by abolishing or taking over trade unions and imprisoning the political Left. Third and more difficult to assess is the mass base of the Nazi movement. Strong suspicion has also been cast upon those elements of the German population who had lost status during the preceding decades because their jobs had disappeared owing to the advance of technology, competition from big business, or the inflation crisis of 1923–24. It was "the small peasant farmers, the independent artisans and the rest of the multifarious mass of individual tradesmen, petty entrepreneurs, salesmen and shopkeepers" (Sohn-Rethel 1978, 131) who were most attracted to the Nazi promise to restore a lost, more orderly and comfortable world.[3]

This powerful reactionary coalition lashed out at all the symbols of the modern era that provoked in them such insecurity and resentment. Nazism revived much of the ultraconservative ideology propagated by the prewar imperial court. Adolf Stöcker, the court preacher attached to the kaiser, had consistently denounced Jews, feminists, liberals, and gay people for creating the ills of German society throughout the imperial regime (Steakley 1975, 37). Now Himmler believed women's organizations to be "a catastrophe," which masculinized women, destroyed their charm, and led the way to gender-mixing and homosexuality (Vismar 1977, 314, my translation). Ironically, the Bund Deutsches Frauenverein, the major women's organization, was already on record as "combating sexual libertarianism, pornography, abortion, venereal diseases, advertisements for contraceptives and the double standard" and could only vainly protest its solidarity with Nazism when it was dissolved in 1933 in favor of the Nazis' own *Frauenfront* (Evans 1976, 237, 254ff.). In the 1930s, women were removed from government and the professions in accord with Nazi policy, which prescribed women's place as being among "children, church, and kitchen" (*Kinder, Kirche, Küche*), but women quietly resumed wage labor during the war years, as they did in the United States, in order to fill the labor shortage created as male workers went to battle (Evans 1976, 262; Millett 1969, 159–66).

For those who nourished illusions about Nazi intentions toward gay people, the Night of Long Knives was a grim awakening. On the weekend of 30 June through 1 July 1934, Hitler, Himmler, and Göring had several hundred political rivals murdered. Among them were the Strasser brothers, who had taken too seriously the "Socialist" claim of "National Socialism" by calling for implementation of such early elements of the Nazi program as abolition of incomes unearned through work, nationalization of trusts, and a ban on land speculation. Also executed where the holdouts from the old imperial regime who balked at the Nazi line. But the best-known victim was Ernst Röhm, who led a "vicious and quite popular struggle against the old order in general" and had dared to call for a "Second Revolution" against "reactionaries [and] bourgeois conformists" in April of 1934 (Gallo 1972, 37; Geyer 1984, 204).

When Adolf Hitler stood before the Reichstag two weeks after the Night of Long Knives, he denounced supposed international Communist and Jewish "conspiracies," Röhm's "plot" against the regime, and his "vice," claiming that some of Röhm's associates had been caught in bed with male lovers on that fateful weekend. Meanwhile the Nazi press defamed Röhm's militia for its "homosexual cliques."

Nazi doctrine constructed homosexuality as an urban corruption and a disease alien to "healthy" village life, but easily spread through seduction and propaganda. With a single-minded pronatalist policy aimed toward producing "Aryan" Germans, sterilization and extermination were reserved for subordinated peoples, including homosexuals. In 1934, Paragraph 175 was extended to include "a kiss, an embrace, even homosexual fantasies," and in 1936, Himmler reorganized the Gestapo to create a division responsible for ferreting out political and religious dissidents, Freemasons, and homosexuals. In 1940, Himmler ordered that everyone completing a prison term under Paragraph 175 was to be sent to a concentration camp if they had had "more than one partner."[4]

Just how many gay people died at the hands of the Nazis will never be known. Concentration camp officials destroyed many of the records as the Allied armies marched into Germany, and other records held in East Germany remain closed. From his examination of extant camp records, Rüdiger Lautmann offers a conservative estimate of five thousand to fifteen thousand camp inmates designated as homosexuals by a pink triangle (1980–81). The Gestapo had a number of ready-made resources for locating gay people when Hitler became chancellor of Germany. One police district alone in Berlin had an accumulated list of thirty thousand names of suspected homosexuals in its files. Some fifty thousand people were convicted under Paragraph 175 during the Nazi period, and judicial files existed on many more convicted before 1933 (Steakley 1975, 110, 113; Herzer 1985; Stümke and Finkler 1981, 263–67). And certainly the many collaborators and sympathizers with Nazism were no more loath to turn in their homosexual neighbors than they were to hand over Jews and the many other victims of Nazi terror.

As Germany invaded other European countries, it cast its deadly net wider. The Nederlandsch Wetenschappelijk-Humanitair Kommittee, which had existed from 1911, fell in 1940, and bar raids took many more, a move welcomed by the Dutch Roman Catholic church, which had been campaigning for the suppression of gay people throughout the 1920s (Tielman 1979; Rogier 1969). Heinz Heger, a twenty-two-year-old Austrian student, was arrested in 1939 on the basis of an intercepted postcard he had addressed to his lover (1980, 19, 39). Those caught by the police network included "unskilled workers and shop assistants, skilled tradesmen and independent craftsmen, musicians and artists, professors and clergy, even aristocratic landowners" (Heger 1980, 9; see Lenz 1979, 29).

Camp prisoners were classified by a set of colored triangles: green for criminals, red for Communists, blue for emigrants, black for "asocials," purple for Jehovah's Witnesses, brown for Gypsies, yellow for Jews, and pink for homosexuals (Lautmann 1980–81). Most camp observers agree that, despite the desperate conditions afflicting all prisoners, an internal hierarchy could be discerned. Greens and reds more often achieved easier jobs, supervisory positions, and thus better diets, while brown, yellow, and pink triangles were subjected to disproportionate violence, hard labor, and starvation (Heger 1980, 32; Kogon 1976, 44). Heger recounts the relentless beatings and pointless labor experienced by pink-triangle inmates, being forced to stand naked in subzero weather, and dawn-to-dusk work moving snow with their bare hands from one side of a road to the other and then back again (Heger 1980, 35).[5] In Sachsenhausen, most homosexuals were included among laborers sent to the clay pits (for brick manufacture) in order to load and push rail carts. Supplied with a diet that fell below the daily minimum necessary for survival and subjected to Gestapo violence, homosexuals suffered an extremely high death rate. Lautmann, Grikschat, and Schmidt quote a survivor who observed: "The SS were glad if several 175ers were left on the road by evening. When in January 1943, the number of dead homosexuals at Klinker [clay pits] reached a total of 24 in a single day, commanding head-quarters became somewhat disquieted. There followed a pause." (1977, 349, my translation). Comparison of the camp records of red-, purple-, and pink-triangle prisoners shows that the death rate for homosexuals was half again as high as for the other two categories (350).

Late in the war, Himmler toyed with the idea of "curing" homosexuals by forcing them to visit brothels. (Heger asked stand-ins to take his place.) Once, he ordered that homosexuals willing to be castrated would be released to fight at the Russian front (Heger 1980, 98; Lenz 1979, 31). Tiring of this, the Gestapo subjected homosexuals and other pris-oners to the notorious "medical experiments" conducted by physicians who mutilated, injected, burned, and froze prisoners to death in the name of science.

Rudolf Höss, the commandant of Sachsenhausen and later of Ausch-witz, wrote this observation in his diary:

Should one of these [pink triangles] lose his "friend" through sickness, or perhaps death, then the end could be at once foreseen. Many would commit suicide. To such natures, in such circumstances, the "friend" meant everything. There were many instances of "friends" committing suicide together. (1951, 104–5)

Perhaps most ironic of all is what little effect the genocide of gay peo-ple had upon homosexuality as a whole. Eugen Kogon observed that "homosexual practices were actually very widespread in the camps. The prisoners, however, ostracized only those whom the SS marked with the pink triangle" (1976, 43; see Heger 1980, 61). Heger could never quite understand why his persecutors would beat him for being homosexual and then force him to commit homosexual acts with them (29)! It was as if a great enough sacrifice to the altar of morality released them from its obligations (see Adam 1978, 69–77, 54–58). Whatever gods the Nazis served, the genocide of a generation of homosexuals, the extermination of gay thought, and the intense supervision of those who might be tempt-ed to homosexuality were not enough to contain the human potential for same-sex love.

The Holocaust then effectively wiped away most of the early gay cul-ture and its movement through systematic extermination and ideological control. Its legacy was a willful forgetting by both capitalist and communist elites who tacitly confirmed the Nazis' work by denying lesbians and gay men any public existence. The doctors, the bishops, and the police could now fully occupy the gay domain. A new generation awoke to homosexual feelings reviled as "sick," "sinful," and "criminal"; they could find one another and their tradition only at great personal cost. But unlike the third- and fourth-world peoples decimated or annihilated by European colonialism, lesbians and gay men emerged in undiminished numbers in new generations. Not reliant on biological reproduction, a gay and lesbian nation grew up again in the very heart of its enemies. No matter how fervent the hatred of judges or psychiatrists, politicians or business people, preachers or patriarchs, same-sex love appeared again among their own sons and daughters as it did in the rest of society.

Chapter Four

The Homophiles Start Over

The McCarthy Terror

When lesbians and gay men organized again after World War II, they faced a new range of repressive forces in Western Europe and North America. Though fascism was defeated in Germany, a reactionary coalition had mobilized in the United States, reaching its height in the early 1950s with the prosecutorial activities of Senator Joseph McCarthy and the U.S. House Committee on Un-American Activities. Though McCarthy's name has come to characterize the whole era, history is never made by a single individual or lone governmental committee. McCarthyism, like its reactionary predecessors, needed supporters in order to assert power. In the first postwar decade, capitalist and governmental elites deployed their forces to restore the prewar social order and hold off the forces of change. Wartime labor needs had overturned traditional pecking orders among ethnic groups, and families had been disrupted by the mobilization for war. National liberation movements in Asia and Africa were challenging Western domination. McCarthyism was simply the most visible aspect of a restorationist trend that was directly to affect lesbians and gay men.

As early as 1945, the U.S. Chamber of Commerce conducted an active anticommunist campaign. Deeply alarmed by Soviet power in Eastern Europe and later by the 1949 revolution in China, the chamber's program directors drew together big businessmen, the Roman Catholic church hierarchy, federal agencies, and veterans' groups, all of whom held "an apocalyptic view of Communism and an unremitting zeal to defeat the Soviet Union and its American supporters" (Irons 1974, 79). The apparently growing popularity of the Communist party, with its program to expropriate the business class, appeared to be the most visible of the menacing changes occurring at home. Strong conservative sentiment often arises among groups of people who feel their standard of living is declining and who, consequently, look back in time toward images of a better world. Social research at the time revealed that McCarthyism appealed most to small businessmen (especially the less educated) and long-term Republican voters; both groups responded to the conservative call to preserve the "American way." As with earlier reactionary movements, McCarthyism drew upon "a wistful nostalgia for a golden age of small farmers and businessmen and [was] also an expression of a strong resentment and hatred toward a world which makes no sense in terms of older ideas" (Trow 1958, 270; see Griffith 1974).

As the nation again prepared for war, this time to "stop communism" in Korea, the federal government set up loyalty commissions to examine any connections between government employees and suspected "subversives." The commissions scrutinized their personal lives for what they thought were "tell-tale" details: "communist associates," "un-American" magazines or books, affiliation with Henry Wallace's Progressive party— even "too great sociability with black people or unorthodox styles of dress" (Goldstein 1978, 299–303). When Wallace was trounced at the polls in 1948, even liberal organizations began to yield in the face of McCarthyite campaigns.[1] Congress responded with new laws to ban the Communist party and register members of "subversive" groups; blacklists were drawn up of persons to be seized in case of national emergency, and plans were made for concentration camps to contain them (Goldstein 1978; 322–24).

On the face of it, there is no reason homosexuality should have been mixed into the anticommunist furor, but in McCarthyism as in other reactionary ideologies, psychosymbolic connections between gender and power assigned a place to homosexuality. For the authoritarian mind, male homosexuality signified the surrender of masculinity and the "slide" into "feminine" traits of weakness, duplicity, and seductiveness. As Leslie Fiedler remarks,

McCarthy touched up the villain he had half-found half-composed, adding the connotations of wealth and effete culture to treachery, and topping all off with the suggestion of homosexuality. . . . The definition of the enemy is complete—

opposite in all respects to the American Ideal, simple, straightforward, ungrammatical, loyal, and one-hundred-percent male. (1954, 77)

Like the German militarists of the Weimar period or the British at the time of Napoleon, the McCarthyites drew together personal feelings of self-esteem expressed in terms of "manhood" with national self-esteem and belligerence. Working within a gender discourse that associated maleness with toughness and effectiveness, in opposition to supposedly female weakness and failure, male homosexuality symbolized the betrayal of manhood—the feminine enemy within men.

A 1949 *Newsweek* article called "Queer People" had already named homosexuals as "sex murderers," echoing a consistent media theme identifying homosexuals as destroyers of society.[2] From there, it was but a small step to brand gay people as traitors and to call for their expulsion from public life (Adam 1978, 46–48).

In 1950, a series of incidents injected homosexuality into the rising anticommunist tide. With loyalty commissions so closely scrutinizing the personal lives of government workers, it is not entirely surprising that homosexuality should be turned up and labeled as one of the suspect behaviors. In March, the testimony of John Peurifoy of the State Department security program identified homosexuals as among the "security risks." In April, Guy Gabrielson, national chairman of the Republican party declared, "Perhaps as dangerous as the actual Communists are the sexual perverts who have infiltrated our Government in recent years." In May, New York State governor Thomas Dewey "accused the Democratic national administration of tolerating spies, traitors, and sex offenders in the Government service." In June, an inquisitorial subcommittee met to investigate "Employment of Homosexuals and Other Sex Perverts in Government" (Katz 1976, 91–94). The subcommittee's December 1950 report projected a right-wing paranoia, claiming homosexuals to be subject to blackmail, emotionally unstable, and of weak "moral fiber." "One homosexual can pollute a Government office," they wrote, calling for a thorough purge of homosexuals from government and revealing that between 1947 and 1950, some 1,700 applicants for government jobs had already been turned down because of homosexuality, 4,380 had been expelled from the military, and 420 were forced to resign or were dismissed from the government.[3] John D'Emilio estimates that 40 to 60 lesbians and gay men were dismissed per month between 1950 and 1953 (1983, 41–44).

Nor was the repression restricted to the federal level. It extended to state and local governments throughout the country and even spilled over to other nations in the Western alliance. Police departments did not hesitate to round up dozens—sometimes hundreds—who dared turn up in lesbian and gay bars; others were entrapped in parks or on the street and pressed to reveal their friends who would then, in turn, be subjected to similar treatment. Local politicians in Miami ordered beach sweeps in 1953 and outlawed the wearing of drag. Following the murder of a gay man in 1954, Miami newspapers "demand[ed] that the homosexuals be punished for tempting 'normals' to commit such deeds" (Taylor 1982, 9)! A 1953 New Orleans bar raid netted 64 lesbians, and a 1955 Baltimore raid got 162 gay men—the list is lengthy (D'Emilio 1983, 50ff). Perhaps the best-documented antigay panic occurred in Boise, Idaho, in 1955. A small state capital dominated by a conservative Mormon elite, Boise erupted in a major scandal (after a teenage boy admitted to engaging in sex with a local man), which resulted in nine men being sentenced to five-to-fifteen-year prison terms for the crime of being homosexual (Gerassi 1966). And in 1958, a Florida senator succeeded in having sixteen faculty and staff members purged from the state university at Gainesville and in having a state committee publish pamphlets "to prepare . . . children to meet the temptations of homosexuality lurking today in the vicinity of nearly every institution of learning" (Fla. Leg. Inv. Comm. 1975; see D'Emilio 1983). In response, many bars and dance clubs developed elaborate defense systems with double doors opened only after patrons were screened. Should the police appear at the door, lights could be turned up to alert everyone inside to act "straight" until the danger passed.

McCarthyism invaded Canada with a decade of antigay witch-hunts conducted in the Canadian Broadcasting Corporation, the National Film Board, and the National Research Council. The Royal Canadian Mounted Police even concocted a scheme to map all the homosexuals in Ottawa, a project eventually abandoned when the map at police headquarters became overwhelmed with red dots (Sawatsky 1980, 112–29). In Britain, police tactics took a similar form, and government attacks included among their victims Alan Turing, the mathematician who broke the Nazi code for British intelligence and established the early principles of the computer (Hodges 1984). Prosecutions peaked in 1954 with the conviction of Lord Montagu and Peter Wildeblood. But in Britain, it was a government commission appointed in the same year to study the "problem" of homosexuality that was to turn the tide of antigay persecution.[4] More on this later.

The McCarthy terror exacted an immense toll from ordinary lesbians and gay men, with thousands being thrown out of work and imprisoned in jails and mental hospitals.[5] Today, with the benefit of hindsight, one cannot but marvel at the speed at which the intelligentsia of the day adopted the official line. The mass media applauded the state-directed purges; medical researchers tinkered with lobotomies, castration, and electroshock to "rehabilitate" gay people; churches sanctioned the persecutions as "Christian"; and Hollywood continued revising history with heterosexualized screen biographies of such notables as Valentino, Hans Christian Andersen, Alexander the Great, Michelangelo, and General Charles Gordon (Russo 1981, 66–90). Even the American Civil Liberties Union abandoned both Communists and lesbians at the time of their greatest peril (Bérubé and D'Emilio 1984, 759). It is a legacy stamped even today in immigration laws that forbid the entry of lesbians and gay men to the United States and in decades of dishonorable discharges from the military (see Williams and Weinberg 1971.)

Homophiles Under Siege

> The right which I claim for myself, and for all those like me, is the right to choose the person whom I love.
>
> —Peter Wildeblood, *Against the Law.*

Gay men and lesbians joined with other minorities in the 1950s in pressing for liberal democratic societies to live up to their self-professed ideals of "liberty, equality, and the pursuit of happiness" for all. Only too aware of the climate of repression around them, the first homophile groups typically adopted a cautious approach to social change, hoping first merely for survival and, only then, for an abatement of the general hostility. The Amsterdam Cultuur-en-Ontspannings Centrum (COC) was revived in 1946 from the subscribers' list to *Levensrecht,* the journal of the Netherlands Scientific-Humanitarian Committee. *Levensrecht* had begun publishing in 1940, but with the Nazi invasion imminent, its editor destroyed its records after committing its five hundred members' names and addresses to memory for the period of the war. In Denmark, Axel Axgil and Helmer Fogedgard organized the Forbundet af 1948, issuing the journal *Vennen* the following year and spawning other Scandinavian chapters which became independent in 1951–52—the Riksforbundet for Sexuellt Likaberattigande (RFSL) in Sweden and Det Norske Forbundet av 1948 in Norway. These were not easy times even in northern Europe. Axgil was fired from his job, evicted from his apartment, and expelled from his political party for his organizing efforts. The Roman Catholic church in the Netherlands, having welcomed the Nazi persecution of gay people in official publications during the war, called for recriminalization after. The Norwegian state church warned against a supposed "world conspiracy" of homosexuals in 1954 (Rogier 1969; Ramsay, Heringa, and Boorsma 1974; Offerman 1984; Kleis 1980). Elsewhere, Arcadie in Paris, Mattachine in Los Angeles, and the Daughters of Bilitis in San Francisco found few allies during the cold war of the 1950s.

Wartime left an ambiguous legacy to women, gay people, and national minorities. On the one hand, it had opened unprecedented employment opportunities and exposed millions to new life-styles both at home and abroad. On the other hand, the end of war brought pressures to restore the prewar social order—or an idealized memory of it—and this restoration sought to roll back new financial and personal freedoms.

With great numbers of male workers at the battlefront and a rapidly rising need for military hardware, new jobs had become available during wartime for women and black people in high-paying industrial manufacturing. Government policy had afforded a respite to Mexican workers from the traditional threat of deportation. Women benefited from state-supported day-care services, which allowed them to work and socialize together in unprecedented numbers and to take for granted the freedoms long enjoyed by men such as going out unescorted and patronizing bars on their own (see Bérubé 1983). With greater independence and access to the public world, women increasingly experienced the opportunities that had long permitted men to create gay places and other supportive environments.

The many men and some women who entered military life also overcame small-town isolation, made new friendships in same-sex environments, and encountered gay life in port cities.[6]

At war's end, however, state and economic elites moved decisively to reestablish their version of the "American way of life." As Jo Freeman points out:

The returning soldiers were given the GI Bill and other veterans benefits, as well as their jobs back. Women, on the other hand, saw their child-care centres dismantled and their training programs cease. They were fired or demoted in droves and often found it difficult to enter colleges flooded with ex-GIs matriculating on government money. Labor unions insisted on contracts with separate job categories, seniority lists, and pay scales for men and women. (1975, 23)

Popular women's magazines of the day extolled the virtues of home, husbands, and babies, reasserting the old gender categories. Along with women and minorities, lesbians and gay men came under renewed attack after the war. Official toleration of special friendships among military men and women during the war yielded to concerted propaganda to suppress, isolate, and eliminate them afterward (see Bérubé 1981, 20; D'Emilio 1983, 24–29; Katz 1976, 637). Allan Bérubé and John D'Emilio state that early postwar navy "lectures project a stereotype of lesbians as sexual vampires: manipulative, dominant perverts who greedily seduce young and innocent women into experimenting with homosexual practices that, like narcotics, inevitably lead to a downward spiral of addiction, degeneracy, loneliness, and even murder and suicide" (1984, 759).

Like other subordinated people, lesbians and gay men experienced acute contradictions in the 1950s. After finding new possibilities through war mobilization, they encountered repression in peacetime. Full employment and urban life had been the unintended consequences of national war preparations. But once the ruling elites were freed from Nazi imperialism, they tended only to reestablish the old order.

Out of this tension between new possibilities and renewed suppression, a homophile movement arose. The first stirrings of movement activity in the United States appeared among recently demobilized men in the Veterans Benevolent Association in New York and among working women in Los Angeles. Both groups developed out of existing friendship networks and made no attempt to go public. When "Lisa Ben" printed nine issues of a circular called *Vice Versa* in 1947 and 1948, it received only private distribution among Los Angeles lesbians (D'Emilio 1983, 32; Katz 1983, 618ff.).

Most important of all was the creation of the Mattachine Society in Los Angeles in 1951. Named for the medieval Italian court jester who expressed unpopular truths from behind a mask, Mattachine originated with a comprehensive vision of social and political change for gay people and a willingness to challenge antihomosexual attacks even in the midst of McCarthyism. The idea for Mattachine was developed by Henry Hay, a music history teacher at the People's Educational Center in Los Angeles. Together with Bob Hull and Chuck Rowland, also center workers, Hay drew on Communist models for inspiration in organizing and effecting social change.[7] In its founding statement of "Missions and Purposes," Mattachine pledged:

- "'TO UNIFY' those homosexuals 'isolated from their own kind. . . .'
- 'TO EDUCATE' homosexuals and heterosexuals" toward "an ethical homo-

sexual culture . . . paralleling the emerging cultures of our fellow-minor-
ities—the Negro, Mexican, and Jewish Peoples. . . .
- 'TO LEAD'; the 'more . . . socially conscious homosexuals [are to] provide
  leadership to the whole mass of social deviates'" and also
- "to assist 'our people who are victimized daily as a result of our oppression.'" (Katz 1976, 412; see D'Emilio 1983, 59ff.)

With its first members drawn from signatories to an anti–Korean war
petition circulated around gay beaches, word spread quickly until Mattachine had more than a hundred discussion groups in southern California
in 1953.

There was occasional cause for optimism. The 1948 Kinsey Report
had made a worldwide impact in revealing how widespread homosexual
experience was among Americans. Edward Sagarin (pseudonym, Donald
Webster Cory) published *The Homosexual in America* in 1951. Though
in retrospect a somewhat weepy and ambivalent book, it presented a plea
for toleration and offered the only publicly available presentation of gay
life by a homosexual writer. Also in 1951, the owners of a San Francisco
gay bar, the Black Cat, established in California Supreme Court the right
to serve gay customers. (The state later attempted again to suppress
gay bars with a 1955 law to remove liquor licenses from "resorts for
sexual perverts" [see Martin and Lyon 1972, 234; D'Emilio 1983, 187].)

In its first years, Mattachine secured a public victory by winning an
acquittal for one of its members, Dale Jennings, on a sex charge arising
from police entrapment. A Mattachine discussion group founded *One,* the
first American homophile magazine to be distributed publicly. (Its editorial board comprised two women and four men including Jennings.) But
One soon had to struggle through the courts to lift a ban imposed upon
it by the U.S. Post Office in 1954. (In 1958, the U.S. Supreme Court
ruled that the post office ban violated First Amendment rights to free
speech.)

But the tense political climate of the 1950s set the tone for Mattachine's first convention in 1953. After a tumultuous weekend sorting
through Mattachine objectives, its founders bowed out in favor of an
anticommunist Coordinating Council led by Kenneth Burns, Marilyn Rie-
ger, and Hal Call. The change in leadership brought a dramatic reversal
in Mattachine policy. In what John D'Emilio calls a "retreat to respectability," Mattachine adopted a low-profile, accommodationist stand that
defined movement strategies for more than a decade.

The approach of the new leadership was premised on the belief that
assimilation into the larger society could be accomplished more readily

by minimizing the "disability" that stood in the way of full participation. The assimilationists insisted that gay people are just the same as heterosexuals except for what they do in bed. The appropriate strategy for attaining equality, then, was to stress the common humanity of homosexuals and heterosexuals and keep sexuality as such private. It was an approach founded on an implicit contract with the larger society wherein gay identity, culture, and values would be disavowed (or at least concealed) in return for the *promise* of equal treatment. The movement would "educate" away the "prejudices" of the ignorant and rely on "goodwill." Tolerance would be earned by making difference unspeakable (see Adam 1978, Chaps. 4–5, esp. p. 121). By 1959, Mattachine had retreated so far from the possibility of open confrontation that it "billed itself as an organization 'interested in the problems of homosexuality,'" not as a gay organization at all (Martin and Lyon 1972, 231). The term *homophile* became virtually synonymous with the assimilationist strategy at this time.[8]

When the Daughters of Bilitis came into being in 1955, the homophile platform was clear in its orientation. Named for Pierre Louys's poems on a lesbian theme, the Daughters of Bilitis (DOB) was founded by four couples in San Francisco and was the first postwar lesbian organization. Under the leadership of Del Martin as president and Phyllis Lyon as editor of the *Ladder* (founded the following year), DOB stated its objectives to be:

- "Education of the variant"
- Development of a library on the "sex deviant" theme
- Public discussions "to be conducted by leading members of the legal, psychiatric, religious and other professions"
- "Advocating a mode of behavior and dress acceptable to society" (see Martin and Lyon 1972, 219; Faderman 1981, 378–79; Katz 1976, 420–26)

Later the association added to its aims "participation in research projects" and "investigation of the penal code as it pertains to the homosexual. . . . and promotion of these changes through the due process of law in the state legislatures."

After the McCarthy terror, accommodation seemed the only realistic choice. Like other minorities facing a seemingly unmerciful oppressor, the homophiles sought to placate the enemy by being law-abiding and deferential and by lying low. The authorities seemed to have become wild beasts; there was nothing to be done but appease them, mollify them, and hope they would exhaust their malicious rage (see Adam 1978, chap. 4, esp. p. 95).

In Europe, the United States and the Soviet Union had settled on a division of the spoils, setting up national governments in their own images: Soviet central bureaucracies in the East, conservative capitalist governments in the West. For gay people, the war's end entrenched losses suffered through the Holocaust. Pink-triangle prisoners released from the concentration camps found that they were still criminals in both the Soviet and American occupied zones and, as such, ineligible for compensation or even recognition as victims of fascism (Hohmann 1982, 27; Stümke and Finkler 1981). The psychiatrists and criminologists, who had gained a monopoly over the public discussion of homosexuality with Nazi sponsorship, retained their dominance in the cold war period. With American occupation, the McCarthyite chill descended over Western Europe, and gay organizations necessarily shared the cautious homophile approach to social reform.

The Netherlands COC sponsored five International Conferences for Sexual Equality between 1951 and 1958, offering support and, most important, hope for lesbian and gay organization in Europe. In West Germany, two decades of Christian Democratic government preserved Paragraph 175 within a larger "God-and-family" social policy, which resisted all attempts at reform despite a 1949 petition by surviving adherents of the Scientific-Humanitarian Committee to abolish it. For gay men, the 1950s offered little improvement over the Nazi era; prosecutions under Paragraph 175 actually *increased* in the period 1953–65 compared with the years of the Third Reich. Among those incarcerated in German prisons in the 1950s and 1960s were former concentration camp victims who now received sentences as long as six years as "repeat offenders" for not renouncing their homosexuality (Stümke and Finkler 1981, 368–70; Schilling 1983). Two of the many testimonials gathered by Joachim Hohmann in *Keine Zeit für gute Freunde* express the mood of the period:

The younger generation can scarcely conceive how gays used to have to live: always fearing for their livelihood, freedom and reputation, always having to play-act in order not to raise suspicions.

Friendships, if they came about at all, were constantly dependent upon the perceptiveness of prudish neighbors, the sharp eyes of the police, on jealous friends, and even the "toleration" of one's own relatives. (1982, 151, 24, my translation)

In 1955, West Berlin confirmed the Nazis' seizure and pillage of the Institute for Sex Research by retaining legal title to its land and property (and remained intransigent in this claim despite gay movement protests in the 1980s). In this political climate, only scattered, clandestine, and very small homophile groups came into existence, often as circles of friends who put out magazines that made oblique references to homosexuality or as human rights groups addressed to general law reform. The expatriate Swiss journal *Der Kreis,* published throughout the period until 1967 (opening the way for the Swiss Organization of Homophiles), and the International Conference for Sexual Equality issued a German newsletter from Amsterdam from 1951 to 1958. As early as 1953, the Hamburg Society for Human Rights (Gesellschaft für Menschenrechte) issued the journal *Humanitas.* Other publishing ventures such as *Der Ring* and *Freond* soon dissolved as their editors were jailed by the authorities. An attempt by Kurt Hiller to refound the Scientific-Humanitarian Committee in 1962 met with little success (Hohmann 1982, 21–27; Stümke and Finkler 1981, 340–409; Baumgardt 1984b, 38; Werres 1973). None could overtly present itself as gay oriented. For Germans, the advent of gay liberation in the 1970s would offer the first opportunity for open organization.

In France, André Beaudry gathered together the subscribers to *Der Kreis* in Paris to found Arcadie in 1951.[9] The free and easy days of the 1920s and 1930s were gone, extinguished through Nazi rule. The conservative governments of the 1950s hedged round gay existence with catch-all laws. A law raising the age of consent to twenty-one was retained from the previous profascist Vichy government. In 1946, a "good morals" law limited the employment of gay people in public service. In 1949, the Paris police chief banned transvestite balls and forbade men from dancing together, ending a tradition extending back into the nineteenth century. In the same year, a new solicitation law criminalized "provocative attitudes" in public places. *Futur,* a "journal of information for sexual equality and freedom," which appeared from 1952 to 1955, was suspended in 1953 and again in 1954 under the same law that had felled *Amitié* (Girard 1981, 13–39).

Arcadie attracted such well-known writers as Jean Cocteau and Roger Peyrefitte and succeeded in issuing a high-toned "literary and scientific review" called *Arcadie* in 1954. Jacques Girard describes Arcadie's approach as a sort of "ministry" to "the profound physical and moral distress of homophiles," linking it to the seminarian background of its founder (44–48, my translation). Like its homophile counterparts in the United States, Arcadie assumed a quietist disengagement from public action in the 1950s, stressing moral discipline and respect for law, morality, and public powers. Indeed, when it opened its clubhouse, CLESPALA (Club Littéraire et Scientifique des Pays Latins), in 1957, it insisted on observing the norms of heterosexist propriety by forbidding kissing on the dance floor (57, 71)!

By the end of the decade, the Mouvement Republicain Populaire, the political arm of the French Roman Catholic church, began to press for further "moral reform," and in 1960, a conference sponsored by the church and the psychiatric profession denounced a supposed "homosexual peril." Soon the Gaullist government had declared homosexuality a "social plague" along with alcoholism and prostitution (15–19; see Hocquenghem 1978, 51).

In the United Kingdom a government commission appointed to investigate the "problems" of homosexuality and prostitution produced an unexpectedly liberal recommendation in 1957. The homophile movement in Britain came about specifically to preserve and promote the commission's recommendation that "homosexual behavior between consenting adults in private should no longer be a criminal offense" (Wolfenden et al. 1962, 25). The Wolfenden Commission resisted the efforts of some of its own members who were physicians to force all gay men into therapy, prompting a minority report from the doctors who decided that anyway "a prison sentence could have therapeutic value" (76). The report reached its liberal conclusion via a tortuous path, reasoning that children must be saved from homosexuality through stiffer penalties on underage sex and that the age of consent be set at twenty-one; that military homosexuality remain criminal for the "preservation of discipline"; and that family breakdown be averted by avoiding the "disaster" of homosexuals marrying.

In an effort to keep the spirit of reform alive, the Homosexual Reform Society and its "charity arm," the Albany Trust, were founded in 1958. Like its predecessors, the society disavowed any identification with being homosexual in favor of prestigious sponsors. Eventually a newsletter, *Spectrum,* appeared; a public forum was held in 1960; and a journal, *Man and Society,* was issued in 1961—all founded squarely on the Wolfenden Report's right-to-privacy argument (Weeks 1977, 168–72).

In the 1950s, then, lesbian and gay organizations were lone voices with little ability to break through the ideological fog generated by the media and the professional and legal establishments. The 1950s generation had been effectively severed from a rich history of gay writing through systematic obliteration of their cultural heritage by fascism. But gay people themselves could not but recognize anew that the official ideologies presented by church, medicine, and police offered, at best, twisted and alien images of their own experiences and elaborate lies about their feelings and intentions (see Adam 1978, 30–53). The homophiles believed that forthright opposition to the official line would invite swift retaliation, concluding that assimilationism would be the safest course of action. The homophiles deferred to the professionals, hoping to engage them in dialogue and believing that conformity would bring toleration.[10]

The lesbian and gay movements were not alone in these dilemmas, and as a new militancy began to sweep black people, students, war draftees, Chicanos, and women in the 1960s, they began to reassess the assimilationist strategy.

The Rise of the New Left

Like members of other minority groups, homosexuals are interested in their rights, freedom, and basic human dignity, as homosexuals.

—Franklin Kameny,
founder of the Mattachine Society of Washington

Lesbians and gay men were not the only casualties of the 1950s restoration of traditionally privileged classes in North America and Western Europe. The pioneering efforts of black people in the American South in challenging the established political order were to galvanize a disparate set of aggrieved social groups through the 1960s. The proliferating social movements of the decade, which came to be known as the New Left, engendered a militancy in the gay community that overturned the homophile approach. Like the early German gay movement before it, the homophile movement of the 1960s expanded and reorganized as part of a larger social upheaval and soon began to question the premises of the assimilationist approach.

Important for the new outlook was the example set by the Beat generation, at first a small group of outlaw poets who rejected the conservatism of the 1950s by reveling in the forbidden pursuits of drugs, anarchism, and hedonism.[11] Among them were Allen Ginsberg and William Burroughs, who did not hesitate to celebrate homosexuality among other taboo pleasures. Ginsberg wrote his famous "Howl" in 1955 as a paean against the bankruptcy of the repressive consumer society of the day. "Howl" came about at a time when Ginsberg had fallen in love with Peter Orlovsky and among its lines were:

> who let themselves be fucked in the ass by saintly
>   motorcyclists, and screamed with joy,
> who blew and were blown by those human seraphim,
>   the sailors, caresses of Atlantic and Caribbean love

—lines that put the poem's publisher in court facing obscenity charges.[12] (He was acquitted.) The Beats gave new life to the artistic and bohemian districts of San Francisco (the North Beach) and New York (Greenwich Village), which developed in the 1960s as free zones for cultural dissidents of all types. Many gay men and lesbians were among those who sought refuge and new lives there.

But San Francisco was not yet ready to recognize its homosexual minority when the subject became an issue in the 1959 city election. By that year, the Daughters of Bilitis had chapters in New York, Los Angeles, Chicago, and, briefly, Rhode Island, as well as San Francisco, and Mattachine had small groups in San Francisco, Los Angeles, New York, Boston, Denver, Philadelphia, and for a time Detroit, Chicago, and Washington, D.C.[13] Both groups were by now holding national conventions and in 1959 Mattachine met in Denver in September, where for the first time it received relatively positive newspaper coverage. It was a short-lived success. In October, Denver police raided the homes of Mattachine leaders, jailing one and procuring the dismissal of another from his job. The *San Francisco Progress* proclaimed, "Sex Deviates make S. F. Headquarters," and the opposition candidate in the city's mayoral election accused the incumbent of tolerating vice. As John D'Emilio remarks, "The San Francisco press criticized Wolden [the opposition candidate] not because he had attacked a persecuted minority but because, as the *Examiner* put it, he had 'stigmatized the city' by suggesting that it tolerated such life-styles" (1983, 121-22; see Martin and Lyon 1972, 227). When gay bar owners revealed to an investigatory commission the following year that they had been forced to pay off San Francisco police officers in order to stay open, the police retaliated with mass roundups of bar patrons through 1960 and 1961 until all the bar owners who had testified were out of business. The upshot was a Tavern Guild of bar owners determined to support one another against police assaults (D'Emilio 1983, 182–84, 189).

In 1955–56, Martin Luther King, Jr., came to prominence as black people in Montgomery, Alabama, boycotted the city's segregated bus system. Like so many other social movements that came to have a profound impact upon their societies, the early black movement had the initially "conservative" intention of enforcing the law and fulfilling the promise of liberal democratic societies. It worked through the late 1950s and the early 1960s to reclaim basic rights to vote and to receive public services; it demanded that black people be integrated into schools and universities, into restaurants and transportation facilities—in short, to be *let in* to American society—and it worked to achieve these ends through nonviolent public action.

It was a struggle that caught the imagination of people around the world. College support for the civil rights struggle coalesced in the Student Nonviolent Coordinating Committee formed in 1960 to work with the voter registration project and participate in the freedom rides to integrate the bus system. Preparation by the Kennedy and Johnson administrations for yet another foreign war to "stop communism"—this time in Vietnam—further impelled both students and blacks (traditionally among the first groups to be drafted for war duty) toward civil disobedience. An anti-war movement began to emerge among once complacent sectors of the population.

Hopeful signs appeared in 1961. Illinois adopted the Model Legal Code of the American Law Institute, thereby becoming the first state to decriminalize homosexuality between consenting adults in private (Gunnison 1969, 119). The Motion Picture Association of America reversed the Motion Picture Code to accommodate Otto Preminger's *Advise and Consent*, thereby lifting the ban on gay themes in the movies. (The homosexual character in *Advise and Consent* nevertheless is obliged to commit suicide [Russo 1981, 121].) A Black Cat drag queen, José Sarria, declared himself a candidate for city supervisor of San Francisco, winning six thousand votes (D'Emilio 1983, 188; see also Adair and Adair 1978, 72–73).

Also in 1961, Franklin Kameny founded the Mattachine Society of Washington, D.C., eventually forcing a confrontation with the homophile old guard and opening the way for a more aggressive assertion of gay rights. Kameny was an astronomer who had been dismissed from the federal civil service in 1957 under the security legislation set in place by the McCarthyites. The Mattachine Society of Washington (MSW) made the rounds of the federal agencies in 1962 and 1963, launching complaints against the Civil Service Commission's discriminatory policies and surviving an attempt in the House of Representatives to "revoke Mattachine's permit to raise funds" (D'Emilio 1983, 156; Marotta 1981, 22ff.; Gunnison 1969, 120–21).

Confrontations between police and the black, student, and antiwar movements intensified during this period. In 1963, hundreds of thousands of black people made the March on Washington to demand their civil rights. By 1964, student civil rights workers returning to class from the Mississippi Freedom Summer had shared the experience of black movement workers and began to question the political system that so strongly resisted the implementation of its own liberal principles. Reflecting upon their own roles in the larger capitalist system, the student movement attacked the complicity of the universities, working toward an analysis that punctured the rhetoric of business and political elites and sought to understand the oppression of people (especially nonwhites) both at home and elsewhere in the American empire. No longer was it a question only of the civil rights of black people; students weighed the moral choices inherent in their own lives, believing "that a political movement is created by thousands of individuals who say 'no' to the structures and politics of the dominant society, who refuse to take part and in so doing create a crisis of legitimacy that stops the machine" (Breines 1982, 23).

When Kameny took his message to the Mattachine Society of New York (MSNY) in 1964, he called for "acceptance as full equals . . . basic rights and equality as citizens; our human dignity; . . . our right to the pursuit of happiness . . . right to love whom we wish," making explicit reference to the black civil rights struggle (1969, 144). Gay people, Kameny argued, had been too long the victims of prejudice and discrimination and had too long tolerated medical domination; they needed to proclaim a pride in being gay.

Increasingly, homosexuals are becoming impatient with the place of their traditional role as that of a mere passive, silent battlefield, across which conflicting "authorities" parade and fight out their questionable views, prejudices, and theories. . . . Homosexuality is . . . something around which the homosexual can and should build part of a rewarding and productive life and something he can and should enjoy to its fullest. (130)

In face of the MSNY president's traditional homophile contention that "we must lose the label of homosexual organizations," Kameny asserted simply that "gay is good!" In its 1964 election, MSNY swept away its old leadership (including Edward Sagarin) in favor of an activist slate (see Adam 1978, 89, 145; Marotta 1981, 31).

The move toward activism provoked turmoil among the Daughters of Bilitis. Barbara Gittings, the founder of the New York DOB in 1958, had become the editor of the *Ladder* in 1962, moving the journal toward an "antisick," mass-movement stance. With new militance emerging among the other organizations, the DOB leadership withdrew from the conference of East Coast Homophile Organizations (ECHO) and removed Gittings from the *Ladder* in 1965. Members of DOB, sharply divided between the homophile and new militant strategies, responded by expelling the conservative leadership in favor of its first black president, "Ernestine Eckstein." When the old leadership regained control in 1966, many activists left the DOB for Mattachine (see D'Emilio 1983, 172–73; Katz 1976, 420–26; Marotta 1981, 49).

Meanwhile ECHO groups took to the streets in 1965 in public demonstrations at the Civil Service Commission, Department of State, Pentagon, White House, and Independence Hall in Philadelphia, attracting the attention of national news media. In New York, the city administration had launched a "clean-up" campaign to close gay bars to "improve" the city's image for the World's Fair. When John Lindsay came to the mayor's office, gay leaders pressed for an end to "Operation New Broom" and MSNY held a "sip-in" in a New York bar to establish the right of gay people to attend bars unmolested by police (Marotta 1981, 32, 39; D'Emilio 1983, 164–65).

In San Francisco, four men organized the Society for Individual Rights (SIR) in 1964, attracting several hundred members in a few years. Soon SIR was holding candidates' nights to review election contenders in its own clubhouse, publishing a magazine called *Vector,* and sponsoring a full calendar of dances, drag shows, bridge clubs, bowling leagues, outings, meditation groups, and art classes (D'Emilio 1983, 190–92). With the assistance of Glide Memorial Methodist Church, a black downtown congregation, a Council on Religion and the Homosexual was organized. A fund-raising ball for the council held on New Year's Eve of 1965 turned out six hundred guests who were forced to cross police lines and face police photographers in order to attend. Experiencing for the first time the routine police harassment long endured by gay and lesbian San Franciscans, the council clergymen and lawyers protested loudly to the local press, which in turn made the first serious effort to communicate that abuse to the public at large (D'Emilio 1983, 193–94; Martin and Lyon 1972, 239). The San Francisco movement went on to set up a Citizens Alert telephone line to serve a gamut of youthful, black, Chicano, and gay victims.

The period from 1965 to 1967 marked a new stage for the New Left. The black movement began to come apart over issues of strategy. In 1964, Malcolm X posed the question "ballots or bullets?" and many, despairing of the slow gains made by the integrationists and alarmed by mounting state repression, opted for abandonment of white society and the construction of a black nation. Others argued for a revolutionary transformation of American society to overturn the military-industrial complex that preserved corporate power against the subordinated peoples of America and the third world. Black people in the northern ghettos revolted in a series of urban uprisings through 1967 and 1968. The Students for a Democratic Society faltered through factional in-fighting, while the antiwar movement reached a new height of mass mobilization in marches on Washington.

Though the impermanence of the 1960s movements has since been much lamented on the Left, the "utopian and 'anti-organizational' characteristics of the New Left were among its most vital aspects" (Breines 1982, 5). These qualities empowered and mobilized millions of people and gave voice to new categories of the powerless and oppressed. Out of the decay of the New Left came the modern feminist and gay liberation movements.

Both women and gay people have long been taught to "know their place," to keep silent before their "superiors," and to believe themselves unworthy of the rights and privileges of men and of heterosexuals. Both now found themselves deeply involved in optimistic affirmative movements that ironically exempted them from their programs. As Judith Hole and Ellen Levine note: "Women had gone to the South to work alongside men in the fight for equality only to find that they were second-class citizens in a movement purportedly determined to wipe out all discrimination" (1971, 110; see also Evans 1979; Breines 1979). New Left ideals called for broad-based, egalitarian, participatory democracy, eschewing bureaucracy and leadership for fear the voices of the masses would rapidly disappear through institutionalization. Still, Stokely Carmichael announced that "the only position for women in SNCC is prone," and Eldridge Cleaver denounced homosexuality as an evil as great as being the chairman of General Motors! Student leaders often exhibited the same mentality. Like the Mattachine's early roots in American communism, modern feminism and gay liberation emerged from antecedents that provided them with both political foundations and explicit rejection. Rumblings of discontent among movement women were discernible in 1964. By 1967, the failure of the National Conference for a New Politics to address women's issues led to a walk-out and the formation of feminist groups in Chicago, Toronto, Seattle, Detroit, and Gainesville, Florida (Freeman 1975, 59).

Gay and lesbian groups were springing up across the United States and Canada, jumping from fifteen in 1966 to fifty in 1969 (D'Emilio 1983, 199). A new politicized generation transformed the homophile movement, often sweeping aside the leadership that had survived Mc-

Carthyism. The homophiles, who had been deeply affected by the McCarthy terror, now seemed too cautious, too fearful. Many homophile leaders nevertheless had been inspired by the changes around them. The 1968 North American Conference of Homophile Organizations (NACHO) resolved that "homosexuality is in no way inferior to heterosexuality as a valid way of life" and accepted the "gay is good" credo (Gunnison 1969, 113). Similarly, in Britain the North-Western Homosexual Reform Committee of the Albany Trust rejected the medical doctrine of homosexuality as the British Labour government at last implemented the Wolfenden recommendations in 1967 (Weeks 1977, 181).

But like the black nationalists, the gay and lesbian veterans of the New Left movements no longer wanted to define themselves in terms left over to them by the heterosexist opposition; rather, they sought to build a new gay culture where gay people could be free. Civil rights and integration seemed like endless begging for the charity of liberals who conveniently ignored the everyday physical and psychological violence exerted by homophobic society.

The student and antiwar movements were already sweeping Europe and gay liberation followed quickly on their heels. Student action in 1968 at Columbia University in New York and at the Sorbonne in Paris nurtured the first stirrings of the new gay liberation. Within three years almost every sizable city in North America and Western Europe would see a gay liberation front in its midst.

Chapter Five

Gay Liberation and Lesbian Feminism

From the Stonewall Rebellion . . .

> Liberation for gay people is to define for ourselves how and with whom
> we live, instead of measuring our relationships by straight values. . . .
> To be a free territory, we must govern ourselves, set up our own in-
> stitutions, defend ourselves, and use our own energies to improve our
> lives.
>
> —Carl Wittman, *Refugees from Amerika: A Gay Manifesto*

On the Friday night of 27–28 June 1969, New York police raided a Greenwich Village gay bar called the Stonewall. Bar raids were an American
institution—a police rite to "manage" the powerless and disrespectable—
and in the preceding three weeks, five New York gay bars had already
been raided. What made the Stonewall a symbol of a new era of gay
politics was the reaction of the drag queens, dykes, street people, and
bar boys who confronted the police first with jeers and high camp and
then with a hail of coins, paving stones, and parking meters. By the end
of the weekend, the Stonewall bar had been burned out, but a new form
of collective resistance was afoot: gay liberation. The Mattachine Action
Committee responded to the Stonewall outbreak with a flier on 29 June
calling for organized resistance, and within a few days radical students at

the Alternative University were providing meeting space for a Gay Liberation Front (Teal 1971, 17–23; Marotta 1981, 72–85).

Still, Stonewall was no isolated event. A police campaign against Los Angeles gay bars in 1967 had sparked a rally of several hundred "on Sunset Boulevard, where they listened to angry speakers intoning the phrases of confrontational politics" (D'Emilio 1983, 227), and student activism, especially on the campuses of Columbia University and the Sorbonne, were associated with the formation of radical gay caucuses. In 1967 and 1968, political tensions were mounting to new heights with clashes between police and black nationalists, hippies, students, and antiwar demonstrators, most notably at the National Democratic Convention in Chicago. In the Netherlands, the Socialist Youth formed a gay caucus, and student groups openly sponsored gay dances on campus (Straver 1973, 170–72). Student Homophile Leagues were formed in 1967 at Columbia by Robert A. Martin and at New York University by Rita Mae Brown. In 1968, the Columbia group picketed a psychiatric seminar on homosexuality held on campus (Martin 1983). In May of the same year, Paris erupted in a general strike and students seized the campus of the Sorbonne in a protest that shared New Left goals. Amidst the "liberated zones," a Comité d'Action Pédérastique Révolutionnaire met, much to the dismay of the orthodox Left (Girard 1981, 80).

The new militants, then, typically came out of student and other New Left movements and carried with them current debates and precepts, which they turned to issues of gender and sexuality. Radicalized by their experiences in black and student organizations, they were now thinking through their own lives with new concepts and were taking a militant message to new constituencies. Feminists and gay liberationists often thought of themselves as revolutionaries rejecting a fundamentally unequal and corrupt power establishment in favor of participatory democracy whereby all the voiceless and suppressed could gain a measure of control over their own lives. Civil rights had become passé: why petition to be let into a social system so deeply riven by racism, sexism, militarism, and heterosexism?

The goal that radical women and gay men shared with the counterculture was "to construct community institutions based on democratic participation": free universities, an underground press, communes, a society of cooperative and nonexploitative relations (see Breines 1982). Deeply suspicious of leaders, bureaucracies, and political parties, the fundamental movement unit was the consciousness-raising group. As explained in

Come Out!, the journal of the New York Gay Liberation Front, it was a deceptively simple mechanism:

A consciousness raising group is a group of gay people who have regular sessions together. By consensus a topic is selected for each session. Each member of the group contributes her personal experiences relating to the chosen topic. When all of the testimony is heard, the group locks into the similarity in the experiences related by all the members. . . . A gay person begins to see that his personal hang-ups, those that he was afraid to divulge to others, are indeed the same hang-ups that other gays were also afraid to divulge. It becomes increasingly difficult to explain this commonness without considering each person's interactions with sexist society. (Gavin 1971, 19)

The group's chairperson would be selected by lot and rotated from meeting to meeting. To limit the formation of elites, every person in the group would be given the floor in turn. Analysis of one's own situation was to flow from the collective experience, owning nothing to received dogmas. Consciousness raising was a technique well known from the "speaking bitterness" campaigns of the Chinese cultural revolution, and, as in China, it helped empower the powerless and grant participation to the masses.[1]

The result of these intense discussions was immense anger, joy, pride, and a boiling over of new ideas. People glimpsed the future and fell in love with a utopia far from the bad old days with their repression and terror, hiding and fear. Gay liberation groups rarely reached the consensus they assumed would come out of consciousness raising, but stimulated outpourings of hopes and ambitions of irreconcilable diversity. Resolutely guarding itself against stasis, gay liberation in its heyday— from 1969 to 1972—functioned as an ongoing catalyst. Like the New Left itself, which had spawned new social movements, gay liberation ultimately was to produce a larger set of gay and lesbian groups.

Sexuality was a yet undeveloped theme in radical thought. In addition to the Beat poets, New Left figures such as Paul Goodman and Daniel Cohn-Bendit had raised it at various times as did a few relatively isolated European intellectuals. Simone de Beauvoir's *Second Sex* raised many of the issues of modern feminism two decades before the revival of the modern movement, and Herbert Marcuse, who had been a youthful participant in the 1918 German revolution and had been steeped in the thinking of the life-reform movements of the Weimar Republic, caught the imagination of many gay liberationists. His *Eros and Civilization,* published in the ideological wasteland of 1955, bridged the prewar and postwar gay movements with its implicit vision of homosexuality as a protest "against the repressive order of procreative sexuality" and as an affirmation of a liberated sensualism (37, 155, 183). As well, Allen Ginsberg, testifying at the trial of black and student movement leaders arrested at the Chicago Democratic convention, invoked the socialist fraternalism of Whitman and Carpenter. In the face of the prosecutor's characterization of the Chicago protestors as "freaking fag revolutionaries," Ginsberg spoke out for

a natural tenderness between all citizens, not only men and women but also a tenderness between men and men as part of our democratic heritage, part of the Adhesiveness which would make the democracy function: that men could work together not as competitive beasts but as tender lovers and fellows. (Tytell 1976, 243; Ginsberg 1974, 14)

Gay liberation never thought of itself as a civil rights movement for a particular minority but as a revolutionary struggle to free the homosexuality in everyone, challenging the conventional arrangements that confined sexuality to heterosexual monogamous families. For gay liberation there was no "normal" or "perverse" sexuality, only a world of sexual possibilities ranged against a repressive order of marriage, oedipal families, and compulsory heterosexuality. It is in this context that Dennis Altman could foresee an "end of the homosexual" because "gay liberation will succeed as its raison d'être disappears" (Altman 1971, 225; see Front Homosexual 1971). Once everyone was free to express her or his latent sexualities, boundaries between the homosexual and the heterosexual should fade into irrelevance and false partitions in the flow of desire give way to personal fulfillment.

Carl Wittman's 1970 "Gay Manifesto" drew together many of the themes of gay liberation thinking. Announcing "we are euphoric, high, with the initial flourish of a movement," it began, "we have to realize that our loving each other is a good thing." Characterizing San Francisco as a "refugee camp" and a "ghetto" controlled by the heterosexist occupational forces of law, police, employers, and capital, Wittman called for rejection of heterosexual standards of gender and monogamy, an end to homophile conformity and closetry, resistance to street violence and police harassment, and confrontation with the "psychological warfare" purveyed by the mass media. "We strive," he continued, "for democratic, mutual, reciprocal sex," affirming the possibility of this ideal even in man-boy and sadomasochistic relationships. Gay liberation also meant coalition with other progressive forces, especially feminism, as well as with black, Chicano, radical, hip, and homophile movements (1972, 157–71).

Gay liberation groups sprang up in the spring and summer of 1969 in the San Francisco Bay area and New York City. Leo Laurence forwarded the radical plank in the pages of SIR's *Vector* and came out with his lover in the countercultural *Berkeley Barb*. The upshot was his lover's dismissal from his job with a steamship company and Laurence's removal from the editorship of *Vector*. They then formed a Committee for Homosexual Freedom, which picketed the steamship company and then a record store that had also fired a gay employee. The Stonewall Rebellion in New York engendered a wave of new groups willing to take immediate direct action against the old array of antihomosexual institutions. In late summer, the New York Gay Liberation Front (NYGLF) and the Mattachine Action Committee picketed in a park where trees had been cut down to eliminate cruising (that is, gay men meeting each other). The GLF joined in antiwar rallies and presented the new platform to the 1969 North America Conference of Homophile Organizations (NACHO) in Kansas City. By fall, GLF dances were regular events in New York, Chicago, and Berkeley, cities where men had often been arrested for dancing or touching in public. Pickets arrived at the *Village Voice* protesting its refusal to print the word *gay* and at *Time* magazine and the *San Francisco Examiner* for their demeaning treatment of gay people. Newspapers such as *Gay Power, Come Out!*, and *Gay* sprang out of movement committees. The GLF confronted Western and Delta airlines about their employment practices, and SIR picketed Macy's for having gay men entrapped by police in its washrooms. Transvestites formed Street Transvestite Action Revolutionaries, and blacks and Hispanics organized Third World Gay Revolution. At the end of the first year, two to three thousand marched to Central Park in New York to commemorate the Stonewall Rebellion as did hundreds in Los Angeles and Chicago (see Teal 1971; D'Emilio 1983; Humphreys 1972b).

In 1970, after "three terrible, joyous days of open, honest battle," conflicts between gay liberation and the old guard wrenched apart a NACHO meeting in San Francisco. In the end, the conference "passed motions supporting women's liberation and the Black Panthers, calling for immediate withdrawal of American forces from Vietnam, authorizing a Gay Strike Day, and calling for memorialization of homosexuals killed in Nazi concentration camps" (Rankin 1970, 4; Humphreys 1972b, 108).

In the same month, the Black Panther leader, Huey Newton, declared his solidarity for the gay movement, stating that "homosexuals are not given freedom and liberty by anyone in the society. Maybe they might be the most oppressed people in the society" (1972, 195). Gay and lesbian delegates, in turn, showed up at the Panther-sponsored Revolutionary Peoples' Constitutional Convention in September to claim their place in the radical coalition that so upset the ruling elites of the United States.

But as early as November 1969, GLF experienced a schism. Jim Owles and Marty Robinson walked out to found the Gay Activists Alliance (GAA) in New York, having found the GLF too anarchic and self-focused, strong on rhetoric but unable to plan effectively, and too preoccupied with revolutionary doctrine to address the day-to-day discrimination occurring around it. The GAA wanted to concentrate on the one issue of gay rights without the diffusion of energy into other New Left causes evident in the GLF. For the GLF, the GAA represented a regression to homophile accommodationism and an abandonment of total social transformation for piecemeal reform. The GAA's adoption of a committee structure and elected leadership, they believed, betrayed the GLF's commitment to consensus and participatory democracy. The movement was facing a transition experienced by so many others before it, when charisma and chiliasm give way to structure and institution. In the end, the GAA proved more durable and effective and the GLF soon exhausted itself (see Altman 1971, 116; Humphreys 1972b, 124; Teal 1971, 106; Marotta 1981, 150).

In practice, many participants flowed between both organizations and the two cooperated on a number of projects. Renewed bar raids in March 1970 brought another round of street demonstrations. Election candidates faced sharp questions on gay rights, and GAA activists forced the New York mayor to address gay issues before television and opera audiences. City hall, the *New York Post, Harper's,* the *New York Times,* and the "Dick Cavett Show" felt the wrath of the GAA in 1970 and 1971 "zaps," or confrontations. The GAA set up task-oriented committees on political action, police, elections, civil rights law for the city, fair taxes, law, news, leaflets and graphics, fund-raising, social affairs, and member orientation—soon accumulating a thick dossier on antihomosexual discrimination.

The GAA's response was often ingenious: "In the summer of 1971, the owner of a credit agency on New York's 42nd Street was questioned about his agency's practice of informing employers of the suspected homosexual tendencies of prospective employees, as well as credit applicants." When questioned about how he determined sexual orientation, he was quoted as saying, "'If a man looks like a duck, walks like a duck, quacks like a duck, and associates with ducks, I'd say he is a duck.' In a short time, a dozen GAA members dressed in duck costumes were waddling around the sidewalk at the entrance to the credit agency, quacking and carrying picket signs" (Humphreys 1972b, 126).

Perhaps the best-known success of the early 1970s was the assault mounted against American psychiatry, which resulted in the 1973–74 removal of homosexuality from the American Psychiatric Association's official diagnostic manual. A century of psychiatric talk in the United States had provided the underpinnings for a range of anti-homosexual practices. After all, what rights could a psychopathology have? If gay men and lesbians were no more than diseased beings, then state institutions had a duty to stamp them out by isolating them in prisons and hospitals, excluding them from a wide range of employment, barring them from entering the country, banning them from bars, and suppressing their voices in the arts and literature. *One* magazine had long disdained psychiatric ideology, but it was not until the militant 1970s that gay people gained sufficient strength and confidence to confront the therapeutic establishment directly. In 1968, even before Stonewall, a contingent of San Franciscans arrived unannounced at a convention of the American Medical Association to speak out against the scientistic extermination of homosexuality. In the same year, students demanded of a medical forum at Columbia University that "it is time that talk stopped being *about* us and started being with us" (see Teal 1971, 293–97; Kameny 1969; Bayer 1981, 92). Gay liberation fronts stormed San Francisco, Los Angeles, and Chicago conventions of psychiatry, medicine, and behavior modification in 1970, where sessions on the "treatment" and "correction" of homosexuality were disrupted with cries of "barbarism," "medieval torture," and "disgusting" and with demands for equal time.

These GLF zaps rapidly polarized the psychiatric profession between such hard-line conservatives as Edward Bergler, Irving Bieber, Charles Socarides, Lionel Ovesey, and Lawrence Hatterer (whom Allen Young characterized as the "war criminals") and a growing liberal contingency including Ernest Van Den Haag, Hendrik Ruitenbeek, and George Weinberg, who had been questioning the psychiatric label for some years. An unprecedented panel of gay people was arranged for the 1971 convention of the APA in Washington, D.C., where Frank Kameny, Larry Littlejohn of SIR, Del Martin of DOB, Lille Vincenz, and Jack Baker, president of the University of Minnesota Students' Association, represented the movement. A 1972 panel included liberal psychiatrists and a gay psychiatrist who appeared wearing a mask. The issue reached a climax in 1973 with a debate between Irving Bieber and Charles Socarides on one side and Judd Marmor, Richard Green, Robert Stoller, and Ron Gold on the other. Gold's paper, "Stop! You're Making Me Sick," represented the gay movement's position.

Official changes were already underway elsewhere as the American Sociological Association passed a no-discrimination resolution in 1969; the National Association for Mental Health called for decriminalization in 1970; the states of Connecticut, Colorado, and Oregon did decriminalize in 1971; a federal court stopped automatic dismissal of gay people from federal employment in the same year; and the National Association of Social Workers rejected the medical model of homosexuality in a 1972 resolution. As the GAA waned through internal dissension (coming to an end, at least symbolically, when its community center was fire-bombed in 1974), leading movement activists reorganized as the National Gay Task Force to press forward the antipsychiatric struggle. When the APA Council accepted deletion of homosexuality from the diagnostic manual in a unanimous vote in 1973, the conservatives forced a referendum on the issue. The result of this curious spectacle of defining pathology by plebiscite was a vote of 58 percent for deletion and 37 percent for retention in 1974. In the end, the new diagnostic manual included a compromise category that continued to allow psychiatrists to "treat" people unhappy with their sexual orientation.

The movement forced debate on homosexuality among a number of professional and scholarly associations in the 1970s, opening the way for the formation of gay and lesbian caucuses within several disciplines: librarianship in 1970; modern languages and psychology in 1973; sociology in 1974; history, psychiatry, and public health in 1975; nursing and social work 1976; and a general Gay Academic Union in 1973 (see Noll 1978, 173–77).

. . . to a World Movement

Within two years from the Stonewall Rebellion, gay liberation groups emerged in every major city and campus in the United States, Canada, Australia, and Western Europe. With a gay liberation press founded in Los Angeles (*Advocate*), New York (*Come Out!*), San Francisco (*Gay Sunshine*), Boston (*Fag Rag*), Detroit (*Gay Liberator*), Toronto (*Body Politic*), and London (*Come Together*), far-flung organizations became much more connected and aware of diverse initiatives. On three continents, gay movements in the early 1970s developed along a similar course, with parallel Left-oriented gay liberation groups forming along with more liberal civil rights organizations. With the general decline of New Left movements in the late 1970s, self-professed gay liberation fronts faded as well, leaving reformist groups in the political field and engendering a new proliferation of gay and lesbian interest groups organized within existing institutions: in the workplace, church, the theater, social services, business, and sports.

The British experience illustrates the process in the early 1970s. The North-Western Committee of the Homosexual Law Reform Society reconstituted itself as the Committee (and then, Campaign) for Homosexual Equality (CHE) in 1969, adopting a platform aimed "to remove fear, discrimination and prejudice against homosexuals, to achieve full equality before the law, and to promote the positive acceptance of homosexuality as a valid way of life" (Marshall 1980, 78). A successful, nonthreatening formula, it attracted sixty local groups by 1972, which offered telephone counseling, regular discos and meeting places, and a concrete political agenda: equalization of the age of consent at sixteen, extension of the 1967 decriminalization to the military, to Scotland, and to Ulster; abolition of gross indecency laws, and freedom of the gay press (see Weeks 1977, 207–13; Galloway 1983).

Gay liberation arrived in London in 1970, when Aubrey Walter and Bob Mellors returned from New York to call a gay liberation meeting at the London School of Economics. Like its American counterparts, the London GLF evolved through high-energy consciousness-raising groups into a collection of workshops focusing on antihomosexual practices in psychiatry, the church, and government. Soon it was working on public education, women's and youth issues, the media, and street theater. Coming out, or public confrontation of its antagonists was always a central feature of gay liberation. As well as forcing its persecutors to become aware of the maliciousness of their actions, coming out had an immensely exhilarating and self-healing effect upon gay men and lesbians who had, for so long, lived a secretive and shamed existence (see Adam 1978, 126). Essential for personal and social change was gay pride, asserting the worth and capability of a people rejected as despicable and weak. For the London GLF, its first act of coming out took the form of a November 1970 demonstration in "Highbury Fields, where a prominent Young Liberal had been arrested by the police and accused of 'indecency'" (Walter 1980, 12). At its height in 1971, the GLF was active in Birmingham, Manchester, Bristol, Cardiff, Edinburgh, and Leeds. But the GLF was all but defunct by the end of 1972, torn apart by tensions between women and men, drag queens and machos, socialists and counterculturalists. By drawing together such a diversity of gay people and engendering such utopian aspirations, the GLF could not resolve the intensely different experiences of its adherents. If male domination was the problem as the feminists and effeminists agreed, then rejection of masculinity was the solution and many GLF men briefly embraced "gender-fuck" drag—mixing beards and dresses, jewelry and leather—in order to parody gender. If sexual repression and the nuclear family were the problem, then public affection and sexual communism could be the answer. In the end, few could so radically rearrange their emotional lives, and such experiments proved more dramatic than viable. At the personal level, many who had come out for companionship and community experienced too much hostility and pain in the GLF cauldron to want to continue devoting so much of themselves to the cause, and GLF yielded to CHE's more sober and limited style.

In Canada, sporadic homophile groups had come about as early as 1964 with the Vancouver Association for Social Knowledge and in 1965 with the Ottawa Council on Religion and the Homosexual. A group of six, who wrote an open letter to Toronto newspapers and to Liberal prime minister Lester Pearson, opened the question of decriminalization in 1964. But it was not until 1967, when the British Parliament approved a new Sexual Offenses Act, that debate in Canada began in earnest. Also in 1967, the Supreme Court upheld the indefinite sentence of a Northwest Territories man, Everett Klippert, as a "dangerous sexual delinquent" following repeated convictions for consenting sexual relations with adult men. The following year, the justice minister, Pierre Trudeau, promised law reform, stating that "the state has no place in the bedrooms of the nation" (Sylvestre 1979, 24), and in August 1969 a new "consenting adults in private" law was proclaimed following passage by the Liberal and New Democratic parties in Parliament. (Many Conservatives and the right-wing Parti Créditiste voted no.)

The modern gay and lesbian movement took the familiar route. Campus groups organized first at the University of Toronto in 1969 and, within three years, across the nation. A Gay Liberation Front formed in 1970 in the well-developed counterculture of Vancouver and then in 1972 in Montreal (Front de Libération Homosexuel) and Toronto (Gay Action). In 1971, a group around George Hislop staked out more moderate ground with the Community Homophile Association of Toronto (CHAT).

When the first march on Parliament was held in 1971, Gays of Ottawa enunciated its law reform program: abolition of the gross indecency law, a uniform age of consent, protection through the human rights codes, equal rights for homosexual couples, destruction of police files, and the ending of discrimination in immigration, employment, custody and adoption, and housing (Jackson and Persky 1982, 217–20). A national meeting in 1972 to plan strategy for a federal election led to annual meetings coordinated by a National Gay Rights Coalition.

As in the United States and the United Kingdom, gay organizations unfolded in Canada throughout the 1970s even in small towns and rural areas where, for the first time, they often *preceded* the commercial infrastructure of bars and public meeting places. In small cities, such as Saskatoon (in 1973) and London, Ontario (in 1974), community-run clubhouses offered the first gay and lesbian places in their regions (see Warner 1976). In sparsely populated areas, such as Newfoundland, northern Ontario, and the British Columbia interior, the urban press provided the catalyst to overcome geography and connect widely dispersed gay and lesbian readers.

In Australia and New Zealand, gay and lesbian organization showed much the same pattern of development as its kin in the rest of the English-language world. With the deepening involvement of Australian forces in the war against Vietnam, an antiwar movement mobilized through the late 1960s, opening an intense political debate and a crisis of confidence in the entrenched Liberal administration. Homophile groups surfaced briefly in 1969 with a chapter of the Daughters of Bilitis in Melbourne and an Australian Capital Territory Homosexual Law Reform Society. A more enduring homophile group, the Campaign Against Moral Persecution (CAMP) formed in Sydney through the initiative of John Ware and Christabell Poll, which stressed the "ordinariness of homosexuality" and sought reform through public education (see Thompson 1985, 10; Johnston 1984; Altman 1979). The group quickly formed chapters in the other state capitals, issuing a journal, *CAMP Ink,* from 1971. In its first demonstration in October 1971, CAMP targeted Liberal party headquarters in Sydney to challenge the preselection candidacy of an opponent of homosexual law reform. When an election was called in 1972, a gay activist ran against the Liberal prime minister, garnering 218 votes. (A similar attempt was made against the New Zealand prime minister to publicize gay concerns.) The ensuing Labour party government decriminalized homosexuality the following year in areas of federal jurisdiction, the Australian Capital and Northern Territories. With gay liberation splitting from CAMP in the mid-seventies, public actions against media, church, and government reached a height only to die down by 1975–76.

The postwar hegemony of the United States, especially among the advanced capitalist nations, as well as among much of the third world, has also had an impact upon the social organization of homosexuality and the development of a political movement. But national traditions and varying arrays of social preconditions have led to different paths of movement development. As argued earlier, a complex set of socioeconomic factors and political possibilities created the crucible in which homosexuality became organized into gay and lesbian subcultures in Western countries. With a shared language, cultural diffusion became an important stimulus for parallel development of the gay world and its movement in the United States, United Kingdom, Canada, Australia, and New Zealand. (Despite its nationalism, Quebec cannot help but be deeply influenced by the Anglo-American culture that surrounds it.) Among other language communities and among nations with different political legacies and economic systems, the movement, although cognizant of the Stonewall heritage, has developed along alternative paths.

In the Federal Republic of Germany, student activism and the coming to power of the Social Democrats preceded the emergence of the modern feminist and gay movements. With the end of the cold war Christian Democrat government, the Social Democrats decriminalized homosexuality in 1969, later lowering the age of consent from twenty-one to eighteen in 1973. Campus action groups (*Aktionsgruppen*) sprang up across the country in 1971–73, often following screenings of Rosa von Praunheim's controversial film, *Not the Homosexual Is Perverse, But the Situation in Which He Lives,* which documented the gay upheaval in the United States. Among the first was Homosexuelle Aktion Westberlin, which adopted an explicitly radical approach (see Stümke and Finkler 1981, 410–14; Danneker and Reiche 1973).

In the Netherlands, a peculiar balance of political forces that has guaranteed a more genuinely pluralistic society than other liberal democracies combined to allow more direct participation of the 1950s homophile movements in the political process and less direct confrontation between the state and homosexuality than in Germany or the English-language countries. The result has been considerable continuity in the national gay and lesbian federations of the Netherlands (as well as Denmark, Norway, and Sweden), all of which have worked well and survived from their

founding in the late 1940s and early 1950s. Gay liberation, although pro-
voking a rethinking of the political agenda, never overturned the early
organizations but instead became largely integrated into them, causing a
partial name change for the COC from the Netherlands Homophile Association COC (selected in 1964) to the Netherlands Association for the
Integration of Homosexuality COC in 1970–71 (see Tielman 1982; Ramsay, Heringa, and Boorsma 1974).[2] Lesbian and gay social integration has
moved toward the elimination of police supervision and censorship, while
the state supports access to the media, funding for social service projects
and scholarly research, and legal accommodation for gay people in immigration, housing, the military, and education.

In France, the "pederastic" committee of May 1968 disappeared as
quickly as it had arisen, along with the barricades of that fateful month.
Not until 1971 was there a second outburst, following an issue of *Tout*
(edited by Jean-Paul Sartre), that called for sexual liberation—free dis-
position over one's own body, free abortion and contraception, the right
to homosexuality, and the right of minors to freedom of desire (Girard
1981, 83ff.; Front Homosexuel 1971). *Tout*'s "call to arms" found
hundreds of adherents—as well as police seizure of the issue as an "outrage to public morals." Here emerged the Front Homosexuel Action Révolutionnaire (FHAR), which issued a *Report against Normality* (also
seized by police) proclaiming a new sexual revolution. Like gay liberation,
FHAR took a spontaneous turn, eschewing leadership for a series of ad
hoc action groups that confronted professional "experts" and the established Left with slogans designed to explode bourgeois morality and sexual repression. The enemy was "le sexisme, le phallocratisme et
l'hétérofliquisme," and FHAR declared to a startled citizenry that "we get
fucked by Arabs. We're proud of it and will do it again. . . . Our asshole
is revolutionary" (Girard 1981, 89–90). By 1972, FHAR had spread to
major French cities, Belgium, and northern Italy as the Frente Unitario
Omosessuale Rivoluzionario Italiano (FUORI), where it invaded a sexology
conference in San Remo to oppose the oppressive practices of penology
and psychiatry.

Again like gay liberation, FHAR soon lost its momentum, to be succeeded by a civil rights–oriented Groupe de Libération Homosexuelle
(GLH), and in Italy, FUORI entered a coalition with other progressive
movements in the Radical party, which took its demands to Parliament.
The GLH soon split into two factions: the Groupes de Base (GLH-GB)
organized in 1975 and 1976 around fighting antigay discrimination in law,
employment, residence, police, and media, and the Politique et Quotidien

(GLH-PQ) which developed a more radical analysis. The first group adopted the single-issue program in an effort to bring together a broad spectrum of gay people with diverse backgrounds and beliefs. It continued to look forward to a time when social distinctions based on gender and sexual orientation could be dissolved and when the commercial ghetto would fade away unneeded. With Trotskyite inspiration, the GLH-PQ argued that homosexual identity was an invention of the bourgeoisie, the better to contain unruly desires in a police-supervised ghetto. Why, the GLH-PQ militants wondered, were antihomosexual practices most concentrated in the institutions of repression—the family, the church, the military, the police, the prison, sports, and the schools? Might the key to a liberated society be a class struggle against the bourgeoisie combined with the liberation of the repressed homosexuality holding together the institutions of repression? Neither of the GLH tendencies survived past 1978, but perhaps most notable was the GLH-PQ's unique development of some tenets of early gay liberation into the late 1970s.

In southern Europe and Latin America, gay organizations have proven much more ephemeral, happenstance traceable to important differences in economy and politics. Traditional gender differences, often labeled Latin machismo, have remained strong in societies where industrial employment encompasses a small portion of the population and women, especially, have not been able to enter wage labor and thereby upset the gender system. So strong are gender codes that gender differences inscribe themselves even within homosexuality, creating two classes of men: the machos, who may with impunity take the "active" role in sex with males or females, and the effeminates (every nation has its terminology), who are stigmatized for "degrading" themselves to the status of women in bed and out (see Young 1973, 60ff.; Carrier 1976; Lacey 1979; Arboleda 1980). With a sexual semiology defined far more by gender than by sexual orientation, a gay world and identity are much less likely to develop. Lesbians, typically, have no public recognition and the power of kin make independent same-sex relationships even less likely for women than men.

In addition, alliances between United States capitalists and indigenous landholding elites have often resulted in semifascist governments aided by successive U.S. administrations. Under such regimes, political organization of any kind becomes perilous. Notwithstanding these factors, small gay worlds have emerged in those sectors of Latin America that most resemble North America and Western Europe: in major cities with large mobile work forces that earn enough money to afford a drink in a bar. Diffusion of the gay idea clearly plays a role, as well, in the commercial establishments that consciously model themselves after American examples.

In Argentina, for example, a Frente de Liberación Homosexual formed in 1973 as part of an alignment of political forces emerging at the end of a dictatorship. Six issues of *Somos* appeared that defined a clear left-liberationist politics and included reports of the massacre of gay people under the Pinochet dictatorship in Chile. Gay liberation was forced to dissolve with the return of right-wing death squads and military government in 1976, when tens of thousands of Argentines identified with progressive movements died at their hands (see McCaskell 1976).

The first of several short-lived gay organizations began in Mexico City in 1971 when a Frente de Liberación Homosexual formed in response to the firing of several gay employees by the Sears store in Mexico City.

By the mid-1970s, gay liberation was in crisis, and out of the malaise and exhaustion after the radical phase of the gay and lesbian movement along with its New Left kin, came a reorganized and diversified set of movement groups. Most central of all the divisions that fragmented early gay liberation was that between women and men, and an autonomous lesbian feminism opened the way for revitalization.

Lesbian Feminism

> Feminism at heart is a massive complaint. Lesbianism is the solution.
>
> —Jill Johnston, in *Ms.*

Intense political debates and dramatic shifts in analysis characterized the emergence of lesbian activism in the early 1970s. Coming out of a flux of rapidly changing and inconsistent movement strategies developing among feminists, gay liberationists, and homophile lesbians, women went through fundamental debates about what a lesbian is and what lesbians should work for. Having a much less extensive public-bar sector than gay men have, many women came out for the first time in the midst of the women's movement and struggled for both a personal and a political orientation in an environment radically different from that of "traditional" lesbians. Because these women had so much on the line and so little anchorage in tradition, their struggles over basic questions often reached a high intensity and were resolved in frequently contradictory ways.

As late as 1970, the New York Daughters of Bilitis was holding to the cautious homophile position, only to be interrupted by the police at one meeting where they had just reaffirmed their political neutrality and had abstained from joint action with the Gay Activists Alliance. They soon reversed themselves and the DOB president, Ruth Simpson, began to invite notable feminists to speak in the ensuing months (1977; Marotta 1981). Del Martin, a DOB cofounder, had joined the National Organization for Women (NOW) in 1967, and many other lesbians were already working behind the scenes for women's rights.

Feminists at this time, however, were not always pleased to find lesbians among their ranks. Betty Friedan, in *The Feminine Mystique* (1963), had endorsed the stereotype of male homosexuality, characterizing it as "shallow unreality, immaturity, promiscuity," while leaving lesbians invisible (276). When Rita Mae Brown attempted to confront heterosexism in the women's movement in 1970 as newsletter editor of the New York chapter of NOW, Betty Friedan, then the national president of NOW, denounced a supposed "lavender menace" threatening the credibility of feminism. Brown and other suspected lesbians were purged from the organization (see Brown 1972; Abbott and Love 1972, 109–12, 127; Carden 1974, 113; Freeman 1975, 99). Similar confrontations occurred among radical feminists in Boston and at the 1971 National Women's Conference in the United Kingdom, where attempts to raise lesbian issues were rejected as "red herrings" and "private problems" (Carden 1974, 53; Walter 1980, 150).

Lesbians received a more sympathetic welcome in San Francisco in February 1970, when Gay Women's Liberation joined with the Bay Area Women's Coalition Conference. In New York, they regrouped with activists from both women's and gay liberation to hammer out the now famous manifesto, "Woman-identified Woman." Calling themselves Radicalesbians, they asserted that "a lesbian is the rage of all women condensed to the point of explosion," and pointed out that feminists could never escape the lesbian accusation. "Lesbian is the word, the label, the condition that holds women in line," they argued, "a debunking scare term that keeps women from forming any primary attachments, groups, or associations among ourselves." Lesbianism was independence from men, freedom from male approval, a matrix of women's solidarity: as such it was at the heart of feminism.

When the Second Congress to Unite Women met in New York in May, participants at a theater evening found themselves plunged into darkness. When the lights came up, they saw at the front of the auditorium twenty Radicalesbians wearing "Lavender menace" T-shirts who presented a list of grievances. The conference was liberated: workshops on lesbian issues were presented the next day, an all-women's dance was a resounding success, and the conference ended with a set of resolutions beginning, "Be it resolved that Women's Liberation is a Lesbian plot" (see Radicalesbians 1971; Teal 1971, 179–81; Hole and Levine 1971, 239–40; Abbott and Love 1972, 113–14).

But the war was not won. In the fall of 1970, when Gay People at Columbia held a public forum, Kate Millett came out as a lesbian in response to a question from the floor. *Time* magazine, which had promoted her as the preeminent feminist thinker, now announced her demise—a classic example of the tactics decried by the "Woman-identified Woman" manifesto. The case became a test of the new solidarity, and in a December press conference, leading feminists, such as Ti-Grace Atkinson, Gloria Steinem, Florynce Kennedy, Sally Kempton, Myrna Lamb, and Susan Brownmiller, rallied to Millett's defense. By 1971, even NOW had turned around, resolving that "N.O.W. acknowledges the oppression of lesbians as a legitimate concern of feminism." In 1973, at the behest of its Lesbian Caucus, the group appointed a National Task Force on Sexuality and Lesbianism (Abbott and Love 1972, 119–23, 134; Abbott 1978).

It had been an exhilarating time, which forged a major realignment of lesbian forces. "This was," remarked Jill Johnston, "a momentous series of steps from self hatred in guilt and secrecy to apologetic pleas for greater acceptance and legal sanctions to affirmation of identity to aggressive redefinition in the context of revolution" (1973, 149). The immediate outcome was a massive mobilization of lesbian energies in a cultural renaissance with the founding of such notable journals as *Ain't I a Woman?* (Iowa City), the *Furies* (Washington, D.C.), *Amazon Quarterly, Lesbian Tide, Sinister Wisdom* (Charlotte, N.C.), *Lesbian Connection* (Lansing, Mich.), *Long Time Coming* (Montreal), *Sappho* (London), and *Unsere Kleine Zeitung* (Berlin) as well as numerous local publications. A series of annual national women's music festivals began in 1973–74, stimulating an outpouring of creative talent, the rise of internationally known artists such as Meg Christian, Cris Williamson, Holly Near, and Margie Adam, and the founding of Olivia Records, devoted to the growing women's culture (St. Joan 1978; Nixon and Bergson 1978).

The redefinition of lesbianism as a form of feminist "nationalism" also spelled the end of the Daughters of Bilitis and secession from the gay movement. Both the New York chapter and the National DOB collapsed in the highly charged days of 1971. Rita Laporte and Barbara Grier seized the *Ladder* from the national DOB in 1970 to publish it as a radical lesbian journal from Reno, Nevada, but they were unable to keep it going after 1972 (see Martin and Lyon 1972, 251; Grier and Reid 1976; Marotta 1981, 263–69; D'Emilio 1983, 230).

From the beginning of gay liberation, lesbians often found themselves vastly outnumbered by men who were, not surprisingly, preoccupied with their own issues and ignorant of the concerns of women. Many women became increasingly frustrated as gay liberation men set up task groups to counter police entrapment, work for sodomy law reform, or organize dances that turned out to be 90 percent male. Men took for granted many of the social conditions that made it possible for them to be gay. But lesbians needed to address fundamental problems facing all women—such as equal opportunity in employment and violence against women—in order to have sufficient independence to become lesbian. Most men had at least the financial independence of wage labor and a well-developed commercial scene to fall back on, whereas many women were struggling to gain a foothold in employment and create places where lesbians could be together. In a movement that was supposed to forward their cause, lesbians grew angry at having to devote time and energy to "reminding" men of their existence. Many lesbians suspected that gay men would be happy to accept the place befitting their sex and class while leaving the system of male domination intact. As Marie Robertson stated to the Canadian National Gay Rights Coalition, "Gay liberation, when we get right down to it, is the struggle for gay men to achieve approval for the only thing that separates them from the 'Man'—their sexual preference" (Robertson 1982, 177).

Early on, a move toward lesbian autonomy was underway. In April 1970, women-only dances were organized through the New York GLF to create a space where women could meet. In Los Angeles, the GLF Women's Caucus became Gay Women's Liberation and then Lesbian Feminism in rapid succession. Women-only meetings were held in CAMP-Sydney for similar reasons. With the apparent embrace of lesbianism by the women's movement in the early 1970s, lesbians around the world began withdrawing from gay liberation in 1972 and 1973. London GLF split in 1972, Lavender September formed in Amsterdam, and the Homosexuelle Aktionsgruppe Westberlin formed a Frauengruppe in 1972 (later becoming Lesbisches Aktionszentrum). Further lesbian organization in Germany usually occurred under the auspices of women's centers sponsored by feminists. Les Gouines Rouges left FHAR in Paris, and the Women's Subcommittee of the New York GAA became Lesbian Feminist Liberation.[3]

Every social movement must choose at some point what to retain and what to reject of its past. What traits and attitudes are the results of oppression and what are healthy and authentic? Which tactics come from the wisdom of forebears in facing the enemy and which merely imitate the established power system? Every movement at some time vacillates between "nationalist" and "integrationist" positions. The black movement divided over whether it wanted to affirm similarity or difference, whether it wanted to abandon Sambo-ism and claim its share of the goods of advanced capitalism, or to affirm all things African and reject a morally bankrupt and exploitative society. Gay liberation encountered similar dilemmas. Were drag queens a heterosexist stereotype acted out by self-hating homosexual men or were they the vanguard of the new gay man, rejecting the violence and misogyny of machismo and proudly coming out with their homosexuality for all to see? Feminists were not immune to the problem. Was motherhood a burden to be collectivized (or avoided) or was it women's unique contribution to humanity? Was housework merely drudgery to be shrugged off for fulfilling and *paid* employment? Was it an essential but unrecognized component in the reproduction and maintenance of the capitalist work force?

The positions taken on these questions by lesbian feminists are inextricable from the debates of the overall women's movement. After an early period of feminist integrationism, many feminists tended toward a socialist feminist camp, which argued for a comprehensive inclusion of women, gay men, and other subordinated people in a broad front against patriarchal capitalism, or toward a certain "nationalism," which aimed for a women's culture and values wherein lesbianism was revalued as the highest expression of women's solidarity and as central to women's struggle. As Ti-Grace Atkinson remarked, "Lesbianism is to feminism what the Communist Party was to the trade union movement" (1973, 14).

Many responded favorably to the new lesbian visibility, declaring themselves "political lesbians" in solidarity without necessarily involving themselves sexually with women. After the initial euphoria wore off, however, it became clear that acceptance was often superficial. Lesbian concerns were once again too often ignored, and few heterosexual women were willing to let go of their "heterosexual privilege"—what Charlotte Bunch called the "actual or promised benefits for the woman who stays in line," or "the small and short-term bribe in return for giving up lasting self-discovery and collective power" (1976, 60). This inaugurated yet another split with the development of "lesbian separatism" in 1972 to

1974. The separatists built within the nationalist position, defining lesbianism as a "woman-identified experience, . . . sharing of a rich inner life, the bonding against male tyranny, the giving and receiving of practical and political support" (Rich 1983, 192; Myron and Bunch 1975). Like other nationalisms, its theorists embarked on synthesizing a transhistorical women's mythology that reordered the universe in terms of gender opposition. Unlike the early feminists who sought to annihilate gender, insisting that such distinctions were social inventions, the nationalists adopted the opposite position, affirming an essential biological difference between men and women and working to rescue a women's culture from millennia of male domination. In contrast to male competitiveness and militarism, women would found a new civilization upon their own traditions of motherhood and nurturance.

So total was the new paradigm that Jill Johnston could claim, "considering the centrality of lesbianism to the Women's Movement it should now seem absurd to persist in associating lesbian women with the male homosexual movement. Lesbians are feminists, not homosexuals" (1975, 85). Mary Daly drew a sharp line between lesbians, whom she defined as "women who are woman-identified, having rejected false loyalties to men on all levels," and gay women, who "although they relate genitally to women, give their allegiance to men and male myths, ideologies, styles, practices, institutions, and professions." The latter group, she claimed, remained male-identified by collaborating with "heterosexist [*sic*] 'gay pride' protests promoted by and for men" (1978, 20, 26). If the pivotal distinction of human civilization is gender, then gay men are simply men and thus of little interest for lesbian politics.

The consolidation of lesbian identity around feminist nationalist precepts was not without problems for many lesbians. Women whose experience of lesbianism had been shaped by the bar community often found themselves rejected as "male-identified." Feminists of the early phase, who defined the core of feminism as the elimination of gender, believed that "all role playing is sick" including the "butch-fem" distinctions that remained an aspect of bar culture (Koedt 1973, 249; see Abbott and Love 1972, 36, 60; Marotta 1981, 250). Others were taken aback by the new "political lesbian" who wanted to "try it out" but knew nothing of the day-to-day hardship experienced by lesbians. Barbara Ponse found that "the self-labeled political lesbian who is bisexual or heterosexual in practice is somewhat of a mystery to women who have always defined themselves as lesbians," and many felt used by apparently bisexual women who had no interest in emotional commitment (1978, 112, 123, 212). Many suspected political lesbianism to be a form of sexual "tourism"—"the one who was going to liberate herself on my body," as Rita Mae Brown put it (1972, 191; see Gay Rev. Party 1972, 179).

Paradoxically, although the redefinition of lesbianism as a form of women's class consciousness gave permission to heterosexual women to experiment with lesbianism, it tended, at the same time, to remove sexuality from lesbian identity. As Ann Snitow, Christine Stansell, and Sharon Thompson state:

In pointing to anger rather than eros as the wellspring of lesbianism, the [Woman-identified Woman] manifesto opened the way for the desexualization of lesbian identity. . . . While the pre-feminist-movement lesbian could not forget her differences from straight women, the feminist lesbian could scarcely perceive them. Ultimately, this homogenization suppressed but could no more eliminate the tensions of difference between lesbian and straight women than it could between white women and women of color. (1983, 33)

For lesbians who decided to stay with the gay movement, feminist nationalism had taken an unfortunate turn. Whereas early feminist writers called for an end to the suppression of female sexuality, later nationalists appeared to be falling back on an image of women as above sexuality. As Jill Johnston wondered, after listening to Ti-Grace Atkinson's pleas for the political lesbian, "in her feminist rationale she had told us that the female dynamic is love and the male dynamic is sex. Translated: Man-Sex-Evil versus Woman-Love-Good" (1973, 117–18). Barbara Gittings and Kay Tobin thought that political solidarity was all very well but that the meaning of lesbianism lay elsewhere: "We believe that the majority of lesbians who come around to any gay group are not looking for analysis or warfare or reconstruction. . . . They want to meet and mix with other gay women in the legitimate pursuit of friendship and love" (1978, 151). And in an article called "Why I Am a Gay Liberationist," Chris Bearchell rejected the "imaginary world where lesbians are pure and gay men are sex perverts," arguing, "Every time a lesbian is a feminist to the world and a lesbian only to her feminist friends she is behaving with the same 'closetry' that characterized much of ghetto life, with the additional betrayal that she is doing so in the name of freedom for women" (1983, 59).

Whereas some feminists denounced the gay movement's failure to take gender abolition as its sole issue and its willingness to embrace such politically incorrect people as drag queens and butch lesbians, others viewed the movement's willingness to embrace such a diversity as a strength. And whereas Rita Mae Brown and Martha Shelley were attacked as male-identified for promoting coalition between lesbians and people oppressed by class and race, others believed that social transformation could not be a question of gender alone. Gittings and Tobin claimed that lesbian separatists had identified the wrong enemy with their "supercharged response to sexism and male chauvinism, to the point that they spend much time and energy attacking the sexism of the handiest men around, the gay men in the movement" (1978, 151). And Bearchell complained:

It is, after all, our sexuality, and the sexual minorities in our community, that are under attack. Here, it seems, is where we must defend ourselves. But suddenly the same radical feminists who had denounced gay liberationists for our concern with such un-radical things as rights, were nervous about being in a coalition with us because we might take some not-quite-respectable position on sex. (1983, 59)

Gay men's reactions to the lesbian secession ranged from breast-beating to confusion and resentment. About the time many feminists became political lesbians, some gay men became "effeminists," taking to heart lesbian criticism of their male privilege and renouncing all personal signs of masculinity. The effeminists recalled the earlier debates over drag in gay liberation and later reemerged as "radical faeries" searching for a tradition of "gay male spirituality" parallel to feminist cultural nationalism. Henry Hay, a founder of the first Mattachine and his lover, John Burnside, figured among its relatively small number of adherents (Collier and Ward 1980; Hardy 1980). Most gay organizations scrambled—often too late—to accommodate lesbian demands, but some groups successfully retained female and male participation by moving toward parity decision making in the organization's day-to-day affairs. Other gay men suspected that many lesbians simply found it more convenient to identify with a large and respectable mass movement than with a group of stigmatized "perverts." After all, feminism offered quick rehabilitation to a reviled sexual identity, and many men were appalled at the willingness of newly respectable lesbians to denounce the lives of gay men as no more than "economic and cultural privilege, . . . anonymous sex . . . pederasty . . . ageism" (Rich 1983, 192).

With the feminist movement continuing to develop inconsistent trends in the late 1970s, debates on the future of lesbian organization went on unabated. Cultural nationalism offered quite a different agenda for lesbian struggle than did integrationist approaches, whether from a liberal civil rights approach or from a more radical socialist feminist model. The immediate outcome of these conflicts has been considerable fragmentation of lesbian energies and a renewed confrontation between these tendencies in the sex debates of the 1980s. But for this story, we must look at the movement in the 1980s.

The Movement and the Grass Roots

The paradox of the 1970s was that gay and lesbian liberation did not produce the gender-free communitarian world it envisioned, but faced an unprecedented growth of gay capitalism and a new masculinity. While debates raged inside the movement, the actions of gay liberationists and lesbian feminists entered a larger political field, which transformed and expanded the gay world in unexpected directions.

The most immediate effect of the movement upon the masses of gay men and lesbians, who were largely unacquainted with its internal debates and struggles, was a new sense of pride, an honest affirmation of a personal emotional life, a sense of relief at not having always to hide or apologize, and a new claim (or reclamation) of the symbols of masculinity. After the "gender-fuck" drag of the early 1970s and the intense critique of gender, both lesbians and gay men began more and more to embody a certain working-class ideal of masculinity; the fashion was "jeans and denim workmen's overalls . . . topped by a man's T-shirt or workshirt . . . [and] heavy men's workboots or sneakers" (Cassell 1972, 83). While heterosexual men were relaxing into a new androgyny in the 1970s, adopting longer hair, brighter colors, and softer fabrics, gay men and lesbians were making a mass commitment to denim, plaid, and leather.

The gender shift is perhaps not so surprising in retrospect. Masculine symbols offer the most ready-at-hand vocabulary of self-assertion. As gay people gained self-confidence and demanded respect, they began to present themselves as serious and tough. Still, it is important not to confuse this artful masculinity with conventional male chauvinism. The new gay masculinity had a specific meaning. It was an open secret among gay men that the apparent motorcyclists and cowboys standing in gay bars were gentle men at heart. Although this cultivated masculinity was a disappointment to gay men of the old school who thought they wanted "real men," for most the apparent inconsistency was attractive and right. Among lesbians, the new dress code rejected the incapacitating delicacy and frilliness vaunted by the heterosexist press in favor of the self-reliant image of the Amazon. Once the new self-confidence was fully internalized, the masculinist style began to wane—but more quickly for lesbians than for gay men.

In another sense, the new masculinity participated in one of the deepest aspirations of the movement, that is, to develop egalitarian relationships free from role playing. In this, the movement was an inheritor of a two-hundred-year trend toward egalitarian ideals in the companionate marriage. Long the victims of male violence and control in families, women had sought to improve their status at home and espouse full equality. It might be argued that homosexual relationships have an inherent interest in shedding gender and that they have, in fact, pioneered work sharing and role flexibility in coupled relationships. Whether ahead of or with progressive trends in heterosexual relationships, Stonewall marked a decisive break with a waning tradition of gender within homosexuality. The masculinization of the 1970s dissolved remnants of the "real man" versus "queer" distinction (described above as the Latin American model), which is so evident in historical documents of gay life in the West. As Rudy Kikel put it: "Up until liberation, I really feel that we were all in love with straight men. . . . what we found was that we could find that [maleness] in each other. And the great benefit was that we became sexual objects for each other" (1981, 12). As well, sex roles (as opposed to gender) largely disappeared in the 1970s in that "the most common set of sexual preferences among gay males is for all roles, both oral and anal and active and passive" (Harry 1976–77, 150). Joseph Harry found only a folk distinction between "versatile" and "not versatile" but not a distinction between sex roles.[4]

None of this is to say that the new trends solved the much thornier micropolitics of day-to-day living or that gender entirely lost its meanings. As women have increasingly entered male-identified jobs and vice versa (and gay people are on the cutting edge of this change), gender has become more and more disarticulated from the division of labor. Still, problems of initiative and response, active and passive, domination and submission, continue to crop up in actual relationships, and discussions of them inevitably become entangled in gender vocabularies, which have so long characterized the differences. In the gay world, drag has been shunted off to the side, becoming a "little tradition" outside a larger mainstream. Transvestism has become a world of its own with many female impersonators developing professional identities and straight audiences. Debates among lesbians about butch-fem relationships have resurfaced to recover what was valuable in the bar dyke tradition and to rearticulate feelings and practices that egalitarian slogans never dealt with.

The other paradoxical outcome of gay liberation was the expansion of the gay ghetto. The success of the movement in beating back state management and repression of gay places allowed for a new generation of businesses oriented to a gay market. Within a decade, every major city in North America and Western Europe had a new range of bars and saunas, restaurants and discos, travel agents and boutiques, lawyers and life insurers, social services and physicians, who catered specifically to a gay clientele. At the same time, there was a remarkable development of many women-owned and operated places, many of which were havens for lesbians.

While gay liberation zapped public institutions, a new class of small businessmen (and some women) began carving out a commercial ghetto that directly touched the lives of many more gay people than the movement itself. While gay liberation theory presumed that the release of homosexuality would explode conventional sexual and familial arrangements, capitalist environments cultivated new institutions compatible with itself. The result, remarked Dennis Altman, was a new masculine gay man who was "non-apologetic about his sexuality, self-assertive, highly consumerist and not at all revolutionary, though prepared to demonstrate for gay rights" (Altman 1980, 52).

The capitalization of homosexuality in the 1970s shaped gay male identity in quite another way. Neither Ginsberg's vision of "tender lovers and fellows" nor gay liberation's democratic gay community could come to pass under such auspices. As businessmen developed efficient sex delivery systems for gay men, a world of adhesive comrades and brothers became a more remote ideal. The unique potential inherent in homosexuality to rehumanize relationships among men became increasingly closed off in favor of orgasm without communication. Relationships among men were participating in the growing sexual reductionism of the current century: male bonding in the commercial gay world tended to implode into its sexual aspect, and those who did manage to make long-term commitments to each other often withdrew from the commercial world to do so. As Laud Humphreys observed: "In the *Wealth of Nations,* Adam Smith postulated the ideal form of human relationship as being specific, depersonalized, short-term and contractual. This capitalist ideal is realized in the sex exchange of the homosexual underworld [*sic*]" (1972a, 66)

The new sexual "freedom" brought a tremendous release of energy and profound exploration of erotics as a value in itself. Early gay and lesbian liberationists looked forward to an era of plural bonding, freed of the oppressive weight of monogamy, jealousy, and sexual boredom. But many gay men began to feel a certain sexual alienation and emotional suffocation. As Robert Patrick bitterly recalled:

> Bars wouldn't make any money if people loved one another. You go to a bar, get drunk, get drugged up and go into the back room and have your sex there. The economic reality is that your cock is being sold by that bar. Your ass is being sold by that bar. But we don't ever think of it that way. (1979, 8)[5]

Thus, whereas the lesbian movement began to submerge sexual topics under talk of sisterhood, thereby slipping back toward traditional definitions of female sexuality, gay men found themselves unable to talk forthrightly of their need for love, confirming traditional male socialization that demands that men be sexual but unemotional. As Andrew Holleran confessed in a perceptive article for *Christopher Street*:

> Last week in the baths I was sitting in a corner waiting for Mister Right when I saw two men go into an even darker nook and run through the entire gamut of sexual acts. And when they were finished—after all these *kisses* . . . and *moans* and *gasps,* things that caused scandals in the nineteenth century, toppled families, drove Anna Karenina to suicide—. . . after all that, they each went to a separate bedroom to wash up. Now you may view this as the glory of the zipless fuck, but I found it suddenly—and it surprised me, for I'd always adored this event before—the most reductive, barren version of sex a man could devise. (1979, 12)

The commercial gay world could provide "fast-food" sex, but it did nothing to nurture lasting relationships among men. It contained and marketed gay male sexuality back to gay men, but reproduced the competitive alienation among men experienced in the larger society. It was, in fact, as Joseph Harry and William Devall found, a satisfactory arrangement for "persons with significant components of heterosexuality in their self-identity" who "vacationed" in the gay ghetto but had no interest in emotional involvement with other men (1978).[6] But for gay men, it was not always enough.

The irony of the 1970s, then, was the ease with which gay and lesbian aspirations were assimilated, contained, and overcome by the societies in which they originated. The gender challenge of the liberation movements (itself imminent in the increasingly complex division of labor of modern capitalism) became the gender affirmation of the end of the decade, whether as gay male masculinity or lesbian feminist nationalism. The socialist challenge of the New Left helped contribute to its opposite: a bigger commercial ghetto. Still, these paradoxes were not simply historical cycles or pendulum swings against an unchanging background. Each social convulsion pulled out, amplified, and rewove disparate discursive strands into different social patterns. Each stage experimented with new combinations of received elements, producing a changed social fabric. But the disarray of outcomes was soon to fall prey to a reorganized enemy as conservative forces in the United States formed the New Right.

Chapter Six

The New Right Reacts

Anita Bryant on the Loose

On 7 June 1977 voters in Dade County, Florida, repealed a six-month-old civil rights ordinance that had prohibited discrimination on the grounds of "sexual orientation." Through 1978, similar repeals grew into a wave striking down equal rights laws across the United States. Emboldened by an increasingly reactionary climate, police and street violence against gay people escalated, television programs appeared resurrecting old stereotypes, and many public leaders shed their veneer of liberalism to attack gay people as immoral sexual predators and threats to the family. A new Holocaust now seemed possible to many when, after a tumultuous year and a half, Harvey Milk, the best-known openly gay public official in the United States, was assassinated.

The reactionary trends of the late 1970s encompassed much more than the rights of gay people. A disparate set of opponents to New Left and liberal ideals was pulling together into a more coordinated force. Segregationists and antibusing groups chipped away at voting rights legislation, affirmative action programs, and health and social services won by the black movement. The Equal Rights Amendment, intended to stop discrimination against women, went down to defeat, and "right to life" groups challenged feminist claims to a right to control one's own body including a right to terminate pregnancy. Under the guise of reducing government regulation, business associations pressed for lowered health and safety standards and for so-called right-to-work legislation designed to contain and destroy labor unions.

The new conservatism appeared primarily in English-speaking countries and preeminently in the United States. In France, southern Europe, and much of Latin America, the 1980s brought social democratic governments or, at least, an end to dictatorship and an often improved political climate for lesbians and gay men. Opposition there tended to come from extremist, neofascist groups enjoying little popular support. In France, for example, a small fascist commando ransacked a gay film festival in 1978, but the far right had little electoral impact or long-term effect upon the civil liberties of lesbians and gay men. In West Germany, as well, gay movement meetings suffered disruptions by neo-Nazis, who, in one incident, assaulted a meeting hall in Munich with tear gas (Girard 1981, 144; Rusche 1984). In the United States, on the other hand, reactionary ideologies gained significant popular support and fueled new repressive moves. What, then, led to the events of the late 1970s and early 1980s and what structural and historical changes gave rise to the New Right?

A look at the Save Our Children organization, which led the Dade County repeal, reveals a profile of the antigay forces. Headed by evangelist singer Anita Bryant, the antigay campaign drew together conservative religious leaders and politicians. Founding the campaign squarely upon fundamentalist church networks, Bryant garnered support from the National Association of Evangelicals, representing more than 3 million people from sixty denominations (Wuthrow 1983, 173). The electronic church through its television programs (such as "PTL Club," "700 Club," and "The Old-Time Gospel Hour") gave Bryant a nationwide platform and raised funds for her, while Jerry Falwell campaigned in person and B. Larry Coy, from the Falwell ministries, became a campaign director. The right-wing Christian Cause, a direct-mail political lobby, also drew on a national reservoir of conservatives, extending its purview to supporters from Jewish and Roman Catholic hierarchies. The archbishop for Miami sent around a pastoral letter to local Roman Catholic Churches, calling on their congregations to vote against civil rights for lesbians and gay men, and twenty-eight rabbis and the president of the Miami Beach B'nai B'rith joined the chorus. Close supporters and directors of the campaign included Florida senators and its governor, antiabortion and anti-ERA activists, police representatives, YMCA and Kiwanis leaders, a football manager, and psychiatrists who had fought to keep homosexuality labeled "sick" (Young 1982, 37; Bryant 1977).

The gay defense campaign, organized as the Dade County Coalition for Human Rights (DCCHR), and the Miami Victory Campaign opted for a "'high-toned' human rights approach of flag-waving and pictures of the endangered American constitution" (Merrill 1977-78, 11). Gay business-men and Democratic party gay club leaders chose a professionally di-rected media campaign for the DCCHR, eschewing door-to-door canvassing and ignoring Miami's large Cuban and black communities. The media campaign ran afoul of pro-Bryant editorials and continual suppres-sion and cutting of progay ads in the Miami newspapers (consistent with their editorial stance in the McCarthy years). Only the Miami Victory Campaign made belated efforts at popular mobilization. On 7 June 1977, equal rights were repealed by a massive margin: 202,319 to 83,319.

Within a few months, Anita Bryant was on tour throughout the United States and Canada. In April 1978, the city of St. Paul, Minnesota, lost its gay rights law in a referendum vote of 54,090 to 31,690; in May, Wichita, Kansas, repealed by 47,246 to 10,005.[1] The Oklahoma state legislature joined in, unanimously passing a law to dismiss teachers who "advocate" or "practice" homosexuality.

When the antigay crusade arrived in Eugene, Oregon, many now clas-sic traits were apparent (Gay Writers' Group 1983). The New Right group, calling itself Volunteer Organization Involved in Community En-actments of the People (VOICE), relied heavily upon fundamentalist churches for its labor, attracting small- and big-business financing and local Republican party organizers. The winning ideological formula equat-ed the no-discrimination law with "child molesting," "gay recruiting," "boy prostitution," "threat to the family," and a "national gay conspiracy," add-ing the argument that "the majority has the right to do business with and rent to people of their choice." Presented as a "freedom of conscience" issue, the repeal campaign asserted the right of local capitalists to employ and lodge only those whom they like, against the right of workers and minorities to earn a livelihood and find shelter. In May 1978, the rights of gay people again suffered a loss by 23,000 to 13,427.

The next confrontation was to come in November. The New Right hoped to consolidate its successes in a fifth repeal campaign in Seattle and in an Oklahoma-style proposal in California to dismiss anyone "en-couraging, or promoting private or public homosexual activity . . . likely to come to the attention of children." In California, the attempted civil rights rollback faced well-established gay communities who understood it as a threat to their very survival. San Francisco—Carl Wittman's "refugee camp of Amerika"—had just gained its first gay city supervisor with the 1977 election of Harvey Milk. Gay neighborhoods had emerged around Castro and Folsom streets; they were "liberated zones" to some and "ghettos" to others, but in any case a territorialization of sexual desire in a political system based on geographical representation. As Manuel Castells remarks, "Many gays were able to live in their neighborhoods because they organized collective households and they were willing to make enormous economic sacrifices to be able to live autonomously and safely as gays . . . a financial and social cost that only 'moral refugees' are ready to pay" (1983, 160-61).[2] While the white middle classes were abandoning the central cores of many cities across the United States, gay people were intent upon building habitable urban communities enriched by street life and indigenous festivals in aesthetic surroundings. In San Francisco, the Castro Street Fair, first organized by Harvey Milk in 1974, had become one such festival.

Gay settlement in San Francisco, Castells points out, filled in city space left over and "opposed by property, family, and high class: the old triumvirate of social conservatism" (153). When Harvey Milk at last entered City Hall after a number of tries, he counted on the support of the dispossessed of San Francisco—a coalition of labor unions, blacks, Asians, Chicanos, feminists, hippies, and, of course, lesbians and gay men.[3] His electoral program opposed the destruction of neighborhoods by big capital and called for a fair tax to force big business to pay its share of city revenue, making a populist appeal for a city governed *for* its inhabitants.

When the Dade County repeal became known in June of 1977, 3,000 had turned out in San Francisco to protest; a year later, as the reactionaries swept toward the Pacific coast, 250,000 rallied for Gay Pride Day in 1978. Public opinion polls in the summer of 1978 revealed a likely win for the antigay initiative sponsored by State Senator John Briggs, which was to expel from the school system gay men and lesbians as well as those who presented homosexuality positively. Some thirty organizations sprang up across California in response, most notably the Bay Area Committee against the Briggs Initiative (BACABI), the Committee Against the Briggs Initiative, Los Angeles (CABILA), and Concerned Voters of California. Whereas the latter group, sponsored by *Advocate* publisher David Goodstein, took the cautious approach pioneered in Miami, stressing abstract principles, the respectability of gay people, and conventional public relations strategies, BACABI and CABILA aimed for mass mobilization and high visibility (see Ward and Freeman 1979; Hollibaugh 1978). They took every opportunity to call out public demonstrations and confront Briggs's supporters in public forums.

Harvey Milk debated with Briggs on television and in town halls, taking on each of Briggs's inflammatory claims by pointing out, for example, that child abuse was an overwhelmingly heterosexual problem (there had been no case of homosexual molestation of children in California schools), that far from removing governmental control, the Briggs Initiative would place the state in the bedrooms of the nation, and so on. In the end, the gay movement succeeded in winning endorsements from a series of unions (teachers, auto workers, steelworkers, Teamsters, culinary workers, postal workers) and from black and Chicano leaders including Angela Davis and farmworkers' leader, César Chávez. Apart from a contribution from the Atlantic Richfield oil company, the Briggs forces relied upon the evangelical churches and fund-raising lists compiled by the Anita Bryant campaign (a consortium that became Christian Voice), winning endorsements from the Los Angeles County Deputy Sheriffs Association, the Ku Klux Klan, and the American Nazi Party (Shilts 1982, 247). California voters rejected Briggs's Proposition 6, 58 to 42 percent.

On that same day in November, Seattle voters retained their gay rights law by 63 to 37 percent. The repeal forces, led by two police officers, had suffered a blow mid-campaign when one of their leaders, Dennis Falk, murdered a black youth while on duty. With sufficient lead time to campaign in a generally liberal city, a willingness to go to the people and build coalitions, and the bungling of its opponents, the three gay defense groups scored an impressive victory.

Many breathed a sigh of relief that the New Right was not invincible, but within weeks, Harvey Milk was felled by an assassin's bullets. His murderer was a former city supervisor, Dan White. White had been a police officer in San Francisco and had won a seat in City Hall in 1977 with a promise to keep a youth home out of his ward. On a city council evenly divided between neighborhood activists representing gay, feminist, black, and Asian concerns on the one side and more traditional pro-business representatives on the other, White soon attracted business interest, eventually taking up an offer to open a fast-food franchise in a major business redevelopment project. His vote on council tipped the balance toward big-business interests with tax breaks and development incentives granted through city legislation. White also cast the only vote against a gay rights ordinance introduced by Harvey Milk and opposed city cooperation with Gay Freedom Day celebrations. After resigning in the fall of 1978 and then wishing to regain his seat, White found Mayor George Moscone unwilling to reappoint him. Believing himself betrayed by the liberal bloc on the council, he shot both the mayor and Harvey Milk in their City Hall offices on 27 November (see Weiss 1984, esp. 100, 126, 158-59).

San Franciscans responded with a massive candle-lit procession to City Hall to commemorate its slain reformers. Five months later, they would return in rage. In the interim, Dan White had gone to trial where police witnesses characterized him as "a man among men . . . [and the] most valuable player [in the] law enforcement softball tournament." Psychiatrists pronounced him "depressed" and suffering from "diminished capacity" owing to a junk-food diet. On 21 May 1979, a jury from which gay people had been excluded convicted White on a manslaughter charge that carried a sentence of seven years and eight months. (In fact, White was released after little more than five years on 6 January 1984.) Though the murder of public officials was subject to the death sentence in California, White had received the lightest possible penalty. The day of the verdict, thousands marched on City Hall, protesting that White had "got away with murder" and that the court had declared "open season on faggots." At City Hall, the insurgents set eleven police cars aflame and smashed City Hall windows; 120 went to the hospital with injuries (Weiss 1984, 407-13; Shilts 1982, 329; McCaskell 1979). The police, many of whom had sported "Free Dan White" T-shirts during the White trial and had invaded a bar a month earlier where they beat several lesbians, now retaliated with a siege of Castro Street, attacking pedestrians and destroying a gay bar.

A tumultuous two years ended with a different kind of response from lesbians and gay men. Before, when Nazis and McCarthyites had targeted gay people, they proved unable to respond effectively. Nearly all attempted to fend for themselves individually by running for cover, adopting the duplicity of closetry, and playing the heterosexist game through marriage and conformity.[4] Individual solutions exacted an immense cost through the psychological suffocation and fear suffered by those in hiding and, more gravely, through the incarceration and murder of thousands ferreted out by the state and its agents. This time, gay people resisted, intending to seize their own destiny and conserve the small spaces they had so laboriously carved out of the cities. When homosexuality was a "vice," an "illness," or a "luxury," it could never resist the depredations of moral entrepreneurs, police, or kin, and Western history is the record of centuries of underground homosexual life. Only by embracing it as an identity could homosexual desire be reorganized as a collectivity capable of defending itself from its enemies.

The Rise of a New Right

But where did these enemies come from and why did they take upon themselves the fight against homosexuality? The answer is not an easy one—no easier than tracing the roots of Nazism and McCarthyism—but like these reactionary movements, a set of constituencies, networks, and alliances can be identified. In brief, three components of the opposition deserve attention. First are the adherents of a number of single-issue groups, many of which appeared in the mid and late 1970s to defend traditional social arrangements against their critics. Most important here are a range of groups focused on "family" and sexuality, such as anti-abortion, anti-ERA, antipornography, and antigay campaigns per se, and also groups with overlapping membership and leadership that oppose gun control and support the military buildup and economic empire building of the United States in the third world. Second are the 22 percent of the United States population who identify themselves as evangelicals and who thereby adopt a religious ideology of general social conservatism and particular homophobia. In many ways, this constituency has been a traditional source of American conservatism, having been the major force behind the temperance movement and the prohibition of alcohol during the 1920s, a bulwark against science and Enlightenment values (best known from the Scopes trial of 1925, where the theory of evolution was condemned as a heresy), and a proponent of McCarthyism and other anticommunist organizations, as well as antifluoridation, antiobscenity, and anti–secular education campaigns in the 1950s (see Gusfield 1963; Hughey 1982). The third component, which has largely distinguished the New Right from the old, is a significant fraction of the capitalist class (from both the corporate elite and small business) and its political organizers who seek to pull together the first two components into a political force supportive of capitalist development unfettered by state regulation, community control, civil rights, or international law.

Having identified three components, it is important to bear in mind that these social formations do not form a coherent bloc. On the one hand, many individuals and groups do not support others in this apparent alliance. Antiabortion groups that draw disproportionately from Roman Catholics, for example, usually show little interest in other portions of the evangelical agenda. Conservative Jews who join with the religious right must contend with a long tradition of anti-Semitism among American evangelicals. On the other hand, important interlocks are evident as the same right-wing ideologues and organizers often appear among the leadership of organizations spanning a diversity of issues.

The "profamily" coalition is one response to a number of social indicators often interpreted as meaning the "breakdown of the nuclear family." Interpretation of rising divorce and abortion statistics, the growing visibility of gay people, and the identification of widespread wife and child abuse have set feminists and gay liberationists apart from the recent single-issue movements. Whereas the former point to dissatisfaction with a family form characterized by male domination and a limiting division of labor as the source of change, the latter typically call for the suppression of the alternatives to the traditional family in favor of state intervention to shore it up. And whereas the liberationists seek to disestablish the legally bound family system that presumes and enforces female dependence in favor of the freedom to choose among domestic alternatives, the traditionalists (who, ironically, condemn big government in the next breath) enlist government to curb working mothers, single parents, and gay and lesbian families along with child-care centers, refuges for battered wives, and child custody for gay parents, all of which provide escape routes from the patriarchal family system. For many people who find that the traditional arrangement of male wage earner and housewife "works," feminism has been experienced as an attack upon their personal worth and an invitation *not* to fulfillment in a professional job but to abandonment in an unfriendly labor market. The statistics on female poverty speak clearly of the casualties of family breakdown as female-headed households make up the bulk of the very poor.

As Anita Bryant worried during her campaign against equal employment rights for gay people, "so many married men with children who don't have a happy marriage are going into the homosexual bars for satisfaction" (Kelley 1978, 76). The core of Phyllis Schlafly's campaign against the Equal Rights Amendment for women shared similar anxieties, claiming in Frances FitzGerald's words, "if women behave themselves sexually, then men will have to marry them, stay married, and support them. That there exists a trade-off between sexual propriety and financial security for women is in fact the underlying theme of all the 'pro-family' groups" (1981b, 25). The Equal Rights Amendment, its opponents worry, "would consign married women to the same unhappy predicament of unwed or deserted mothers, by lifting from husbands and fathers any special obligation to support their families" (Boles 1979, 106). Ironically, as advocates of the free market, the New Right appears to believe that the traditional trade-off could not survive a free market of alternatives and that too many would abandon it without state institutionalization.

For inhabitants of advanced capitalist societies, families have been charged with emotional meaning as havens in a heartless world. Especially for male wage-earners, the competitive, impersonal labor of capitalist employment contrasts with the promise of trusting, nurturant relationships at home. Given this symbolic opposition, any threat to the family portends a completely contractual world where sex, food preparation, and child rearing would all presumably become only impersonal paid services. As Linda Gordon and Allen Hunter remark of the profamily movement, "the images of the aborted fetuses, the emphasis on the cruelty of abortion, reflects a fear for the withdrawal of motherly compassion" (1977–78, 14; see also Luker 1984, 163). For the traditionalists, "sexual freedom has dissolved the bonds of the society, leaving nothing but a quasi-criminal anarchy in the home, the workplace, and the school" (FitzGerald 1981b, 25). There is a need then that sex not become too easy; allowing abortion and contraceptives, especially to youths, or sex education in schools all contribute to lowering the double standard. Indeed sociological research on the profamily forces frequently reveals their strongest support comes from women who are housewives without advanced education (and thus limited job prospects), with more than three children and with strong church participation: prochoice groups more often include women who are "educated, affluent, liberal professionals" (Luker 1984, 194–98; see Conover and Gray 1983; 111). For many whose options appear to be the continued dependence and security of the patriarchal family or abandonment upon a heartless labor market, ERA and gay rights apparently symbolize a future fraught with difficulties.

The irony of the New Right position is its fervent support of American capitalism at the same time as it struggles against modernity. Like the racists who observe black ghetto poverty and then conclude that black people cause urban decay, the profamily people confuse cause and effect, problem and solution. Black history shows that impoverished sharecroppers, attracted northward by the promise of a better life in industrial employment, found instead residential segregation, unstable employment, and a white capitalist class with little interest in investing its profits back into black neighborhoods. The ideology of the Right has done no more than blame the victim by making a myopic identification of blacks with their economic plight while clinging to the national dream of frontier capitalism where anyone could become rich through enough entrepreneurial know-how. Similarly, the modern gay and lesbian communities, which have created new styles of community and intimacy in modern, anomic societies, are instead identified with the loss of community that is characteristic of modern capitalist societies. What is missing from the New Right analysis is the entire social mechanism that engenders the changes they so fear, for it is capitalist economic development that opened alternatives to kin-controlled livelihoods; that offered medical, food, and domestic services on a cash market; that employed women as a cheap docile reserve of labor; and that constructed the heartless labor market that dissolved kin obligations, thereby creating new pressures and opportunities that have made new forms of intimacy possible.

Caught in this symbolic vortex, homosexuality for the New Right as for the Nazis, signifies the modernity, the sexual freedom, and the dissolving underpinnings of traditional domesticity. The reactionaries have never been interested in the *experience* of gay people or in hearing their voices, often priding themselves in their ignorance of the subject and demanding that gay and lesbian speech be silenced as "obscene," "immoral," or "subversive," thereby giving free reign to their own projective fantasies of child molesters and sex fiends. Perhaps what is most remarkable about modern homosexuality is, in fact, the refounding of intimacy and community on the very sites of advanced capitalist development: in the commercial sex scene (bars and baths), in declining urban districts used up and abandoned by investors, and in the workplace.[5] Like the racists, whose short-circuited analysis jumps over the social and historical antecedents of black poverty, the heterosexists protect the causes of their anxieties and blame those who are trying to cope with the same difficult environment. Like the Nazi anti-Semites who found it much easier to attack a visible but relatively powerless symbol of modernity, heterosexists displace their fear and anger of modern society upon lesbians and gay men.

Evangelical churches figure prominently in the profamily movement both in leadership and in popular support. Symbolic of the once dominant rural white Protestant class in the history of the United States, evangelicals have been fighting a century-long campaign to retain moral and political influence in an increasingly diverse and secular society. Since the split of American Protestantism in the 1920s between a liberal majority, which has accommodated itself to the exigencies of urban capitalism, and a conservative minority, intent upon preserving the moral absolutism characteristic of the agrarian roots of Christianity, Evangelicals have manifested several strategies to conserve tradition. When faced with a world where old cognitive maps prove inapplicable, people can revise their worldviews (as did the liberal Protestants), withdraw from the larger society, or attempt to preserve or restore the old order. Each strategy has a very different political impact and the Anabaptist and Pentecostal tendencies usually choose to insulate themselves from secular cultures and abstain from mainstream politics, some building communities dedicated to preserving antiquated life-styles in their entirety (see Hunter 1983).

It is among the Baptists that political activism combines with Christian traditionalism, but even here there are important divisions. Black Baptists have always been much more impressed by biblical themes of brotherhood, freedom, and the promised land than by the moralism and authoritarianism of the white churches, and Baptists have been central in the struggle for black civil rights from Martin Luther King, Jr., to Jesse Jackson. It is conservative white Baptists who tread the fine line between disengagement from a world of secular humanism and political engagement. Biblical injunctions alone, then, explain very little about religious responses to homosexuality, as their interpretation is as diverse as the political spectrum itself. White fundamentalist Baptism has developed a peculiar ideology that George Lipsitz calls a mixed "cult of self-improvement," and "religion of upward mobility, encouraged adjustment, amicability, optimism, and conformity" (1983–84, 101). Its preachers rage against the heterogeneity of American society, which has dislodged the absolutist vision of fundamentalism from its once privileged status and forced it to retreat into being no more than one private confession among many. Their fervent identification with the American state and its imperial ambitions, their adoration of nineteenth-century capitalist ideologies of frontier individualism, and their zealous belief that God is on their side are a unique construction of Christian doctrine paralleled only by the other essentially nativist American church, the Mormons.

The peculiarities of white fundamentalist beliefs stem from the sociological base of the Evangelical churches. When compared with other denominations, Evangelicals are more often older, married, and female, have lower education and income, and live in rural areas especially in the southern states (Hunter 1983, 49; Lienesch 1982; Simpson 1983, 188, 195). At the opposite extreme, those with no religion are more often male, single, skilled workers or professionals, and live in urban centers in the western states. The demographic profile bears comparison with supporters and opponents of women's and gay issues. Opponents of the gay equal rights ordinance in Eugene, Oregon, were disproportionately older, Evangelical, less educated, and members of traditional families; supporters were younger, single, well educated, and unreligious (Gay Writers' Group 1983, 23). The profile of opponents to the Equal Rights Amendment (when compared with supporters) shows trends toward women with lower education and income, white middle-aged men, and rural dwellers who attend church regularly. Black people supported ERA overwhelmingly.[6] Psychological studies of homophobia have also found it correlated with measures of racial prejudice and endorsement of traditional gender roles, and the contours of antigay dogma show many of the same traits as other racisms (MacDonald et al. 1973; Henley and Pincus 1978; Adam 1978, 42–51).

This is also a very well organized constituency. Of all the religious groups in the United States, Evangelicals attend church most frequently and give it money most consistently, also turning out to vote in elections at the highest rate. This gives Evangelicals political influence that extends well beyond their numbers, and new gains in television have greatly increased their apparent strength. Because time and space in communications media in the United States are commodities like any other, access to the nation is a simple question of money. Whereas religious broadcasting was once a public service given to a variety of local viewpoints, by "1980, ninety per cent of all religion on television was commercial," bought by the new religious right (FitzGerald 1981a, 59). Most notable of these are Jerry Falwell's "Old Time Gospel Hour," Pat Robertson's Christian Broadcasting Network, and a host of smaller electronic evangelists who campaign for money with images of the starving in Ethiopia and Kampuchea, or the scare tactics of lesbian and gay teachers in the classroom. In addition to the television church, Falwell's Moral Majority and Robertson's Christian Voice issue regular direct-mail appeals. A 1981 letter from Falwell warns, "Please remember, homosexuals do not reproduce! They recruit! And, many of them are out after my children and your children"; a Christian Voice fund-raising letter cries, "Can't let militant gays, ultra liberals, atheists, porno pushers, pressure Congress into passing Satan's agenda instead of God's" (Young 1982, 307, 309). More recent letters exploit the fear of AIDS to raise funds for antigay campaigns. The relentless stream of antigay propaganda forms but one component of a political lobby for school prayer and against union rights, affirmative action, and science teaching. It includes support for United States client states such as Israel, South Africa, Taiwan, South Korea, Chile, and El Salvador. In 1979, Moral Majority, the Christian

Broadcasting Network, and Christian Voice along with National Religious Broadcasting, Campus Crusade, and others formed the (Religious) Roundtable, a cartel to further coordinate national and international efforts (Liebman 1983).

If *Jews* or *Legionnaires* or *bankers* were substituted for *homosexuals* in religious right literature, it would be immediately recognized for the hate propaganda that it is. In 1979, the gay movement succeeded in temporarily removing television preacher James Robison from the air in Dallas and New York, arguing that gay people should at least have equal time to refute the endless barrage of vilification. Because the television networks refused gay people *any* time, they canceled Robison's show rather than apply the equal-time principle. Before long, however, Robison was restored as is.

Finally, the group that has attracted most recent attention is a set of corporate families and political organizers who hope to harvest the social conservatives for the advancement of corporate capitalism and have scored notable successes in shaping U.S. government policy. Best known is Richard Viguerie, a fund-raiser for the George Wallace presidential bid, who compiled a massive mailing list of American conservatives and has proven successful in direct-mail fund-raising for various New Right causes. Viguerie, Paul Weyrich (Committee for the Survival of a Free Congress), Terry Dolan (National Conservative Political Action Committee), and Howard Phillips (Conservative Caucus) have attracted significant capitalist backing to create a set of political lobbies and policy institutes with which to cultivate the profamily, single-issue, and religious right organizations for the capitalist class.

Most evident among the funding sources is the Joseph Coors family (breweries). The Coors corporation has a lengthy record of intimidating employees with lie-detector tests to root out Communists, gay people, and union sympathizers, and it has a reputation for excluding women, blacks, and Chicanos from advancement in the corporation. One of Harvey Milk's early political accomplishments was to forward Howard Wallace's campaign to remove Coors beer from San Francisco gay bars. The financial linkages between the American corporate elite and New Right organizations are not easy to discover, but well documented is the backing of the Scaife Foundation (Mellon fortune in steel, Gulf Oil, and banking), Pew Freedom Trust (Sun Oil), billionaire Nelson Bunker Hunt, the Marriott family (hotels and amusement parks), the Hearst family (newspapers), Amway corporation, California industrialist Robert Fluor, and according to the *Washington Post,* donations from Weyerhaueser, Ford,

Reader's Digest, Potlach, Mobil, Coca-Cola, Consolidated Foods, Ashland Oil, Citibank, Republic Steel, General Motors, Morgan Guaranty Trust, and IBM.[7] All this political maneuvering occurred against a strongly supportive backdrop of events directly shaped by the same elite actors. The economic recession of the late 1970s and the retrenchment of major industries increased unemployment, creating greater defensiveness in a population anxious for its livelihood. As American capitalism continued its trend toward capital-intensive high-technology production at home while relying on third-world sources for its cheap labor supply, American workers, women, and minorities were forced toward "concessions" and "conservation" of their positions and away from the struggle for greater equality. As the capitalist class maintains a near monopoly over mass communications media in the United States, it can as well provide interpretations, frame debates, and set agendas for social problems and their solutions, including explanations for economic rollbacks and the deployment of force both at home and abroad. With overt McCarthyites returned to power in the Nixon and Reagan presidencies, it has been possible to foster the impression of a popular "shift to the right" (though public opinion polls do not show a change on women's or gay issues [Mueller 1983]) and to present jostlings among conservatives of various stripes as the totality of legitimate debate. The state and media have played upon the general sense of beleaguerment, finding the culprit first in the national defeat in Vietnam, next in the "humiliation" experienced by diplomats and CIA agents at the hands of Iranian students, and, then, in the Sandinista revolution in Nicaragua. With a president since 1980 who is directly identified with Hollywood mythologies, well-worn militarist formulas have enjoyed yet another revival. Combining slighted national self-esteem with masculinist ideology in a rhetoric of football, war, and western movies, the Reagan presidency has appropriated the military hardware to arm guerrilla and state armies in Nicaragua, El Salvador, Angola, and Mozambique where thousands of peasants are the usual victims.[8] The reconsolidation of a national fantasy of obsessive anticommunism and suppression of movements for self-determination both at home and abroad augurs badly for the gay and lesbian movement and its friends. The Reagan presidency has created a uniquely effective union of state and media to legitimize the dismantling of state services and civil liberties. The Right has, for now, successfully checked the popular movements that would extend democratic control and civil liberties to the disenfranchised.

Treatment of the New Right cannot conclude without a note on the participation of apparently homosexual people *within* reactionary organizations. In several instances, New Right adherents have been exposed in homosexual activities through police entrapment or by the press. Congressmen Jon Hinson, a Mississippi ultraconservative, and Robert Bauman, once president of the far-right Young Americans for Freedom, are cases in point. Both had voted against progay legislation in Congress. Others include the Reverend Leo McKenzie, communications director of the archdiocese of Philadelphia and vocal opponent of gay rights; Billy James Hargis, a prominent fundamentalist preacher of the 1950s; and Nixon Supreme Court nominee Harold Carswell.[9] All were drawn from the same groups as other New Right followers and no doubt had had no contact with the gay world, experiencing their homosexuality as a guilty secret scarcely admitted to themselves, much less to other people, and carefully concealed behind what Laud Humphreys calls a "breastplate of righteousness."

More problematic is the case of Terry Dolan, director of the National Conservative Political Action Committee, a major New Right force, who apparently takes a libertarian position, regretting the moralism of the religious right while opposing civil rights legislation of any kind in the hope that big government might be reduced in general.[10] Emboldened by the gains of the 1970s, gay conservatism came to the fore most notably in the formation of Republican party gay clubs and in gay business organizations. Nearly always white (upper) middle-class men, whose class position has apparently overcome the implications of their homosexuality, they fervently wish for an exception in conservative ideology to allow them the place appropriate to their backgrounds.

Hard times often stimulate cautious or conservative responses among those under attack, as the homophile movement of the 1950s demonstrates. And certainly repression causes social movements to reevaluate their tactics and wonder if everything would be different had they taken another course of action. In 1932, a member of the Nazi militia wrote to the Scientific-Humanitarian Committee in Berlin to condemn its law-reform policy, claiming that if only the committee had presented gay men as "healthy, regular guys, boy scouts, army officers, or athletes," instead of talking so much about sex reform, then homosexuality would not have had such bad press. The Nazis, he assured the committee, were willing to ignore one's private life—only the real deviants like pedophiles would be sterilized (Stümke and Finkler 1981, 103–10, my translation)! It is perhaps not surprising that in periods of intensified persecution accommodationist and conservative strategies should again come forward and voices should again be raised to argue that everything would be all right "if only" gay people would get good press through effective image making, acting respectably, and abandoning leathermen, boy-lovers, and butch dykes (e.g., Severin 1983; Kirk and Pill 1985).

Under Attack in the United Kingdom, Canada, and Australia

In the nations of the British legal tradition, there is less reason to talk of a New Right than in the United States. With much smaller evangelical populations, fewer single-issue groups, and none of the trappings of the central power of the capitalist world, antigay practices of the later 1970s and early 1980s show considerable continuity with earlier periods and little, if any, distinction need be made between old and new conservatism. All three nations, nevertheless, have been subject to the same trends of the world capitalist economy and, with a shared language and cultural tradition, have not been impervious to developments in the United States. The rightward drift of the United States emboldened moral entrepreneurs, the police, and conventional conservatives in the United Kingdom, Canada, and Australia.

In the United Kingdom, Evangelicals formed the Festival of Light as early as 1971, but they have not succeeded in becoming more than an irritation in the body politic. In 1976, Mary Whitehouse, a long-time campaigner against "declining morals" on the British Broadcasting Corporation, had *Gay News* charged with "blasphemy" for publishing a poem on Christ. Though the blasphemy law was virtually moribund, not having been used since 1921, she won the conviction of its editor, who received an eighteen-month suspended sentence and a £500 fine; *Gay News* itself was fined £1,000 plus court costs. A *Gay News* defense fund eventually paid costs after the House of Lords upheld the conviction in 1979 despite massive public demonstrations and outrage at the absence of press freedom revealed by the conviction (see Weeks 1977, 205, 268; Weeks 1981, 277, 281; Tracy and Morrison 1979, 9–17).

Whitehouse's attacks varied little from those made by the press on *The Well of Loneliness* in the 1930s. Those attacks displayed the usual preoccupations of the homophobic mind: the appeal to disease metaphors, equating lesbianism with "leprosy"; the claim to childhood innocence (presumably young people are unable to think of such things themselves so must be "seduced" by adults); the shock that lesbians would dare show themselves at all ("they flaunt themselves in public places with increasing effrontery"; "they take a delight in their flamboyant notoriety"); and the pious appropriation of God to do antilesbian work for the prosecution (the book is "moral poison") (Brittain 1968, 54–56; see also Adam 1978, chap. 2).

In Canada, a wave of police raids from 1975 to 1981 owed much to conservative governments already in power for more than a generation, the first being the Drapeau administration of Montreal and the second, the Conservative government of Ontario. Following widespread practice in North America, Montreal police launched a "cleanup" campaign in the months preceding the opening of the 1976 Olympic Games, descending on seven bars and a bathhouse in four raids to intimidate the city's gay men and lesbians. Using nineteenth-century bawdy house laws that permitted the arrest of everyone "found in" a place "resorted to for the practice of acts of indecency," police could undermine the 1969 decriminalization law by allowing judges to define gay conduct as indecent. In 1976, a bath raid in Montreal seized 89 men and a membership list of 7,000 and another in Ottawa netted 27 men and 3,000 names. The raids reenergized the flagging gay and lesbian movements in Quebec, leading to the formation of the Association pour les Droits des Gai(e)s du Quebec (ADGQ). When Montreal police struck again at a popular gay bar in October 1977, arresting 145 as "found-ins" and 8 for "gross indecency," the ADGQ mobilized demonstrations that paralyzed the city core and organized a defense committee that fought each case through years of litigation. (Those who refused to plead guilty were ultimately acquitted after six years in court.)

The Drapeau administration was a hold-over from an earlier era of Quebec politics, taking its cues from the Catholic right. In the 1960s, Quebec's own New Left formed as a nationalist movement intent on preserving French-language culture in North America without the patronage of the Roman Catholic church or the domination of Anglo-Canadian capital. As a participant in the nationalist alignment, the ADGQ pressed the Parti Québécois, which had recently come to power as the provincial government, to remedy the Montreal persecution. Clearly not averse to tweaking the noses of the old guard, the government added "sexual orientation" to the Quebec Charter of Human Rights on 15 December 1977 (see Sylvestre 1979, 57–60, 141–47; Jackson and Persky 1982, 229–30).

In Toronto, police invaded the offices of the journal, the *Body Politic*, on 30 December 1977, ostensibly to seize evidence on a charge of "using the mails to transmit immoral, indecent and scurrilous material." The charge arose from the November publication of an article called "Men

Loving Boys Loving Men," which took a sober look at pedophilia. Though the prosecution needed only a single copy of the journal to press its case, the police carried away twelve packing crates of material, including the journal's financial records and subscription lists, leading to fears that police were compiling "pink lists" of gay Canadians for further persecution. Legal proceedings continued through 1978 as Renaissance International, Canada's Evangelical moral crusaders, sponsored Anita Bryant on a national tour and Toronto police began the first of several bath raids in December. In February 1979, a Toronto court acquitted the journal but the Conservative provincial government appealed, keeping the *Body Politic* in the courts with appeals and new charges until its ultimate acquittal in 1983. Perhaps more significant than the charges themselves was the province's ability to curb a dissident press by imposing a six-year financial drain upon a largely volunteer and nonprofit collective.

In 1979, the progressive mayor of Toronto, John Sewell, spoke out against the provincial prosecution of the *Body Politic,* creating a furor that spilled over into the 1980 city election. With George Hislop, the city's first openly gay candidate running with the mayor's endorsement, the campaign attracted antigay pamphleteering from Renaissance International, the city police, and the ultraright fringe. Both Hislop and Sewell went down to defeat in November. (Sewell increased his popular vote from 39 to 47 percent but lost to a single conservative candidate; two candidates had split the conservative vote in the previous election, which had brought him to the mayor's office [Casey 1981; Jackson 1980–81; Fleming 1983].)

Three months later the Conservative provincial government called an election for 19 March 1981. On 5 February, the same week of the election call, 150 Toronto police officers arrested 286 "found-ins" and 20 "keepers" in a massive raid on several bathhouses, thereby arresting the largest number of Canadians in a single action since the declaration of the War Measure's Act in 1970 to stem the activities of the Front pour la Libération du Québec. In a cynical bid to capitalize on the preceding municipal election, the Conservatives succeeded in winning away seats from the New Democratic party (a long if ambivalent supporter of civil rights for gay people) in Toronto, returning to power with a parliamentary majority.

It was also at the height of the Anita Bryant campaign in North America that Australian police took an unexpectedly harsh turn. Police attacked a Gay Mardi Gras rally of about 2,000 people in Sydney on 24 June 1978, beating demonstrators and arresting 23 women and 30 men.

Demonstrators who had not been arrested maintained an overnight vigil at the Darlinghurst police station in solidarity with those who had been seized. With Mary Whitehouse arriving at the invitation of the local Festival of Light, a Gay Solidarity Group formed to defend the Mardi Gras 53. With sympathetic protests directed against New South Wales tourist offices in Melbourne, Adelaide, and Brisbane, the Gay Solidarity Group marched on the Darlinghurst station on 15 July where 14 more were taken by police. By the end of the winter, the toll had risen to 184 when courts threw out most of the charges.[11]

In Canada and Australia, the unintended consequence of police actions was the revitalization of gay organizations that had fallen into some disarray in the 1970s. The day after the bath raids in Toronto and again two weeks later, 3,000 marched on the #52 Division police station, spawning a Right to Privacy Committee that became the largest gay organization of the city in the 1980s (Hannon 1980).

Chapter Seven

The Movement in the 1980s

The gay and lesbian movement unfolded such a wealth of interests and initiatives in the 1980s that this chapter can offer only a cursory inventory of its diversity and range. Modern scholars have delved into the various linkages between sexuality and family on the one hand, and professions and state on the other, to sort out the contexts that shaped homosexuality into a people with a social movement in the modern world. The movement has inevitably varied with world conditions and according to the tasks thrust upon it by its political adversaries. Here we take account of several external and internal stresses: the confrontation with government and their agents and participation in the political process; organization around religious issues, ethnicity, and other social statuses; the development of movements in the third world and Eastern bloc nations; the advance of debates about gender and sexuality among feminist and gay activists; and the need to meet the demands posed by the sudden new epidemic of AIDS.

Civil Rights and Electoral Politics

German sociologist Max Weber once defined the state as "an association that claims the monopoly of the legitimate use of violence" (Gerth and Mills 1958, 334), and it is state power that has primarily preoccupied the gay and lesbian movements of the 1980s. It is perhaps a sign of the maturity of the movement that activists have sufficiently learned the rules of the game to have begun to make significant headway through law reform in many countries. No longer unorganized individuals easily

121

controlled by the state, gay people have, in the modern era, followed some well-tested routes toward political efficacy. Like the Irish and Italians in the United States in the first decades of this century, or the blacks of today, gay people have taken on many of the traits of ethnicity to assert their political will. Increasingly organized through an indigenous press, in neighborhoods, at work, and at church, lesbians and gay men have forged a social movement that—like all others—seeks to give them a voice in their own future and to defend themselves against the violence of the state and of others.

In the modern liberal democracies of Western Europe, North America, and Australia, issues and struggles have developed common patterns, such that annual conferences of the International Gay Association (founded in Coventry, England, in 1979) can provide a useful forum for sharing experiences and developing new policies. The late 1970s and early 1980s have also seen the unprecedented emergence of fledgling gay organizations in several state socialist and third-world societies. The political rules and social priorities of these new groups in Eastern Europe, Latin America, Asia, and Africa differ sufficiently from the mature movements such that fruitful world comparisons shift from comparisons among advanced capitalist nations to comparisons among first-, second-, and third-world countries.

This section on civil rights and electoral politics focuses, then, on political gains in liberal democracies. The cutting edge of legislative change has been the introduction of sexual orientation into human rights codes, which outlaw discrimination in employment, housing, and state services. Notable accomplishments in civil rights law, however, cannot distract attention from the fact that many jurisdictions—especially in English-language countries—continue to criminalize sexual contacts between men and subject gay men to arbitrary police and judicial harassment for the expression of mutually consenting acts of sexuality and affection. (Lesbians are typically ignored in these laws.)

Lesbians and gay men now have brief but extensive experience in holding elected office in city, intermediate, and national assemblies on three continents. Still, despite these developments, conservative and neoconservative sectors of modern governments continue to play out local "sex scandals" through moral frameworks that show little change since 1897. Medieval Western presumptions about homosexuality live on, especially in the practices of police and military organizations, orthodox churches, New Right lobbies, and aristocratic remnants.

Just what the gay civil rights movement "wants" is summed up in this exemplary statement of the French Comité d'Urgence Anti-Répression Homosexuelle (CUARH) adopted in 1979:

- Abolition of the law fixing a higher age of consent for homosexual relations than for heterosexual
- Addition of "sex" and "sexual orientation" to the antiracism laws that ban discrimination
- No discrimination in employment or housing
- Custody and visitation rights for gay parents (which would "suppress the paradox which wants homosexuals to be reproached for not having children, then takes them away when they do have them")
- Recognition of "social, administrative, judicial and fiscal rights of two people living together as a homosexual couple"
- Right to adopt children
- Destruction of police files on lesbians and gay men
- An end to isolation of gay people within prisons
- Deletion of "homosexuality" from the World Health Organization classification of mental illness
- An end to medical research and therapy to change sexual orientation
- Compensation for gay victims of Nazism and recognition of them in memorials
- Right of asylum to persons persecuted in other countries because of their homosexuality
- International recognition of the problem of antigay intolerance[1]

The struggle for the inclusion of "sexual orientation" in human rights legislation is an attempt to provide legal recourse for people denied employment or shelter because of their homosexuality. It is a law reform that demands no more than the realization of the self-proclaimed principle of liberal democracies that everyone receive equal and impartial treatment before the law and that people be evaluated according to their job performance and not by criteria irrelevant to their competence. By the mid-1980s, more than fifty cities in the United States and four in Canada had affirmed this right. Since the 1977 amendment in Quebec, the province of Ontario in 1986, two states, Wisconsin and New South Wales in 1982, two nations, Norway in 1981 and France in 1985, and the European Parliament in 1984 have made the same affirmation. Several state governors in the United States have also issued executive orders covering employment in state governments themselves.

These civil rights gains deserve some attention and reveal a diversity of approaches. In Wisconsin, the gay movement succeeded in forging an unprecedented consensus, even drawing endorsements from the whole range of religious authorities. With even Roman Catholic and Baptist officials seeing the virtues of no discrimination, despite their rejection of homosexuality itself, the reform became a no-risk proposition for Wisconsin politicians. The New South Wales reform, on the other hand, faced stiff opposition from church officials. As early as 1975, a Homosexual Rights Coalition of state groups formed to organize a Tribunal on Homosexuals and Discrimination and succeeded in meeting with Labour premier Neville Wran. In 1977, a church coalition of Anglican, Salvation Army, Roman Catholic, and New South Wales Council of Churches officials campaigned through the pulpits to suppress the antidiscrimination bill. The Labour government, nevertheless, passed the bill despite the shrill claims of television evangelist Fred Niles that homosexuals would be seizing children from school classrooms as a result.

The Norwegian law owes much to the unflagging work of Conservative parliamentarian Wenche Lowzow. Her discovery of her own lesbianism and relationship with Kim Friele (who is general secretary of Norway's major gay organization, DNF-48) no doubt explains much, and her participation in the coalition Labour, Centre, and Conservative government, much more. The Norwegian law, drafted on the model of legislation protecting women and minorities, extends beyond protection against discrimination to include a provision against the propagation of hate literature. The law bans "statements of an aggravated insulting nature" and "statements inciting violence" against "homosexual tendencies, way of life or orientation" in addition to the standard safeguards against discriminatory acts.[2]

The French sexual orientation law fulfills one of the demands of CUARH and results from a series of reforms introduced by the Socialist government elected in 1981 (which is discussed further below).

In 1981 the Council of Europe passed an equal rights resolution, and in 1984 the European Parliament adopted perhaps the most comprehensive statement on the civil rights of gay people to date. Introduced by Italian Communist member Vera Squarcialupi, the resolution received support from all the Socialist and Communist parties and all but one of the liberal and centrist members. Conservatives and Christian democrats split on the measure resulting in a vote of 114 to 45 (Pronk 1985). Though nonbinding on the member nations of the European Economic Community, the resolution establishes an important precedent for them.

For every legal breakthrough, however, there have been dozens of legislative bills and referenda that have turned down equal civil rights for lesbians and gay men or even abolished existing protections. Though the glare of publicity faded with the defeat of the Briggs Initiative in California and of the repeal proposition in Seattle, another sexual orientation ordinance fell in a 1980 referendum in Santa Clara County, California. There, the New Right coalition led by the Moral Majority proclaimed in their campaign leaflets that equal rights for gay people would allow homosexuals to molest children and would lead to the mass murders of boys and the infection of the community with venereal diseases. Citing medical authorities, they claimed that homosexuality is a "curable" behavioral "choice" and that, anyway, gay people are affluent and do not need equal rights protection![3] Texans voted no in the 1980s, sending out conflicting messages on the same issue: Austin voters rejected an initiative in 1982 that would have legally established a *right to discriminate* against gay people in housing, while Houston voters repealed a no-discrimination ordinance in 1985. In California, civil rights legislation passed by the state house and senate suffered a veto by Republican governor George Deukmejian who claimed the law was "not needed"!

While a gay rights bill languishes in Congress, the federal government remains a center of antigay policies. After 200,000 people marched on Washington on 14 October 1979 to demand fundamental rights for lesbians and gay men, Congress continued to reduce their limited civil liberties by vetoing a decriminalization law passed by the District of Columbia and by banning federal funding for any legal proceeding that might confirm the civil rights of gay people.

The judicial record is equally mixed. Lower courts have generally upheld students' right of assembly when universities have refused to recognize gay and lesbian campus groups, even overturning a 1981 Florida law that would have cut off state funding to colleges that tolerated gay campus organizations. In 1985 the U.S. Supreme Court struck down the Oklahoma law that banned the favorable mention of homosexuality in schools as an unconstitutional interference with free speech after seven years of court battles sponsored by the National Gay Task Force and the National Gay Rights Advocates. The decision came on a perilous 4–4 tie vote which resulted in the upholding of a lower court ruling. But as the judges who presided over the civil rights era of the 1950s and 1960s retire, their successors have been more and more conservative, dimming the prospects for any new gains over the next generation; and in June 1986 the court ruled in a 5–4 decision that states retain the right to criminalize private sexual conduct between consenting adults. The Bowers v. Hardwick case began in 1982 when a police officer arrested Michael Hardwick, an Atlanta gay man, in Hardwick's own bedroom and charged him with violating the Georgia law that declares "any sexual act involving the sex organs of one person and the mouth or anus of another" to be a felony punishable by up to twenty years imprisonment. Even more disturbing are the repeated cases across the United States and Canada where the lower courts have handed out very light sentences or outright acquittals to the murderers of gay men after they claimed their victims had made sexual advances to them. In some cases of "queer bashing," the "respectable" middle-class background of the murderers has sufficed to convince judges to give probationary and suspended sentences even where sexual approaches were not alleged but the victim was thought to be gay.[4]

In Canada, the single gay rights case to reach the Supreme Court resulted in the quashing of a decision by the British Columbia Human Rights Commission that had ordered the newspaper, the *Vancouver Sun*, to pay $500 in damages for refusing to print an advertisement for the paper *Gay Tide*. Using an "etcetera" clause in the British Columbia human rights code, the commission originally ruled that gay people did have equal rights and that the *Vancouver Sun* had acted discriminatorily. In 1979, the Supreme Court of Canada, however, held in a 6–3 decision that only those who own presses have the freedom to determine their content and that no one else has legal access to the pages of the nation's newspapers.[5]

Despite the apprehensions of the New Right, the actual record of sexual orientation provisions is far less dramatic. In the first few years in Quebec:

- A hospital employee, fired for being a homosexual, obtained a $10,000 settlement and a favorable letter of recommendation.
- Two women teachers in private schools received settlements of $3,000 and $4,000 after they were fired.
- The Montreal Catholic School Commission was ordered to allow a gay organization to meet in a school after school hours on the same basis on which other voluntary organizations were permitted to meet.
- The *Progrès-Dimanche* newspaper was fined $800 for refusing to print a paid notice for a gay conference.

(Jackson 1981; see also Sylvestre 1979, 134-37)

The Supreme Court of Norway delivered its first conviction under the comprehensive antidefamation law in 1984, ruling in a 4–1 decision that television evangelist Hans Bratterud had violated the law by demanding in a radio broadcast the dismissal of all homosexuals from leading positions. The court reasoned that "it is no encroachment on the freedom of worship that qualified insults to vulnerable minority groups are forbidden" and that Bratterud's remarks were "concretely aimed at homosexuals in an area where they may be hurt badly and where it will be difficult for them in a satisfactory manner to prevent major harmful effects."[6]

Against the expectations of many, openly lesbian and gay candidates for political office have been able to be elected in a wide variety of places, and a number of political parties have endorsed the idea of at least basic equal rights for all regardless of sexual orientation. Party support has come almost exclusively from Social Democratic (or Green) and Communist parties and occasionally from traditional liberal or centrist parties. Lesbian and gay activists have often had to work against entrenched homophobic policies in left as well as center and right parties in order to bring about a policy change. Many, however, have remained intransigent.[7]

In 1977 the French Socialist party, as well as the French and Italian Communist parties, adopted gay rights planks. By 1985, the president of Communist Youth in Italy was gay activist Nichi Vendola. In 1981 the Spanish Socialist Workers (PSOE) and Communist (PCE) parties followed suit (Mirabeti Mullol 1985, 446-48). With the French Socialists and Spanish PSOE in power in the early 1980s, both nations moved forward to equalize their laws. An early act of the French government was to extend amnesty to 156 gay men convicted under a discriminatory age-of-consent law and to abolish the "homo squad" of the Paris police. In 1982, the age of consent was equalized for all at fifteen, and under a general plan to regularize dozens of pirate radio stations, the government licensed Fréquence Gaie, the first full-time gay radio station in the world (but not until the station's listeners demonstrated in force through Paris streets to support its mandate). In 1985 the National Assembly added sexual orientation to the antiracism law. The Spanish Socialists removed homosexuality from the notorious "Social Danger" law in 1979. Passed in 1970 by the previous fascist government of Francisco Franco, the law had declared gay people a social danger in the manner of the Gaullist law of 1960, thereby providing a warrant for police persecution. In 1984 homosexuality was removed as an offense from the Spanish Code of Military Justice.

In Italy and the United Kingdom, where leftist parties dominated city politics and conservatives held national power, lesbian and gay organizations won municipal support for community centers in several cities. Both the 28th of June Cultural Centre in Bologna and the OMPO gay center and museum in Rome opened with the assistance of Communist city administrators (Virgil 1984). Labour city councils in Manchester and London also funded lesbian and gay community centers in England in the 1980s.

In Canada, on the other hand, the New Democratic party (NDP) agreed to press for an equal rights amendment in 1976, but in subsequently elected governments in three provinces, it failed to implement its own policy. A similar resolution adopted by the Liberal party in 1978 did not prevent Liberal members of Parliament from joining en bloc with Conservatives to exclude sexual orientation from the Charter of Rights entrenched in the Canadian Constitution of 1982. (Sex, however, was added.) In a 12–2 vote, only the two NDP committee members supported inclusion. Still, there remained a question whether the comprehensive wording of Section 15 of the Charter might nevertheless include protection for gay people, and in 1986 the Conservative minister of justice opined that it probably did, while refusing to formalize it in the Canadian Human Rights Code.

As early as 1972, Jim Foster addressed the convention of the Democratic party of the United States with a list of gay grievances; in 1980, it endorsed an amendment to the Civil Rights Act to protect lesbians and gay men. The 1984 convention, held in San Francisco, brought out 100,000 marchers who demanded:

- Immediate, increased funding for AIDS research
- Provision of social services for lesbian and gay youth, aged, disabled, prisoners, and poor
- "An end to violent attacks against lesbians and gay men"
- An executive order prohibiting discrimination in federal employment
- A national lesbian and gay rights law
- Child custody, adoption and visitation rights
- Enforcement of civil rights legislation, including within the lesbian/gay community
- Passage of the Equal Rights Amendment for women
- An end to discrimination in immigration and naturalization laws
- The right of women to choose "if and when to bear children" including the right to choose abortion
- Legal recognition of lesbian and gay relationships
- Repeal of sodomy and solicitation laws

In fact, the convention did adopt several of the demands. The 1984 convention saw black presidential nominee Jesse Jackson embrace lesbians and gay men in his "Rainbow Coalition" and bring a call for their civil rights to the convention floor and the nation at large; as well, some forty-six gay and lesbian Democratic clubs met to give a voice to their constituents.

Openly lesbian and gay politicians have demonstrated, against the pessimists, that homosexuality is not an insuperable barrier in gaining the confidence of the people and that in many instances, majorities of voters are willing to understand the concerns of gay people and understand the relationship of those concerns to their own interests. To see just how such successes have been achieved, it is best to distinguish among three styles of publicness: (1) those elected primarily in Europe as part of a party list, (2) incumbents who come out after winning at least one election, and (3) those winning elected office as openly gay candidates in district elections.

The key to public office in party list systems is to win the approval of the party, which is allocated parliamentary seats according to its proportion of the popular vote. Both Angelo Pezzana, elected on the Radical party ticket in Italy, and Herbert Rusche, with the West German Green party, were nominated to parliament by parties formed from coalitions of progressive social movements (such as feminist, ecological, peace, student, and civil rights movements) where the gay and lesbian movement is an explicit participant (see Rusche 1984b). The inclusion of Eveline Esthuis as one of two Communist representatives in the parliament of the Netherlands follows the party's adoption of a stronger feminist orientation in the early 1980s.

The experience of incumbent parliamentarians who either came out voluntarily or were exposed is more mixed. Wenche Lowzow was retained, after coming out, on the Norwegian Conservative list through one election, but dropped in 1985 following the dissolution of the Conservative alliance with the social democrats. Maureen Colquhoun, a British Labour member of Parliament, endured a press exposé of her relationship with the editor of the lesbian journal *Sappho* and lost her seat in the 1979 Conservative sweep of the United Kingdom (see Colquhoun 1980; Hemmings 1980). In the United States, Allan Spear, Democratic-Farm-Labour state senator in Minnesota, won reelection several times following a voluntary coming out. Gerry Studds, Democratic congressional representative from Massachusetts, also won reelection in his district following exposure by a congressional investigating committee in 1983. Unlike other congressmen revealed before him, who typically pleaded diminished responsibility owing to "drinking problems," Studds declared to Congress that he is gay and suffered a congressional censure because of his relationship with a congressional page (see Goldsmith 1983). In 1984, British Labour M.P. Chris Smith came out while protesting an antigay ordinance passed by the city of Rugby; at the time of this writing he had not yet faced reelection.

Since the breakthrough election of Elaine Nobel to the Massachusetts House in 1974, a number of state and local politicians have employed the same winning formula. Almost never sponsored by business, privilege, or wealth, openly lesbian and gay candidates have won on popular platforms pieced together from the concerns of subordinated people in the United States: racial minorities, feminists, tenants, the aged, neighborhood activists, labor union members, environmentalists, and, of course, gay people themselves. David Scondras's election to Boston City Council is a classic example. A long-time activist in tenants' organizations, health centers, and food co–ops, Scondras had been instrumental in exposing a massive arson-for-profit conspiracy where land speculators and landlords had been burning down their buildings (dispossessing and sometimes killing tenants in the process) in order to collect insurance payments (Lachman 1978; Goldsmith 1981; Brady 1983). The populist formula brought Harvey Milk and his successor, Harry Britt, to the San Francisco Board of Supervisors, Karen Clark to the Minnesota state house, and John Laird to the Mayor's office in Santa Cruz, California. When Sue Harris gained a seat on the Vancouver (British Columbia) parks board in 1984, she did so from a background in lesbian activism and through work with the Solidarity Coalition of 1983, which formed to resist sweeping cutbacks imposed by the right-wing Social Credit government of the province (Larventz 1985). By the mid-1980s, several cities, namely, Laguna Beach, California, Key West, Florida, and Bunceton, Missouri, in the United States and Fitzroy, Victoria, in Australia, had elected gay mayors. Manchester, England, inaugurated its first openly lesbian mayor in 1985.

In 1984, West Hollywood, California, voters chose an unprecedented *majority* of gay and lesbian candidates for their city council with lesbian activist Valerie Terrigno as mayor, and voters in Sydney, Australia, added three gay men to that city's government.[8] While the traditional triumvirate of capital, property, and family continued to look with suspicion and alarm upon the political mobility of gay people, major labor unions were joining with the gay rights movement to adopt sexual orientation resolutions: in 1979, the Canadian Union of Public Employees; in 1980, the French Confédération Générale du Travail; in 1982, the Irish Congress of Trades Unions and the American Federation of State, County, and Municipal Employees; in 1983, the American Federation of Labor–Congress of Industrial Organizations (AFL-CIO); and in 1985, the Trades Union Congress of the United Kingdom.

Still, despite a notable record of gains, all same-sex erotic contact, especially for men, remains outlawed in half of the states of the United States, concentrated largely in the more conservative southern and Rocky Mountain regions. Half of the Australian states (Queensland, Western Australia, and Tasmania) have failed to decriminalize, and the United Kingdom extended decriminalization to Scotland in 1980 and to Ulster in 1982 only after a lawsuit launched by the Northern Ireland Gay Rights Association, which led the European Court to declare the old law a violation of the human rights treaty of the European Economic Community. The Republic of Ireland remains the unique holdout in Western Europe, while New Zealand decriminalized in 1986 following an acrimonious debate fueled by New Right campaigners from the United States.

Conservative institutions have conceded little, showing unflagging loyalty to doctrines established in the nineteenth century and before.

- When the Christian Democratic government of West Germany suspended one of its generals for having allegedly appeared in a gay bar, it indulged itself in the symbolic brew of the 1907 Eulenberg scandal. As in 1907, the government failed even to establish that General Kiessling was gay. The Social Democrats this time, however, agreed that sexual orientation should be no bar to professional competence.
- The queen of England summarily dismissed her personal bodyguard of nine years, Commander Michael Trestrail, without concern for his distinguished work record when his sexual orientation was discovered.
- The right-wing Social Credit government of British Columbia simply abolished its human rights commission, which had rendered the decision favorable to *Gay Tide,* for "budgetary reasons" and vetoed the sexual orientation ordinance passed by Vancouver City Council.[9]
- The Australian state of Queensland saw fit to precede the 1982 Commonwealth Games in Brisbane with a "cleanup" which netted twenty-three men.
- The Roman Catholic bishop of Strasbourg, France, evicted the International Gay Association from a hall it had rented well in advance of its scheduled meeting.

• Belgian officials fired schoolteacher Elaine Morissens for daring to discuss lesbianism on television, a decision upheld through three years of litigation.

Such incidents could be recounted indefinitely.

Finally, the police and military remain centers of antigay violence in many countries, even acting with a certain relative autonomy from the states that employ them. Jeffrey Weeks observes that in the first years following decriminalization in England "between 1967 and 1976, the recorded incidence of indecency between males doubled, the number of prosecutions trebled and the number of convictions quadrupled" (1981, 275). It is a pattern reproduced elsewhere with suspicious regularity. Dramatic police raids are often staged soon after the passage of liberalized laws and "sex scandals" are manufactured for eager press consumption. Even so, mass roundups of gay men and lesbians are only the most visible aspects of a systematic surveillance machine that routinely processes thousands more. As Doug Wilson points out, although the mass arrest of more than three hundred men in raids of Toronto bathhouses attracted considerable press attention in 1981, the routine arrest of eight hundred others on indecency charges in the same year went unnoticed (1984, 9). What was most unusual about the Toronto raids was the massive mobilization of gay people in response to them, not the raids themselves. Bath raids are virtually endemic practices in Western nations.[10]

The military hierarchies of the United States, the United Kingdom, and West Germany continue to dismiss thousands of men and women each year who are accused of having "homosexual tendencies," often officially labeling them as gay in the process, thereby making them targets of employment discrimination. A 1981 Pentagon edict insists that the presence of gay people in the military "seriously impairs the accomplishment of the military mission," "adversely affects the ability of the armed forces to maintain discipline . . . [and] the system of rank and command," invades conditions of minimal privacy, lowers "public acceptability of military service," and opens the military to "breaches of security." The Royal Canadian Mounted Police repeated the same litany to a Canadian parliamentary committee on equality rights in 1985, revealing the heterosexist fantasy that links homosexuality with sexual predation and treason.[11]

These police ideologies are not without effect, sometimes leading to police challenges to civilian administration of the legal apparatus.

- On Gay Pride Day in 1980, Fred Paez, the secretary of the Houston Gay Political Caucus and an active investigator of police violence, died of a gunshot wound to the back of the head while in police custody. Two Houston policemen, subsequently tried for "negligent homicide," claimed that Paez had made sexual advances to them and had been shot "accidentally." Both were acquitted. When a reform city council came to office with gay support in 1984, police responded with a series of eleven raids on gay bars and bookstores in Houston.
- A series of police raids and arrests in Sydney occurred in the months following adoption of the 1982 New South Wales civil rights law. The movement responded by parking a trailer emblazoned with the words "Gay Caravan Embassy" across the street from the house of Premier Neville Wran. The gay "diplomatic mission" to the premier pressed for a decriminalization bill to follow the human rights law and for an end to police harassment. (Decriminalization was won in 1984.)
- In Almeria, Spain, the murder of three young gay men found handcuffed together and burned beyond recognition in the back seat of their car, was determined to be the work of the Guardia Civil. Three officers were subsequently sentenced to twelve to twenty-four-year terms for the murders.
- Paris police instigated a new round of harassment of gay bars in 1984 as the Socialist government moved forward with liberalization of the law.
- In New York, police pillaged a bar frequented by black gay men the same night that Vice President Walter Mondale addressed a fund-raising dinner for gay civil rights a few blocks away.

The videotape surveillance and entrapment of men caught masturbating in washroom stalls or the discovery of boys having sex with men is the kind of evidence often accumulated by police over several months for eventual release in a single dramatic press conference identifying "sex and prostitution rings" or "white slavery rackets." The publication of the names, addresses, and occupations of the accused following such press conferences has often preceded the presentation of police budgets before city councils in the United States and Canada. Publication of names frequently preempts any penalties imposed by the courts by exacting a wave of job dismissals, evictions, and sometimes suicides of the accused.

Mindful of the use to which police files were put in identifying gay people for the Nazi genocide, gay leaders have petitioned governments to eliminate police "pink lists" of gay and lesbian citizens who have committed no crimes but are documented solely because of their homosexuality. The West German police even succeeded in winning the conviction on libel charges of gay activist Gerd Blömer, who had accused them of keeping such lists, only to be exposed some months later as being guilty of Blömer's accusation (McCaskell 1980). The Canadian solicitor-general announced that police files on gay people were ordered destroyed in 1984; the issue has arisen, as well, in the United States, France, Israel, Italy, and Switzerland. These are events that call to mind Guy Hocquenghem's wry observation: "The law is clearly a system of desire, in which provocation and voyeurism have their own place" (1978, 49).

Coming Out Everywhere

In the 1980s, lesbians and gay men have organized around the diverse aspects of their lives to meet new needs and problems and to create communities in new places. Almost every sizable Christian denomination and Jews as well now have assemblies of gay people seeking reconciliation of religious doctrine with same-sex bonding. National organizations have formed in smaller European nations, such as Finland, Iceland, Austria, and Greece, and have begun even in East Germany and Yugoslavia. People of Asian, African, and Latin American descent have come together to confront racism in the gay world and homophobia within racial communities, often organizing first in countries with well-established gay and lesbian movements to reach out to compatriots in the third world.

Furthermore, lesbians and gay men sharing age or disability in common have begun to meet together. Youth groups are widespread and older people have formed support groups, most notably New York's Senior Action in a Gay Environment (SAGE) founded in 1979. The Rainbow Society for the Deaf, begun in 1976, has chapters around North America; a gay student group received college recognition in 1984 from Gallaudet College for the deaf. The Gay and Lesbian Blind organized in New York in 1978 and a Chicago Lambda Resource Center for the Blind began making cassette books on gay topics in 1980. Physically disabled New Yorkers organized Mainstream in 1984, and few sizable communities lack a group affiliated with the Gay Alcoholics Anonymous Acceptance Network.

The status of gay people in religion has been perhaps most problematic of all, given the intense hostility of most Judeo-Christian officials toward homosexuality since the thirteenth century. It is likely no accident that the first gay movement group called itself the Scientific-Humanitarian Committee, thereby clearly separating itself from religion and staking its claim on the territory of the Enlightenment. Although religion has been dislodged from geology and astronomy and has been forced to content itself with religious pluralism and freedom of conscience, it continues to occupy sexuality and to launch rearguard actions to preserve its hold. Whereas most of the liberal democracies have developed a separation between church and state and have accepted a plurality of political viewpoints, the idea of sexual pluralism has yet to escape the weight of religious occupation. Christian, Jewish, and Islamic organizations have long been primary sources of antigay ideologies. When exercising punitive power of their own, churches have subjected sodomites to death and mutilation; when closely interlocked with modern states, they have often harassed, imprisoned, even executed, gay people for daring to love persons of their own choosing.

In Ireland, where Roman Catholicism is written into the constitution, repressive sexual policies remain law: divorce, contraception and abortions are banned, customs seizes gay publications, and gay men remain outlaws. But when an Irish court sanctioned the murder of a gay man in 1983 by handing out suspended sentences to the man's five attackers, the small gay movement succeeded in attracting seven hundred protesters to its first public demonstration.

In Israel, the institutionalized power of the rabbinate led to the eviction of the 1979 International Jewish Conference of Gay Men and Lesbian Women from three meeting places as each in turn was threatened with suspension of its kosher license should it tolerate the meeting of gay people. Israel retains a law prescribing ten-year jail sentences for homosexual acts, but a gay and lesbian defense group has met since 1975 as the Society for the Protection of Personal Rights (Sofer 1985).

The theocratic state of Iran executed a number of men for homosexuality in 1978 and 1979, sparking demonstrations in Paris and San Francisco and prompting Italian activist Vincenzo Francone to chain himself to the gate of Tehran prison in protest in 1980.

Christian Democrat parties in Europe and the evangelical Right in the United States have been major forces blocking recognition of equal rights for lesbians and gay men and have frequently shown a willingness to endorse or lead persecutory campaigns against them. In New York City, a consortium of Roman Catholic, Jewish, and Salvation Army officials have been willing to pursue a lengthy court challenge to nullify the mayor's executive order banning discrimination against gay people, but in 1986 City Council transformed the order into municipal law. In Ontario, the Conference of Catholic Bishops insists on the right to dismiss anyone from the provincially supported "separate" school system who "indulges in homosexuality as a morally acceptable way of life." It is also noteworthy that in the Netherlands, where a third of the population identifies itself as without religion and that portion of the population has organized itself as a significant political force, lesbians and gay men live with considerable state acceptance. It is also in the Netherlands that Pope John Paul II in 1985 met the most vocal public resistance to the antigay and antifeminist pronouncements of his worldwide tours. Little wonder that a Gay Atheists League has formed in the United States.

The churches, of course, do not form a monolith. Few have been able to escape the gay rebellion of the 1970s, and in general, liberal Protestant congregations where policy is determined democratically, have moved toward a variety of compromises with gay protests against injustice, while conservative Protestant, orthodox, and Roman Catholic churches, with authoritarian structures, have persisted in enunciating policies frozen in medieval theologies. Best known is the papal pronouncement of 1976 that labeled homosexuality as "intrinsically disordered" and "the sad consequence of a refusal of God," a position condemned by forty-six French theologians, meeting in the same year in Lyon, as "worn-out philosophy and abusive authoritarianism . . . without truth, justice, or the love of God" (Girard 1981, 153; Mirabet i Mullol 1985, 266, 273, my translation).

For gay people with no wish to abandon their religious beliefs, few churches have been willing to extend the hand of friendship. Troy Perry, an expelled Pentecostal preacher, decided to found a ministry to the gay community in 1968; growing from a congregation of twelve in Los Angeles, his group by 1983 became the center of a Universal Fellowship of Metropolitan Community Churches (UFMCC) of 195 congregations in ten countries. Dr. James Tinney founded Faith Temple in Washington, D.C., in the black Pentecostal tradition; the Centre du Christ Libérateur, founded in 1976 in Paris, also serves as a general Protestant ministry to lesbians and gay men. The independent gay churches have earned reputations for social service work such as telephone hot lines for the troubled and support groups for parents and alcoholics. The UFMCC, for example, operated a Cuban Refugee Relief Fund to resettle gay and lesbian Cubans among the "Marielitos" of 1980 (see Humphreys 1972b, 149-52; Teal 1971, 278-79; Perry 1973; Swicegood 1974). Jews organized gay and lesbian synagogues as early as 1970 in New York, and since then, across the United States, Canada, Australia, the United Kingdom, France, and Israel (Brick 1979; Teal 1971, 280).

A very few have found a place for themselves within the church through liberal Protestant theologies holding that the gender of participants in human relationships is not at issue, only the quality of the relationship. The influential 1963 statement *Towards a Quaker View of Sex* opened the way with the proposition "homosexual affection can be as selfless as heterosexual affection, and therefore we cannot see that it is in some way morally worse" (Heron 1966, 41). The Unitarian Universalists called for an end to discrimination in 1970, opening an Office of Gay Concerns within the church in 1973 (Gearhart and Johnson 1974, 69; Humphreys 1972b, 152). When the Golden Gate Association ordained William Johnson, an openly gay candidate for the ministry, it forced a wary acceptance of the issue in the United Church of Christ and the formation of a gay caucus (Early 1977; Johnson 1979). The 1976 ordination of Ellen Barrett as an Episcopal priest created a similar dilemma, but the Episcopal church refused to take a pro-ordination stand. And in 1972, the Evangelical Lutheran church of the Netherlands held that "there is no obstacle" to gay ministers (Mirabet i Mullol 1985, 323, my translation).

The experience in other Protestant denominations is far more mixed. When Affirm, the organization of gay people in the United Church of Canada, challenged official homophobia, a church commission recommended the adoption of the Quaker position. The 1984 general assembly of the church, however, resolved to oppose discrimination against gay people and to refuse them ordination at the same time (Rodgerson 1984)! Gay caucuses among Methodists, Lutherans, and Presbyterians have encountered considerable resistance. Most others are gay organizations "in exile" from churches such as Brethren/Mennonite Council on Gay Concerns, Gay People in Christian Science, Affirmation (Mormon), Kinship (Seventh-Day Adventist), American Baptists Concerned, and Integrity (Anglican Church of Canada).

Dignity, the organization of gay and lesbian Catholics founded by Father Pat Nidorf in San Diego in 1969, functions uneasily with the Roman Catholic hierarchy. Its theorist, Father John McNeill, was reprimanded and silenced by the Vatican; clergy who have willingly ministered to the gay community have been withdrawn and disciplined. Despite church officials, Dignity has sprung up across the United States, Canada, Mexico, and Spain. David et Jonathan, the French equivalent, has also spread rapidly since 1972.

The "delayed" development of gay and lesbian movements in other countries can be attributed to the absence of some of the social conditions that support the growth of a gay and lesbian ethnos or to political suppression or both. In Austria and Finland, decriminalization laws in 1970 and 1971 were coupled with press muzzle rules providing jail sentences for "incitement" to homosexuality and for membership in a gay group. This direct suppression of basic rights to freedom of speech and assembly resulted in an almost complete blackout of gay topics in the Finnish media and the censorship of even university textbooks and picket signs. When the Finnish gay organization Sexuaalinen Tasavertaisuus (SETA) demonstrated publicly against the law in 1981, twenty were arrested—but no charges were laid. Austrian authorities have shown similar embarrassment in applying such a clearly undemocratic law; in 1979 lesbians and gay men organized Homosexuelle Initiative (HOSI) in Vienna (and later in four other cities), published a journal, *Lambda-Nachrichten,* and in 1982 opened a gay community center (Rosa Lila Villa) with assistance from the Vienna city council.[12]

In the least industrialized zones of Europe, such as southern Italy, Portugal, and Ireland, gay organization has been sporadic. In Iceland, Samtoken was founded in 1978 to counter incidents of antigay discrimination. The Greek gay organization, AKOE, first demonstrated publicly in 1981 against a solicitation bill, which subsequently banned sexual propositioning whether for money or not; the group has attempted to defend the journals *Amphi* and *Kraximo* against repeated prosecution for "offending public morals."[13]

In Spain, a gay and lesbian movement sprang forth at the death of caudillo Francisco Franco. During the dictatorship, two Barcelona lawyers, Armand de Fluvià and Mir Bellgai, circulated a letter to protest the 1970 social danger law and pulled together six Spanish subscribers to *Arcadie* to form an underground Agregación Homófilo para la Igualdad Sexual (AGHOIS). During this time, the group developed contacts with other European organizations, having the AGHOIS bulletin mailed back into Spain through *Arcadie* and then, following a complaint to the French government by the Spanish foreign minister, through the Swedish *Revolt* (Fluvià 1978; Mirabet i Mullol 1985, 244-45).

Following the death of Franco, gay liberation went public in 1977 in Barcelona as the Front d'Alliberament Gai de Catalunya (FAGC), soon followed by Euskal Herrico Gay Askapen Mugimendua (EHGAM) in Bilbao, and a number of groups in Madrid, Malaga, and other major cities. After its first gay pride demonstration in 1977 had been dispersed by police firing rubber bullets, FAGC returned to the Ramblas section of Barcelona in 1978, despite a government ban, with two thousand supporters drawn from feminists, leftist parties, labor unions, and Catalan nationalists. Emerging in the late 1970s, with a wide range of other antifascist leagues, gay liberationists felt assured of broad-based support and, in turn, struggled with their coalition partners for an inclusive plank of democratic reforms. By 1979, six thousand marched through the streets of Barcelona for Gay Pride Day.

The FAGC manifesto melded the radical utopian and civil rights demands of the gay and lesbian movements of the 1970s, arguing for "sexual liberation in its totality" through "struggle with other oppressed sectors," "suppression of the concepts of marriage, monogamy, and family," "an end to the gay ghetto," "suppression of ideological categories such as 'homosexual/heterosexual' . . . 'masculine/feminine,'" as well as for amnesty for those imprisoned because of their homosexuality, abolition of the social danger law, age of consent at fourteen, equality between the sexes, right to make use of one's body as one wishes, right to "personal intimacy" and the "public expression of affection," right to dress as one pleases, separation of church and state, an end to censorship, free treatment for sexually transmitted diseases, right to abortion, rights for prostitutes and transsexuals, and so on (Mirabet i Mullol 1985, 334-37). As elsewhere, lesbians organized within FAGC and then dissolved into the feminist movement before finally setting up an autonomous Grup de Lluita per l'Alliberament de la Lesbiana in 1981.

The state socialist nations of Eastern Europe and Cuba share many of the fundamental social conditions that have made gay and lesbian worlds possible in advanced capitalist societies. Because for the most part they are urban industrial systems with much of the population engaged in wage labor, official equality of the sexes, and employment opportunities for women, many of the nations structured on the Soviet model could be expected to have autonomous homosexual networks from which gay and lesbian identities emerge. These are also societies that have broken with feudal formations, where kinship has declined as a principle in the allocation of life chances, centers of feudal ideology (such as churches) have been disestablished, and decisions about family and reproduction have largely devolved upon individuals. Indeed, persistent reports from these societies suggest the existence of social networks in major cities defined and motivated by homosexual interests and not infrequently self-identified as "gay" and aware of gay and lesbian cultures in the West. In East Berlin, Prague, and Budapest, gay bars and coffeehouses have existed for some years, and in East Germany and Yugoslavia, incipient gay and lesbian movements are in the making.

Yet all these social formations are severely compromised by the immense power of the central bureaucracies, which regulate so many aspects of life and suppress public organizations that lack explicit state approval. With monopolistic control of communications systems and state administration of personal mobility, commercial meeting places, and housing, movement formation is largely suppressed.

Despite the frequently monolithic treatment of state-managed societies in the Western press, there is considerable variation among them. Apart from the USSR and Romania, most have followed along or preceded the legal liberalization of the West. Poland and Bulgaria have never criminalized homosexuality and East Germany decriminalized in 1948 (abolishing the antihomosexual law altogether in 1976), Czechoslovakia and Hungary followed in 1961, and Albania and the Yugoslav republics of Croatia, Montenegro, Vojvodina, and Slovenia in 1977. The USSR and Romania continue to exact five-year prison sentences, another situation challenged by Italian activist Vincenzo Francone, who chained himself to the Kremlin's St. Basil's Cathedral in protest. One letter written from Romania and published in the gay Esperanto journal *Forumo* states that gay men are often sentenced to one to five years and

degraded as cheap, almost slave laborers. . . . Often to hide the political motives for arrest, homosexuality is used as a pretext. If necessary, state security agents plant "evidence," generally pornographic pictures. . . . All citizens over twenty-five who are still unmarried must pay a special tax. [15]

A comparison of East and West Germany abounds in paradoxes. While the Communist government, true to its early commitment, ceased prosecuting men for homosexual acts at the end of World War II, it seized control of businesses in the country, thereby dissolving the lesbian and gay bars that flourished from 1945 to 1947 and pushing gay people out of the public sphere (Klimmer 1969; Kokula 1983, 17). The government of the Federal Republic on the other hand, maintained a policy of persecution through the 1950s, but small businesspeople opened a number of unofficial gay and lesbian bars out of which a public gay community and movement emerged. As early as 1973, a Homosexuelle Interessengemeinschaft Berlin applied without success for permission to meet in East Berlin. In 1982, a modern gay and lesbian organization arose under the auspices of the state-approved Evangelical Student Congregation. Out of a lecture given by Dr. Jürgen Ziemers on "Homosexuality in Theology, Church and Society" attended by three hundred people came a series of workshops on poets, writers, history, and parenting and the formation of the Leipzig Arbeitskreis Homosexualität. By 1984, gay work groups had formed in six more cities including an all-lesbian group in Berlin. This development is clearly regarded with suspicion by the state bureaucracy. The laying of memorial wreaths at two concentration camps for gay people killed in the Holocaust prompted a decree forbidding memorials to "individual groups" of Nazi victims (though Jewish and other groups are, in fact, recognized) and a ban on the wearing of pink triangles as a symbol of solidarity (Hauer et al. 1984, 28, 105-18).

In Yugoslavia, gay people went public with conferences in 1984 and 1985 called "Magnus—Homoseksualnost in Kultura" organized through the Student Cultural Centre of Ljubljana. The films, speakers, and exhibitions presented at the conferences received positive coverage on local radio.

Finally letters from an underground Gay Laboratory in Leningrad have recently appeared in the West European Communist press concerning the development of clandestine seminars and support groups in the USSR, which rely, in turn, on information gleaned from the Euro-Communist press.

Certainly black, Hispanic, and Asian gay men and lesbians have actively participated in gay and lesbian movements from its earliest days. In 1978, a National Coalition of Black Gays (NCBG) was founded, and largely as a result of the 1979 march on Washington, a National Third World Lesbian/Gay Conference was organized. A 1985 issue of the NCBG journal *Habari-Daftari* lists sixty-six groups of gay and lesbian people of color in nine countries ranging from women's poetry and publishing collectives to the San Francisco–based Gay American Indians. Explicitly interracial coalitions have arisen across the United States since the founding of Black and White Men Together in 1980 and in South Africa through the Gay Association of South Africa (GASA). Its publication, *Link/Skakel,* has been banned from public distribution by the white minority government, and a GASA leader Tseko Simon Nkoli faces treason charges under the notorious state-of-emergency decrees of 1985.

Asians, as well, have pulled together support groups in major cities of the United States, Canada, and England, and there are stirrings in Japan, Hong Kong, and India. Indonesians founded the first organization in Asia in 1982 in Solo and branches started in three other Javanese cities, one of which edited the journal *G.* Indonesia is also unique as the site of the only existing movement of homosexually interested people who are not identified as "gay" or "lesbian," but are organized around the indigenous, transgenderist *waria* identity. Even today, some potential exists for organization of other nongay-identified peoples for whom homosexuality makes up a significant part of their selves, such as the surviving North American berdaches or Indian *hijras* (see Translation Group 1984; Nanda 1986; Williams 1986). Each of these peoples have a particular place in the division of labor, often as performers or holy persons, and consistent with their intermediate status between men's and women's work, show gender-mixed characteristics. They are commonly known to have homosexual relationships with people in the larger society but not with each other.

Gay and lesbian organization has often been more tenuous in Latin America than in Europe, but most major nations developed an organized presence in the late 1970s and in the 1980s. As mentioned earlier, the gay world itself encompasses only a small portion of the homosexually interested population, as so many (as in Asia and Africa) remain in agrarian production characterized by traditional kinship and gender systems and precapitalist codes of homosexual desire. Nevertheless, the wish to realize deeply felt emotional and sexual preferences has motivated many in the urban sector to embrace gay and lesbian identities and to stand up for the right to experience pleasure, form households, and make friends without interference from the state, church, or families. The collapse of military dictatorships and restoration of civil rights in several nations throughout the region has boded well for gay people, as gay and lesbian groups have emerged among a general proliferation of women's, workers', minority, native, and socialist formations.

In Mexico, gay liberation revived as the Frente Homosexual de Acción Revolucionaria (FHAR) "in response to numerous anti-gay assaults and murders and police harassment in the Federal District."[16] They first appeared publicly as part of a 1978 demonstration in support of students arrested after the 1968 Olympics; by 1979, FHAR and the new lesbian group Oikabeth drew 1,500 in a gay pride march through Mexico City. By the mid-1980s, groups had grown up in several sizable cities, most notably Guadalajara, in response to a state social danger law and a series of police roundups in 1983. In 1982, the Revolutionary Workers party even ran an openly gay candidate, Rosario Ibarra, for president.

In Brazil and Argentina, the gay and lesbian movement organized in the waning days of dictatorship to develop relatively rapidly with the restoration of parliamentary democracy. As early as 1961–64, an underground gay press circulated in Rio de Janeiro and São Paulo until its suppression following the United States–backed coup that replaced the democratically elected president with a military dictator in 1964.[17] With the regime's promise of an "opening" toward democracy in the late 1970s, a gay journal, *Lampião,* began and a group called Somos formed in São Paulo amid widespread agitation for democracy from many sectors of the Brazilian population. Soon *Lampião* was in court on a public morals charge and police had imprisoned 1,500 in sweeps through the gay ghetto following a 1980 national conference held in São Paulo. More than a thousand turned out to protest the police roundups in June of 1980. When the military regime stepped down in 1982, the Workers' party fielded eight gay candidates including an incumbent, João Baptista Breda (who had come out on national television), and Brazil experienced an unprecedented national discussion of gay life in the media and the arts. In Argentina, as well, the fall of the military regime allowed a small gay and lesbian movement to revive, to march first in a 1984 demonstration demanding the trial of the previous dictators and then to fight laws that still permitted police to arrest 250 at one party in Buenos Aires and allow the death of fourteen gay men at the hands of death squads in the preceding two years.[18]

Elsewhere organization has been comparatively short-lived, dependent on the efforts of a few individuals. In Colombia, gay studies groups held meetings in 1976 and two newspapers, *El Otro* and *Ventana Gay,* appeared sporadically from Medillín and Bogotá. The first public gay pride parade occurred in the capital in 1983. In Venezuela, Edgar Carrasco and Luis Alvarez produced *Entendido* from 1980 to 1984, attempting to organize around a large-scale police raid on a Caracas disco in 1982. In 1983, the Grupo Autoconciencia Lesbianas y Feministas became active in Lima following a meeting of the Latin American Women's Conference, and began to issue a newsletter, *Al Margen.* Along with the Movimiento Homosexual de Lima, founded in the same year, the aims of the Peruvian movement have attracted the support of the opposition United Left party. The retirement of the military regime in Uruguay in 1985 has opened new possibilities, while the continued suspension of civil liberties in United States–backed dictatorships in Chile, Paraguay, and parts of Central America preclude the development of popular movements in those countries.[19]

The Sex Debates

As the cultural feminist position gained ground in the women's movement, the apparent reorientation of the feminist program around the suppression of pornography began to cause consternation among many movement participants. While a widespread presumption about the fundamental unity of purpose of feminists and gay liberationists had prevailed through much of the 1970s, a certain disillusionment with the alliance set in among many men in the 1980s, while lesbians figured prominently on both sides of the sex debates. Several events began to polarize the discussion. In 1980, the Lesbian Rights Committee of the National Organization for Women succeeded in having the national convention adopt a resolution that "NOW does not support the inclusion of pederasty, pornography, sadomasochism, and public sex as Lesbian rights issues, since to do so would violate the feminist principles upon which this organization was founded" (Ehrenreich, Hess, and Jacobs 1982, 88). In 1982, the ninth Scholar and the Feminist Conference focused on sexuality and had to face a concerted campaign of denunciation by antipornography feminists as well as seizure of the conference planning book by the administration of host Barnard College. Also in 1982, the Cambridge (Massachusetts) Women's Center expelled a lesbian sadomasochist (S/M) support group by a vote of 9–1 on the grounds that it was contrary to feminist principles. In 1984, prominent leaders in the antipornography campaign convinced the cities of Indianapolis and Minneapolis to allow for the prosecution of sexually explicit publications as violators of women's rights. (The Indianapolis law was subsequently blocked by a court ruling citing First Amendment rights; the Minneapolis ordinance was vetoed by the mayor.)

The cultural feminist challenge (which, I have argued, displays many of the presumptions of a nationalist argument) forced many in the lesbian and women's movements to wonder—were dirty books and unconventional sex practices the enemies of women's liberation? Why was the *depiction* of sexuality consuming so much movement energy when the *real* subordination of women by the state, churches, employers, and families was falling out of sight? Was there a parallel to be found with the Victorian suffragist movement, which imperceptibly left off its critique of major patriarchal institutions of society to adopt an agenda approved by the political establishment? Had the problems of sexism been reduced to pornography as they had been reduced to temperance at the turn of the century?

By the end of 1984, feminist anticensorship groups had organized across North America. A set of magazines, presenting sexual images made by and for lesbians, appeared only to face a new round of banning imposed this time by women's bookstores. (Gay bookstores, on the other hand, stocked the new magazines only to come under considerable pressure, especially in Philadelphia, from the culturalist wing of lesbian feminism.) The gay movement, with a long history of resistance to state censorship from *The Well of Loneliness* case to the *Body Politic* trials, reacted with dismay to the nationalist thrust.

For many feminists, the nationalist view evolved out of a series of experiences in attempting to gain rights for women. The way to end male exploitation made possible by women's relative powerlessness was to develop defenses and alternatives to the violence experienced day to day by so many women in society. The perpetuation of wife abuse depended upon the inability of women to flee male violence at home, so the move-ment organized refuges for battered wives. Rape would never be con-trolled while prosecution depended on police who believed sexual coercion to be a male right, so activists opened rape counseling centers. Low status on the employment market left women vulnerable to sexual harassment on the job, so feminists pressed for legal protection from it. The organizational wave among women in the 1970s was toward forming groups of "women against violence against women." Here, it seemed, was a social realm in which the concrete daily effects of women's oppres-sion could be relieved at least in part.

While most feminists retained more liberal or socialist analyses of women's oppression, the ongoing struggle against violence and the col-lective solidarity engendered by the struggle began to lead to the con-solidation of another feminist worldview. Like so many previous social movements, this nationalist tendency elevated the feminist conflict into a cosmic battle that revalued itself as the unqualified good against an implacable enemy, a position that, in Angela Miles's words, "asserts a feminine essence, which contains all that is good in humanity, in opposi-tion to the oppression and destruction of civilization which is ascribed to maleness itself; it posits as its aim the establishment of a free and good all-female society" (1981, 485). It is perhaps not surprising that theorists with strong theological backgrounds, such as Mary Daly and Sally Gear-hart, played such major roles in the formulation of this Manichaean cos-mology. Women's culture is fundamentally different from men's, the nationalists argued, because of women's unique commitment to life through their procreative potential. They claimed that "feminist analysis is founded in the central aspect of reproduction for all species. . . . Re-production is the epitome of creativity, the ultimate creative act, belong-ing particularly to women" (Hughes 1985, 96-97).

In this context, pornography loomed large as a primary indicator of what was wrong in the relations between women and men. Not the harbinger of sexual liberation as claimed by the editors of *Playboy,* pornography so often duplicated and intensified the most reactionary images of women as willing objects of male sexual predation, seemingly expressing and reinforcing a male culture of violence. Images of dominated and mistreated women abounded in pornography, leading many women to read these images as a form of hate literature inciting men to all the behaviors they were working to overcome. Patricia Hughes summed up the anxieties of many women in asking, "is it possible for that man to treat me . . . as a human being when he received gratification from seeing someone who looks like me bound, beaten, humiliated?" (100). Many suspected that the proliferation of pornographic images in popular culture represented a male backlash against the rise of feminism. As Eileen Manion notes, "insofar as it blatantly sneers at us, tediously insists we are nothing but cunts, bunnies, pussies, and chicks, it seems like the grandiose ravings of the (male) infantile imagination" (1985, 69). For Andrea Dworkin, a leading theorist of the nationalist position, pornography epitomized male culture and identified the enemy. In the opening lines of one of her polemics on the subject, she proclaims: "Men love death. In everything they make, they hollow out a central place for death, let its rancid smell contaminate every dimension of whatever still survives. Men especially love murder" (1978, 10).

But the war against pornography had subtly shifted the contours of feminist discourse. In a decade, feminist reasoning had seemingly come full circle: from arguing the artificiality of gender and demanding its transcendence, it now asserted an unbridgeable chasm between the sexes and the need to obliterate "death-loving" male values. The new nationalism, or cultural feminism rang with echoes of nineteenth-century argumentation that women are essentially more pure, more temperate, and more moral than men, and that women's mission is to battle male lustfulness and corruption. Antipornography literature implicitly endorsed some very traditional assumptions about the nature of women and their roles in society. As Carole Vance notes, "through a culturally dictated chain of reasoning, women become the moral custodians of male behavior, which they are perceived as instigating and eliciting" (1984, 4; see Snitow 1985, 143). Here was the revival of the view that women are essentially caring, peaceable, and nurturant, and therefore want only "muted, diffuse, and interpersonally oriented" sex, whereas male sexuality is "driven, irresponsible, genitally oriented, and potentially lethal" (Echols 1983, 449; see also Echols 1984). As Ellen Willis complained of the propositions advanced by Women Against Pornography, the cultural feminists argue that:

> lovemaking should be beautiful, romantic, soft, nice, and devoid of messiness, vulgarity, impulses to power, or indeed aggression of any sort. Above all, the emphasis should be on *relationships,* not (yuck) *orgasms.* This goody-goody concept of eroticism is not feminist but feminine. (1983, 464)

Debates over the direction of modern feminism were now progressing beyond in-house differences over policy, as antipornography forces moved to enlist the state in enforcing their views. Purges of politically incorrect groups from women's centers and bookstores and confrontations at conferences had been troublesome signs to liberation feminists, but entry into the political arena galvanized them to organize in opposition. A legal initiative, written by Andrea Dworkin and Catherine MacKinnon, to declare pornography a violation of women's civil rights was now appearing before legislative bodies, and dissidents to the nationalist orthodoxy were appalled by its symbolic linkages presuming "that sex is degrading to women, but not to men; that men are raving beasts; that sex is dangerous for women; that sexuality is male, not female; that women are victims, not sexual actors; that men inflict 'it' on women; that penetration is submission" (Duggan, Hunter, and Vance 1985, 143). Had women come to feminism only to uphold the old gender orthodoxy dressed up as the strategy of the 1980s?

None of these debates had the luxury of isolation from the larger political context, and no one could ignore the gains of the New Right, which had stopped ERA, rolled back lesbian and gay rights, and curtailed hard-won social services. Once introduced into a wider political context, the Dworkin-MacKinnon proposal drew enthusiastic support in Indianapolis from a city councillor active in the Stop ERA movement, from the mayor who was a Presbyterian minister, from the police, and from the Christian Right. It passed by twenty-four votes cast by Republicans to five cast by Democrats on the council (Duggan, Hunter, and Vance 1985, 131-33). And in the same year, Dworkin showed no hesitation in coming to Toronto to join with the FBI and the United States Surgeon-General to lecture Canadians about the evils of sexual deviance.[20] In 1986 the Conservative government introduced a parliamentary bill to ban all visual depictions of sexuality, citing feminist demands.

Nationalist initiatives were coming up, as a conservative trend was emerging elsewhere in the women's movement. Leading theorists such as Betty Friedan, Alice Rossi, and Jean Bethke Elshtain were now arguing that motherhood and family values deserved a new prominence in feminism and that divisive issues such as sex, abortion, and lesbianism should be downplayed in the feminist agenda. Accommodationist conservatism was becoming a growing response to the assault from the right, and vituperative denunciations of gay people from within feminism followed not far behind (see Stacy 1983; Willis 1981; Elshtain 1982-83).

For many gay men, the antipornography trend was especially alarming, given constant pressure from the state to muffle gay voices and suppress their sexuality.[21] The gay and lesbian movement was in continual contention with the New Zealand Indecent Publications Tribunal, which included a wide range of sexual and nonsexual publications on its prohibited list. Canada Customs routinely scissored out pages and inked out paragraphs of magazines which conflicted with individual officer's notions of "decency" and Toronto police won a conviction of Glad Day, the city's gay and lesbian bookstore, for stocking "obscene" material that had already passed through Customs' screening. At the same time, the Ontario film censorship board was invading art galleries, cutting or banning gay films (among them, the exuberant West German classic *Taxi zum Klo*), and even banning *Not a Love Story,* a film made by feminist antipornography activists. In 1984, British Customs seized eight hundred books from Gay's the Word, London's gay and lesbian bookstore, including yet again *The Well of Loneliness* and Edward Carpenter's works, later admitting in court that its prosecution relied on criteria no more sophisticated than the simple equation of "gay" with "obscene."[22] (Charges were eventually dropped in 1986.)

Pornography has a very different meaning for gay men (and some lesbians) than that offered by cultural feminism. Whereas women in observing pornography found a medium made *about* them but *by* and *for* (heterosexual) men, gay men found a medium that presented images of themselves for their own consumption. Where many women found the depiction of coercion to be a form of hate literature, gay men typically read consent even into portrayals of S/M sex, for both sexual partners, at least prima facie, shared the same status as men and were being presented to viewers who likely shared their sexual tastes. For feminist nationalists, S/M looked far too much like a male fantasy of beating and humiliating women in complicity with the general subordination of women in the larger society. (But these analysts never comment upon the S/M genre embodied in Sacher-Masoch's own classic text, *Venus in Furs,* where women dominate men, and the camera in *Not a Love Story* resolutely guards this image out of focus during a scene in a sex magazine shop in order to lead the viewer *away* from this possibility.) For gay men, where consent is presumed, S/M represents no more than a sexual drama where, one might say, Halloween masks are not confused with real devils. For most gay men, then, pornography filled a relatively benign role of offering their sexuality in the midst of a sex-phobic society and in offering aesthetic images of men as pleasurable and playful in contradiction to the predominant imagery of men as instrumental and controlling. Feminist nationalists typically relegate gay pornography to footnotes, thereby subsuming it under a supposedly universal analysis and, in the tradition of all good imperialists, dismiss gay experiences as too unimportant to take into account. While these feminists were finding a legitimation of male dominance in pornography, gay men were finding its subversive potential in its allowing men to express tenderness and make love with each other in opposition to deeply held taboos of patriarchal society.

Certainly as antipornography groups were first mobilizing among feminists in the 1970s, one strand of gay liberation thought was striking out in quite another direction. Exemplified in the diverse writings of John Rechy, Guy Hocquenghem, and John A. Lee, the libertarians celebrated a sexuality shorn of the encumbrances of love, family, and morality and affirmed the value of giving mutual pleasure without "higher" justifications. As Allen Ginsberg once argued, "I think orgies should be institutionalized; impersonal meat orgies, with no question of personality or character or relating to people as people" (1974, 34). While some defended the tenderness, the human connection, and emotional depth of even casual sexual encounters, Hocquenghem offered the vision of the "primary sexual communism" of the baths where "the plugging in of organs takes place subject to no rule or law" (Hocquenghem 1978, 97; see also Rechy 1977; Lee 1978; Adam 1980). In a polemic aimed at feminism, Hocquenghem insists, "we are pleasure machines; we've been reproached enough for it" (Borg and Hocquenghem 1977, 106; my translation). But ultimately, the sex freedom position fell into decline with the advent of the very real threat of AIDS.

In the 1980s, a growing number of lesbians began, as well, to speak up for the right to unorthodox pleasures, to question the demand for sex legitimated by romance, and to claim a renewed solidarity with gay men and sexual minorities. In 1981, a self-proclaimed Lesbian Sex Mafia turned up in New York to raise such forbidden topics as S/M and butch/ fem, and many concurred with Gayle Rubin's remark, "I, for one, did not join the women's movement to be told how to be a good girl." After the publication of a lesbian sex book on sadomasochism and other taboo sexualities by the Samois collective in San Francisco, many lesbians rethought a good deal of their own sexual experience and the meaning of power within their relationships. To distance themselves from the cultural feminist complex where lesbianism had its valued but asexual role, Monique Wittig remarked to one conference, "I am not a woman, I am a lesbian" and Sue Golding announced to another, "I am a sex pervert!"[23] Taking up the challenge to create a nonexploitative erotica by and for lesbians, four publishing ventures *(On Our Backs, Bad Attitude, Power Exchange, Outrageous Women)* appeared in 1984 and 1985.

In the end, what the sex debates demonstrate perhaps is the hold that Victorian parameters continue to exert upon the modern era. As Rosalind Coward (1983) points out in her review of feminist thinking, so much of modern discourse on sex and gender pays homage to the nineteenth-century delineation of the issues. Yet despite their fallback into a morass of unexamined signifiers, the cultural feminists did initiate a critique of sexual imagery and raise the possibility of alternative worlds of erotica potentially subversive of patriarchy. The gay movement, perhaps preoccupied with defending what little erotica exists, has yet to challenge the limitations of gay pornography that infrequently presents the beauty of Asian or black men, reproduces Hollywood icons of male muscularity, and seems unable to contextualize sexuality in broader emotional contexts. The growing market in gay male gothic romances suggests a widespread interest in a richer vision of intermale relationships than the strictly sexual. The libertarian position tends to limit itself to the cherished liberal principle of the right of individuals to do as they see fit as long as they hurt no one else. Despite its radical pretensions, it is an argument that abstains from any critique of the ways in which sexual representations and alternatives have already been shaped by the logic of capitalism, where sexuality is increasingly marketed as a commodity like others, split off and contained in sex ghettos, and encoded with the competitive individualism of the market economy. Like other arguments for individual freedom, it throws comparatively powerless and unorganized individuals into prestructured social settings where they have to make do with the possibilities presented by entrepreneurs and governments.

The failure of imagination on the Left opens the way for the New Right simply to harvest unarticulated feelings of discontent with contemporary forms of intimacy into tired formulas of sexual discipline and medieval morality. In patriarchal capitalism, the New Right promises, lies sex respected as a sacred and meaningful trust, intimacy preserved in traditional families, and caring relationships embedded in a secure social order. Though the Right embraces the cause of its problems, thereby turning its promise into a cruel hoax, it claims that such previous values can only be jeopardized by feminism and gay liberation, for the sexual liberationists have yet to show how trusting and solidary human relationships can be built anew, how intimacy can arise on the sexual frontiers, and how pleasure can be indulged with good conscience. Part of the problem is the abstraction of debates on sexuality from the dynamics of its social environment and the not fully conscious recognition that the sex debates are not just about sex. As Eileen Manion observes,

Sexuality has shouldered an enormous weight of expectations in our culture, expectations that sexual "fulfilment" will compensate for the sensual impoverishment of urban life, the emotional impoverishment of a culture that promotes thin sociality at the expense of long-term deep connection.[24]

In truth, individuals, couples, and groups, here and there, have often accomplished just that, but await recognition in a society that forbids its discussion.[25]

Most contentious of all is the issue of sexual contact among adults, youths, and children. Gay people, who are again and again painted as "child molesters" by the religious right, have, sometimes unwillingly, had to consider the question. So emotionally charged is the question that discussion has only infrequently attained the level of "debate" with even the possibility of considering it being choked off, shouted down, or censored in most instances. Very little scholarly attention has been given to pedophilia, nor have its participants, young or old, been given forums to explain their experiences, at the same time as a wave of antipedophile hysteria has swept across the English-language countries, France, and West Germany in the 1970s and 1980s. In this period, an unrestrained public campaign fed by the police and press has discovered "sex rings" in unlikely places, led to the widespread passage of repressive legislation, and the imprisonment of pedophiles for terms exceeding those meted out to murderers.

These campaigns are made possible only by a complex net of presumptions about children, gender, and sexuality that is peculiar to these societies. For the Melanesian peoples, who hold that the insemination of boys is *necessary* for them to attain sexual maturity, the antipedophile complex is inconceivable, and for the many societies where sexuality is an integral component of the pedagogical relationships of older and younger men, current Western attitudes would be thought puzzling or reprehensible. Accounts of how the genitals of the French dauphin were publicly admired in court in the eighteenth century show how drastically Western ideas about children's sexuality have changed in two centuries.[26] But today, the notion of the pedophile vampire preying on children, who are supposedly completely innocent of any erotic thoughts, is a cultural staple and the social control establishment insists upon making it true.

Part of the international variation in the treatment of the sexuality of pedophiles and of children can be easily explained by legislation on age of consent. In countries that have equalized the age of consent for homosexuality and heterosexuality and have lowered the age to fifteen or sixteen (for example, Netherlands, 1971; Denmark, 1976; Sweden, 1978; and France, 1982), large categories of "pedophilia" have been rendered unproblematic. For the United Kingdom and Canada, which maintain twenty-one as the age of consent and for the United States and Australian states with more restrictive laws, pedophilia escalates into a major problem.

For all nations with liberal democratic traditions, the issue revolves around the question: at what age can people give consent for sexual relations? Anthropological and historical comparisons are of limited value here as individual consent rarely emerges out of the larger social complex of collective decision making to become a primary issue. In the advanced capitalist nations, where individual sexual choice is founded on financial independence, entry into wage labor underlies individual mastery over his or her own domestic arrangements and the law typically follows along. It can be no accident that age of consent laws governing sexuality approximate the age when young people are permitted employment (and in those countries where the discrepancy between the two legal ages is wide, the tension between practice and the law is greatest).

The sexual practices of those under these ages opens another, more trenchant, set of conflicts. The New Right has effectively played upon parental anxieties by typifying gay men and lesbians as child molesters intent upon seizing children from parental jurisdiction. Intergenerational sexuality also reopens the dialectic between pleasure and danger that has divided feminists on pornography and sadomasochism. For many feminists, all too aware that the relative powerlessness of women and children deprives them of the conditions in which consent is possible, age of consent laws form a necessary bulwark against sexual abuse. The voluntary motherhood plank of the Victorian women's movement struggled simply for the right to say no to sex, a right not already guaranteed because of the subordination of women in marriage. Children, without the resources to determine their own living arrangements, schooling, finances, or even diet, seem similarly defenseless against the structural power of adults, especially when the relationship is between female children and male adults. Lorenne Clark enunciates the widespread feminist objection "because the sexual behaviour . . . violates the requirements of mutuality and/or equality which are the hallmarks of permissible, non-coercive, sexual conduct which does not violate the physical integrity or rights of some of the participants" (1980, 10).

For the gay and lesbian movement, as well, pedophilia has provoked considerable uneasiness. Whatever their putative roots in ancient Greece, the modern gay and lesbian worlds have, in fact, developed in accord with the mainstream cultural valuation of relationships between equals and have fundamentally differentiated themselves from gender- and age-inscribed models of intimacy. Practically, the gay and lesbian movement, already chagrined by the child molestation charge of its opponents, has vacillated over including the demands of boy lovers that age of consent laws be abolished. While some groups have taken up the call as a basic civil liberties issue founded on the right of all persons to control their own bodies, others have pushed pedophile groups out of community centers, conferences, and marches as an embarrassment to gay people.

The modern pedophile movement has, for the most part, accepted the framework of the current debate, contending that consent is possible among youths and children and asking that their relationships be evaluated by the same criteria as others: when coercive or exploitative, let them be banned; when mutually pleasurable, caring, and desired, let them be.[27] Few social scientists would disagree that child abuse, including sexual abuse, occurs overwhelmingly *within* families and that unrelated adults account for only a tiny proportion of the cases, though media presentations and public perception insist upon the opposite view. Once again, the New Right would displace a problem built into the patriarchal family upon a powerless minority while preserving intact the actual power relationships that do lead to child abuse. The result has been such causes célèbres as the 1980 condemnation of seventy-seven-year-old Alexander Ebbinghaus in West Germany to an indefinite sentence of preventive custody, though "the judge took particular pains to ascertain that the children had 'a good relationship with the accused' and that they felt at ease with him" and knew that Ebbinghaus had already been tortured by the Nazis at Esterwagen and Buchenwald from 1936 to 1944 and had spent eleven years in prison in the 1950s and 1960s all for consensual relationships with children (Witzel 1985, 105). Similarly, Swiss author Alexander Ziegler, who wrote "Die Konsequenz" spent three years in prison for "unnatural acts" (Hohmann 1982, 33).

The research literature is remarkably silent on demonstrably untoward effects of nonfamilial pedophile relationships upon children as they grow up, but the effects of police interrogation and months of litigation may not be benign upon the young people involved. A 1975 announcement of the discovery of a "homosexual vice ring" by Ottawa police stimulated weeks of press speculation about "white slave prostitution rings" with boys as "young as eleven," and the publication of the names of the sixteen accused led to a round of dismissals, suspensions, evictions, and one suicide. The subsequent trial revealed that the sixteen-year-old chief prosecution witness had his testimony coached by police who suggested names and addresses of "clients." The young man attempted suicide during the trial and subsequently succeeded in taking a drug overdose at the trial's end (Sylvestre 1976, 40-46; Hannon 1976).

In the same year, a district attorney, facing reelection in a Boston suburb, indicted twenty-four men on more than one hundred felony charges and set up an anonymous telephone hot line inviting the community to denounce their neighbors as child molesters. The trials subpoenaed young men in their twenties to testify against men they had had sex with when they were teenagers. This time, members of the gay movement formed a Boston Boise Committee to rally a defense for the accused, a group that became the nucleus for the North American Man-Boy Love Association (NAMBLA) in 1978 (Mitzel 1980).

In the United Kingdom, a Pedophile Information Exchange (PIE) grew out of gay liberation in Scotland in 1974. Its attempts to open a public discussion on children's sexuality were met by evictions, dismissals, and angry crowds recruited by lurid headlines in the Sunday press. In 1981, PIE's most visible advocate, Tom O'Carroll, was imprisoned for sixteen months for "conspiracy to currupt public morals" for involvement in publishing PIE's journal, *Magpie*. Both PIE and *Magpie* dissolved in 1984.[28] In 1983, eight members of the Australian Pedophile Support group were arraigned in Melbourne on the same charges that were later overturned by the court. Ironically, the major casualty of the arrests was Alison Thorne, a local schoolteacher, who happened to remark on radio that the arrests were a violation of civil liberties and lost her job for saying so. In Canada, the six years of the *Body Politic* in the courts had started off with the 1977 publication of a sober account on pedophilia called "Men Loving Boys Loving Men" (Hannon 1982).

These prosecutions occurred in the larger context of the sex panic of the late 1970s (discussed in Chapter 6) when the media and professionals united to alert everyone to the dangers of child abuse. Laws were passed forbidding the depiction of the sexuality of people under the age of eighteen, and police incarcerated hundreds accused of mutually voluntary sex with underage people. Members of NAMBLA endured invasions of their homes, arrests, interrogation, and imprisonment through the 1980s.[29]

The pedophile movement itself has endured relatively unmolested only in the Netherlands and Denmark. While NAMBLA understands itself as an integral part of the movement, other groups have diverged from the gay and lesbian movement in their search for self-definition. Many activists, recognizing Kate Millett's critique that abolishing the age of consent will not address the real subordination of young people, have moved toward children's rights advocacy. The "old-style" pedophile-support position appears in *Paedo Alert News,* an English serial published in Amsterdam. The Netherlands Paedophile Workgroup, NAMBLA, and a British publishing group, *Minor Problems,* have evolved toward a program of making sexual self-determination possible through a comprehensive empowerment of the young, including rights to work, design their own education, choose their domestic arrangements, and have full legal rights.[30] The boldest experiment of this type is the Nürnberg Indianerkommune, a collective of young adults and runaway children operating a bicycle repair shop, which attempts to practice complete social equality without regard to age. Aligned with the Green party,

the Indianerkommune fights for a life with children and youths, against grownups' lovelessness, sexual suppression, and the alienation of school. It arouses consciousness of [the addiction of consumerism], for children's rights, against possessive relations, and for nonviolent sexuality without legal age limitations.[31]

But this has not been accomplished without significant police harassment.

Reorganization around sexuality defined by age has led to attempts to build a movement of both sexes and all ages, and away from gay and lesbian identities premised on (overcoming) the importance of the gender of the beloved.[32] Here, perhaps, the pedophile/children's rights movements merit their own chronicler apart from the mandate of this book.

The AIDS Crisis

The primary crisis facing the gay movement in the 1980s came from an entirely unexpected source with the discovery of a hitherto unknown fatal virus, which by 1985 claimed more than seven thousand lives, three-quarters of whom were gay men. Lesbians, who were swept along in the discriminatory tide that afflicted gay men following identification of the syndrome, were nevertheless spared from the disease itself. That a disease should apparently pick out certain social groups and not others is no surprise to epidemiologists. Despite the lack of public awareness, many groups defined by social class, age, and ethnic characteristics have their particular disease profiles. Jews are especially vulnerable to Tay-Sachs syndrome, blacks to sickle-cell anemia, women to toxic shock syndrome and breast cancer, and, indeed, middle-aged white men to diseases of the heart and the digestive, respiratory, and genitourinary systems. The virus apparently responsible for acquired immune deficiency syndrome (AIDS) flourishes in blood and semen, leaving gay men uniquely vulnerable to it through semen transmission from man to man. These transmission routes also expose intravenous drug users (through direct blood contact in sharing hypodermic needles), hemophiliacs (through massive blood transfusions), and women who are the sex partners of men carrying the virus. Thus lesbians remain uniquely free. The incidence of AIDS among certain tropical peoples such as heterosexual men and women from central Africa and Haiti was still not well understood in 1985, and, indeed, most of the AIDS cases in Belgium and half in Quebec were counted among these groups.

The first indication of the existence of the new disease was a note in the medical press published in 1981. By 1982, 471 cases of AIDS had been identified in the United States, and by 1985, more than 15,000. Awareness of this new syndrome, which so damages the immune system that normally minor illnesses become fatal, spread through the gay community through 1982, and support groups formed to offer assistance to people with AIDS and to lobby for treatment and research funding. For a year, while gay people watched their friends and lovers dying around them, neither governments nor the media would respond with interest to the pleas of movement groups. Only when the American Broadcasting Company (ABC) ran a news story in the spring of 1983 on *children* with AIDS (typically acquired congenitally from mothers with the disease) did media interest rise, and then media attention focused primarily on the 1 to 2 percent of cases considered to be "innocent victims" of AIDS—female partners of men with AIDS, people with AIDS transmitted through blood transfusions, and children (see Baker 1985). After several months of coverage, national media and governmental attention waned until the announcement in the summer of 1985 that popular Hollywood actor Rock Hudson was seriously ill with AIDS.

From the beginning, AIDS was socially constructed along a series of moral oppositions that defined gay men as disease carriers polluting an innocent population. Homosexuality, which had only recently been de-labeled as an illness, became quickly remedicalized, with gay men labeled as responsible for their own plight and thus undeserving of sympathy. In reviewing the press coverage Edward Albert notes, "Not only is the disease construed as self-caused but, in its presentation on the page, cannot but be read as brought upon us all by 'those' same persons in a causally witnessable way" (1985). AIDS had become the leprosy of the modern age. As Susan Sontag remarks, "In the Middle Ages, the leper was a social text in which corruption was made visible; an exemplar, an emblem of decay" (Sontag 1978, 58). The syndrome was replayed through the moral drama of nineteenth-century cholera, where "disease in the poor retained the power of moral stigma—the slothful poor attracted their diseases—while the . . . same disease in the wealthy was caused by microbes unleashed by *others*" (Patton 1985, 57).

The Christian right was quick to exploit the new opportunity. Jerry Falwell, promoted as an instant expert on the topic by an obliging television network, announced that AIDS was God's punishment upon homosexuals, called upon people with AIDS to be quarantined (or imprisoned if they had sex with anyone), demanded mandatory blood tests for AIDS antibodies and a central file of those testing positive, and urged the closing of gay bathhouses.[33] Fred Niles, on his Sydney television show, demanded that gay Australians traveling to the United States be quarantined on their return.[34] And Republican congressman William Dannemeyer hired professional homophobe Paul Cameron (a psychologist expelled from the American Psychological Association for unethical conduct) as an "AIDS consultant" to advise on how best to exploit the AIDS issue. Little wonder that rumors began circulating in the gay press that AIDS was a virus developed as a biological weapon by the CIA from the swine fever virus that the CIA had already used to damage hog production in Cuba (Chomsky and Herman 1979, 69).

The result of media exposure was the beginning of research funding and the development of a public panic. With very little understanding of the specific means of transmission, Tulsa city officials drained a municipal swimming pool following its rental to a gay group in 1983, a New York co–op attempted to expel a physician treating people with AIDS, a Florida hospital dumped a person with AIDS on an airplane with a one-way ticket to San Francisco, some medical personnel refused to work with AIDS patients, some police and ambulance workers would not assist people who "looked gay," and a number of funeral directors declined to accept the bodies of people who had died of AIDS.[35]

With national attention focused on the problem of protecting the blood supply, the first research result was the identification in France and the United States of the AIDS virus (LAV/HTLV-3) and the development of a test for antibodies occurring from exposure to the virus. Although the AIDS-antibody test substantially reduced the risk of transmission through blood transfusions, it did not distinguish among people with AIDS, people who carried the virus, people in early stages of AIDS, and people who had recovered from exposure to the virus without developing the disease itself. As with many other diseases, apparently only a minority of those exposed to the virus, in fact, suffered from the disease; many others testing positive remained healthy. Nevertheless, the AIDS antibody offered a new and more effective weapon in identifying large numbers of traditionally stigmatized classes of people, initiating a new round of discriminatory practices. The U.S. military led the way with the announcement that all military personnel would have to take the test and those testing positive would be expelled without benefits. Life insurance companies and employers of food handlers began to press for compulsory blood tests the better to discriminate against (for the most part) gay clients and employees. AIDS-antibody tests were becoming the pink triangles of the 1980s as public labeling procedures setting up gay men and other risk categories as targets for public abuse. In 1985, only San Francisco, Los Angeles, and West Hollywood had legislated against discrimination against people with AIDS. Though some courts elsewhere ruled that the disability category already covered them, the U.S. Justice Department stated publicly that it did not.

In 1983, a national Federation of AIDS-Related Organizations formed in the United States to coordinate public education and support services for people with AIDS. Amid the earlier confusion of the epidemic, even many gay movement organizations accepted the medicoreligious definition of "the" problem, leading to publicity campaigns against promiscuity, arguing that gay men should cut down on the number of their sex partners. Many nongay "experts" did not hesitate to echo the pope in demanding complete celibacy, denying gay men their sexuality altogether. In New York, a sexual compulsion program aimed to convince gay men to get over the sexual freedom of the 1970s, and many were counseled to get a lover—something many would have gladly done long ago if the opportunity had arisen! In San Francisco and then in other cities, public health officials suppressed bathhouses and sex clubs in the belief that AIDS was being spread there (see Levine 1985; Murray and Payne 1985; Altman 1986). But the sex-control policies owed more to entrenched Western mythologies than to scientific logic.

There are some lessons of history to be gained from the study of control measures adopted against sexually transmitted diseases, as Allan Brandt's recent work, *No Magic Bullet,* shows. Sexually transmitted diseases have been wrapped so long in moral reasoning that dispassionate analyses of truly effective means of control have often been pushed aside in the past. As Brandt demonstrates, the control of sexually transmitted diseases has very often been confused with the control of sexuality itself, a conceptualization which overlooks more pragmatic means of prophylaxis, and has led to the unintentional increase of the problem. During the 1910s and 1920s, public health authorities expended a great deal of energy and money attempting to counsel men (especially soldiers) to remain chaste and in closing down "red light" districts across the United States. The results were ever-increasing rates of syphilis and gonorrhea. Infection rates were not brought down until the implementation of quite another policy by the federal government in the 1930s—and this was accomplished in the days before penicillin. The new policy abandoned the daunting task of trying to make sex unpopular in favor of a more practical approach of making condoms readily available and instructing men in their use. By separating the issue of infection (basically a question of placing a barrier between oneself and the infective agent) from the question of sexuality, significant headway was made in controlling disease.

Bathhouses have existed for more than a century in the United States and have evolved as one of the central institutions of gay male culture. They have offered sexual meeting places, but more importantly, have also served as places for talk, play, and intimacy—in short, for courtship. In societies traditionally antagonistic to male bonding, bathhouses, along with bars and voluntary associations, have had a significant role to play in providing relatively secure and positive locations for courtship and sociability. From a public health viewpoint, they offer a unique opportunity for encouraging unsensational education about AIDS and other sexually transmitted diseases.

Yet even as the AIDS-related movement consolidated around the safe-sex message, the antigay opposition mobilized to obstruct its efforts. With speech by gay people about their sexuality still targeted by censors, police, and preachers as obscene, safe-sex literature encountered obstacles across the United States and Canada, as a number of local and national jurisdictions confiscated or cut public information fliers intended to limit the spread of AIDS. And the greatest tragedy of all is the approximately five years in which the AIDS virus proliferated with almost no one knowing of its existence.

It is a story in which only the opening chapter has been written. Unrecognized by the larger public are hundreds of stories of individual heroism both of people with AIDS and their supporters—such as the Gay Men's Health Collective in New York, the Shanti Project in San Francisco, and the National Gay Task Force crisis line—who have struggled to make the idea of gay *community* a reality and have ministered to the needs of the beleaguered. In another era, AIDS may have been the occasion for yet another deadly campaign against gay people. In the 1980s, thousands rallied to demand research funding and health care, spoke out to bring the safe-sex message to all, and set up AIDS support committees in every sizeable city. Movement groups often developed their first regular contacts with government agencies to work in common toward containing the virus.

Chapter Eight

Conclusion

It must first be noted that book writing contains its inherent limitations, and this book, too, cannot escape them. The act of marshaling evidence around a topic, such as the gay and lesbian movement, inevitably induces a retrospective coherence into a subject and hides the very real history of fits and starts, fragile initiatives and collapse, and individual feats of boldness that characterize the formation of any social movement. Despite the rewards of comparative historical sociology, this organizational principle for texts cannot but even out the diversity of experiences and aspirations that go on under the label gay/lesbian movement and give the movement an apparent life that would supposedly transcend the personal dilemmas, decisions, projects, and retreats that make it up. The problem is especially acute in conjuring forth a lesbian movement. Lesbians have fundamentally shaped the course of both the women's and the gay or gay-lesbian movements and have shifted back and forth between the two, at times debating with each other from within the two camps, as well as flowing through autonomous lesbian organizations. The identification of a lesbian movement per se, then, is particularly problematic and not parallel to the more singular movement that has occupied gay men.

Comparative and dialectical approaches do, however, offer particularly beneficial vantage points for discovering where movements come from, how they work, and why they change. In this closing section, I would like to consider some of the prospects and issues that might occupy the movement further (presuming that AIDS does not overwhelm everything else).

An enduring issue will certainly be the battle for the right to love and live with the person of one's choice and to disestablish the state-supported patriarchal family currently shored up and administered through tax and family laws, municipal zoning regulations about who may live with whom, policies of social welfare and therapeutic bureaucracies, and the conceits of insurance agents and businesses. Gay parents, especially lesbian mothers, have been fighting to retain children from previous marriages as well as to create households with new children. For lesbians for whom procreation is a relatively easy technical issue, children are possible, and many have created families of their own, despite the obstruction of the medical and artificial insemination establishments. For heterosexuals, infertility is a difficulty solved by adoption and by an increasingly sophisticated range of research options; for gay men, reproductive rights are absolutely denied by the state. When lesbians and gay men do adopt or provide foster care, they remain subject to the hysteria of the state as when two preschool boys were seized from David Jean and Don Babets in Massachusetts (and a law passed in 1985 forbidding the placement of children with gay people), though their parenting capabilities were unquestioned.

There are, as yet, very few instances where gay people can nominate their lovers for the benefits enjoyed by spouses. In 1982, San Francisco mayor Diane Feinstein vetoed a law that would have allowed domestic partners spousal rights provided there was a "one-year relationship between two people who 'share the common necessaries of life,' [and] declare their relationship in a signed statement . . . [and] each [is] the principal domestic partner of the other."[1] On the other hand, in 1985, West Hollywood did pass a domestic partners law and the Netherlands offers gay and lesbian couples access to subsidized housing, welfare benefits, and immigration, with gay people able to sponsor their partners for citizenship. There are other scattered instances: the Australian Broadcasting Corporation recognizes domestic partners for "employee travel, accommodation, [and] bereavement leave"; Air France permits airfare discounts for the lovers of employees as well as for spouses; *Village Voice* (New York) employees won medical benefits for "spouse equivalents"; the Wisconsin Automobile Association switched from marriage to "household" rates; and Berkeley (California) did pass a domestic partners bill to give city employees equal health benefits.[2] In Sweden, a parliamentary commission proposed recognition of lesbian and gay cohabitants as well as an antidiscrimination law, political asylum for gay refugees, and state support for gay groups and public education on gay issues (Petersson 1985).

Also among fundamental problems are the communications media reproducing and distributing ideas and images of lesbians and gay men to the public. The predominance of exploitative imagery of women provoked feminists toward their antipornography drives, though sexual images form only one small sector of the problem. And certainly the gaylesbian movement also showed itself sensitive to the issue of defamatory treatment in picketing the movies *Cruising* and *Windows*, which reasserted vampire images of predatory homosexuals. Calls for state control through censorship rest on the naive conviction that white, heterosexual, (upper) middle-class, male judges will somehow begin to represent the concerns of women and gay people against a class of image producers who very much resemble themselves. The problem of symbol production runs deeper. In state socialist societies, the state monopoly on public discourse largely precludes gay people from speaking for themselves; in liberal democratic societies, capitalist and state communications channels shunt lesbians and gay men aside, preventing them from speaking to the mainstream of society. In recent years, a virtual cultural renaissance has led to a boom of gay and lesbian publications. Local and national periodicals, fiction and nonfiction, radio programs, films and visual art have flourished—but almost entirely outside the established mass communications system. And in almost every sizable town in North America, Western Europe, and Australia, anyone can look up "gay" in the telephone book to speak to people in the local movement group. But in the United States, where television, radio, and city newspapers lie almost exclusively in corporate hands, the much-vaunted constitutional guarantee of freedom of speech gives way to a narrow ideological spectrum defined by the interests of big capital.

The remarkable tradition of toleration and pluralism in the Netherlands likely owes a debt to the "pillarization" of the communications systems, where a set of voluntary organizations, separated on political and religious lines, "all have at their disposal their own schools, universities, and broadcasting facilities (i.e., broadcasting time on a proportional basis on the state-run radio and television)" (Grubb and van der Heer 1979, 23). At any one time, people in the Netherlands can sample opinion from the left or the right, the religious or humanist, and from five nations in four languages. Gay and lesbian programs are available in the mass media, especially on the left and humanist networks. In France, the state system has been recently supplemented by noncommercial radio collectives that represent a variety of interests; under their auspices, "Fréquence Gaie" becomes possible. In English-language nations, gay programming remains typically confined to the occasional community access channel, and media gatekeepers manipulate the presentation of lesbian/gay issues in the mainstream. The ongoing task of women and gay people, as well as many other subordinated peoples, can only be to push for the democratization of the communications industry in order to overcome the capitalist or state administration of ideas and to critique media discourses so deeply infused with machoism, militarism, and consumerism. While American television viewers can watch men killing men every hour in the name of entertainment, men expressing open affection toward one another remains largely taboo!

The problems of lesbians and gay men living in modern societies will not be simply solved through public education or goodwill—where it exists—but necessarily involve the fundamental restructuring of some of the basic institutions of society. These problems are not always unique to gay people and are certainly beyond resolution by any one social movement. Any group of people seriously interested in social change must consider its place in the larger political context and the potential for coalition with other peripheralized peoples. The fading away of the idea of a common front of oppressed peoples, so enthusiastically endorsed by gay liberation, and the continuing tendency of movements to develop toward nationalist exclusivity have contributed to the easy containment of reform movements by established authorities and thus to the reproduction of the status quo. The successes of lesbian and gay politicians are instructive: they have always pulled together coalitions of the dispossessed and disenfranchised to win power and have rarely won concessions from established power blocs with the assistance of corporate, church, or elite forces. By conceiving of the issues as a public relations campaign to be fought in isolation, little headway is likely. But by showing people how gay issues are general issues and by understanding and contributing to the struggles of other subordinated peoples, coalitions become possible. In an era of political pessimism, when the Right has restored its hegemony and each social movement comes to believe it stand alone, coalitions fail to form.

Again, comparisons offer a wider perspective. Revolutionary coalitions would offer the purest point of contrast but have yet to form in any society in which gay movements have become a presence, but local nationalist movements among submerged peoples have succeeded in places where gay people are organized. It is noteworthy that in Quebec and Catalonia (and, to some degree, Euskadia), gay self-organization has occurred within a larger nationalist and social democratic ferment and that gay groups have been embraced in these alliances. The subsequent reform won for gay rights and the ensuing solidarity of labor, women, and national minorities with lesbian and gay issues in these places is remarkable. In the United States, as well, gay and lesbian alliances with black movements have proven fruitful. It is black (and Jewish) members of the U.S. Congress who have been among the most consistent backers of civil rights reforms for gay people, and "rainbow coalitions," whether at the city level (for example, Mel King's Boston campaign) or nationally, have offered far more solid commitments to gay rights than the vague concessionary statements dispensed by mainstream candidates.

Nor need this principle be confined by national boundaries. When Mexicans march on Gay Pride Day, they include support for the self-determination of the Salvadoran people, and the Farabundo Marti National Liberation Front (FMLN) in turn sends supportive statements to the gay movement. A gay support group for the Nicaraguan revolution was organized in 1979 in San Francisco (and later elsewhere).[3] For the most part, national gay and lesbian organizations and even the International Gay Association have refrained from commenting on foreign policy issues that do not appear directly to involve gay people. But can this abstention be extended to ignore the subsidization of dictatorships that make gay organization impossible, as in Chile or El Salvador, or to ignore governments that so easily finance the export of military technology from napalm to nuclear bombs while limiting research and medical funds for AIDS?

Perhaps most important for the future of gay people are the neighborhood groups that have formed in the last decade in London, Paris, New York, and San Francisco, which have the strengths of fully developed communities with their long-term social networks and day-to-day concern about local living space. Here are the nuclei of democratic self-organization and real self-determination away from the prying eye of repressive agencies. It is at this level that one might anticipate "a resurrection of local, popular, and disqualified knowledge through the production of critical discourses" (Smart 1985, 135).

Perhaps most difficult of all is to remember not to let oneself be defined by one's enemies. Michel Foucault once mused about

the common fear that gays will develop relationships that are intense and satisfying even though they do not all conform to the ideas of relationship held by others. It is the prospect that gays will create as yet unforeseen kinds of relationships that many people cannot tolerate. (1982–83, 10)

It is the rush to appear "respectable," to have continually to justify one's existence, and to cope with the "scandals" invented by the opposition that mire lesbians and gay men in traditional frameworks and fetters the full creative potential of relationships that are at once pleasurable and entirely voluntary.

Notes

Chapter One

1. See Foucault 1980 on the development of knowledge in order to control.

2. This section telescopes a great deal of family history better developed in Foreman 1977 and in the work of Philippe Ariès, Jean-Louis Flandrin, Lawrence Stone, Mark Poster, and others.

3. This section condenses several stages of capitalist development that are treated in more detail in Adam 1985b.

4. See Thompson 1980 on the British "counter-revolution."

Chapter Two

1. This section is heavily indebted to the pioneering research of James Steakley (1975), John Lauritsen and David Thorstad (1974), and Hans-Georg Stümke and Rudi Finkler (1981).

2. See Fredrik Silverstolpe's forthcoming book on "Gay Stockholm, 1860–1960."

3. The rendering of *Eigene* into English has caused translators headaches. Its closest approximations are: "the special," "the particular," "the essential," "one's own."

4. For an incisive discussion of the implications of the Eulenberg affair, see Steakley 1983, 42–47; Hull 1982.

5. (My translation.) Unfortunately, "monstres sacrés" loses much in translation.

6. Philip Dyer, "Origins," "World of Art," and "Widening Horizons," in Spender 1974, esp. 35, 67.

7. Bonnet 1981, 96–165, 207. Baudelaire had gone to trial charged with obscenity for publishing poems with lesbian themes in *Les Fleurs du Mal.*

8. Much of this section is indebted to the fundamental work of Jeffrey Weeks.

9. F. B. Smith (1976) argues that the Labouchere Amendment was almost unintentional, having been slipped into an antiprostitution bill with almost no debate. This does not explain why the amendment would be seen as so "natural" that it did not occasion opposition.

10. Wilson 1974, 265, drawn from Ernest Hemingway, *A Moveable Feast* (New York: Charles Scribner's Sons, 1964), 20.

11. See Baritz 1960, 33 on the activities of Ford Motor Company.

12. For an examination of coping strategies among subordinated peoples, some of which contribute to that subordination, see Adam 1978.

13. U.S. Senate, Committee on Naval Affairs 1975, 11, 30; see Katz 1983, 398. The entrapment squad reported to then Acting Secretary of the Navy, Franklin Roosevelt.

Chapter Three

1. Steakley 1975, 88; Isherwood 1976, 18; Kokula 1984; Bleuel 1974, 5; for the most complete history of this period see Stümke and Finkler 1981.

2. Personal communication from James Steakley.

3. See Abraham 1981; Blackbourn and Eley 1984; Dobkowski and Walliman 1983; Moore 1966; Hamilton 1982.

4. On Nazi ideologies of homosexuality, see Schilling 1983; Herzer 1985; Stümke and Finkler 1981; Bock 1983; Mosse 1982; Steakley 1975.

5. Much of this was dramatized in Martin Sherman's 1980 play *Bent*.

Chapter Four

1. Wallace's Progressive message clearly interested some gay people. F. O. Matthiessen made the seconding speech for Wallace's nomination as presidential candidate at the party convention (Hyde 1978, 362) and Henry Hay toyed with the idea of a Bachelors for Wallace group to organize gay people (see Katz 1976, 408).

2. See Katz 1976, 586, 610, 639, 643–46, 651–52. The West German press took a similar line at this time, a direct inheritance of Nazi precepts. See Stümke and Finkler 1981, 373–86.

3. U.S. Senate, Committee on Expenditures in the Executive Departments, Subcommittee on Investigations 1975.

4. Weeks 1977, 159–61; Wildeblood 1955, esp. 35, 42, 46. For the antigay campaigns of the British press, see Pearce 1973.

5. On some of the personal stories about living through these times, see especially Katz 1976, chap. 2, and Adair and Adair 1978.

6. See also Christopher Isherwood's comments in Praunheim 1980, 32.

7. It should be noted, however, that the Communist party itself was opposed to homosexuality in line with the Stalinist position and Hay was obliged to leave the party to do his Mattachine work.

8. Jacques Girard attributes the coining of the word to the Dutch activist de Arent Van Sunthorst in 1949. See Girard 1981, 49.

9. *Der Kreis* was the only prewar gay publication to survive into the 1950s by publishing in Switzerland. In 1951 it was a trilingual journal with a circulation of eight hundred.

10. See Martin and Lyon 1972, 238, for a defense of this policy.

11. See D'Emilio 1983, 177–80; Tytell 1976. Catharine Stimpson (1982–83) points out that the Beat style, like most of the New Left, contained no challenge to sexism.

12. On his new relationship with Peter Orlovsky, Ginsberg remarks:

We made a vow to each other that he could own me, my mind and everything I knew, and my body, and I could own him and all he knew and his body; and that we would give each other ourselves, so that we possessed each other as property, to do everything we wanted to sexually or intellectually, and in a sense explore each other until we reached the mystical "X" together, emerging two merged souls. We had the understanding that when our (my particularly) erotic desire was ultimately satisfied by being satiated (rather than denied), there would be a lessening of desire, grasp, holding on, craving and attachment; and that ultimately we would both be delivered free in heaven together. (1974, 23)

13. At its height DOB included chapters in New Orleans, Reno, Portland, San Diego, Cleveland, Denver, Detroit, Philadelphia, and Melbourne, Australia. See Martin and Lyon 1972, 227.

Chapter Five

1. On consciousness raising, see Altman 1971, 113; Teal 1971; Freeman 1975, 124–25; Evans 1979, 214–23; Breines 1982.

2. A branch of the COC was also founded in Antwerp in 1965 as the Belgische Vereiniging voor Sexuale Rechtvaardigheid COC (Maroey 1969). I am grateful for conversations with Rob Tielman, Judith Schuyf, Kim Friele, and Wenche Lowzow on the Netherlands and Norwegian movements. They are, of course, not responsible for my interpretation.

3. Teal 1971, 58; Abbott and Love 1972, 116; Jay and Young 1972, 292–320 passim; Kokula 1975, 64, 72–79; Girard 1981, 103; García Gaudilla 1981, 45; Marotta 1981, 275–82; Thompson 1985, 58.

4. On the new masculinity, see Humphreys 1972a; Hocquenghem 1979, 67; Girard 1981, 115; White 1980; Chesebro and Klenk 1981; Blachford 1981; Marshall 1981. Renaud Camus put it this way, "Well, I like fake butch types better than real ones; the real ones are a pain in the ass. Besides, I like fakes. I like guys who look very male, physically, but who are actually very sweet and nice, and not aggressive at all" (1981, 108–9).

5. Harvey Fierstein's Broadway play *Torch Song Trilogy* wrestles with similar dilemmas.

6. On the sexual ghetto argument, see also Altman 1978; Dahmer 1978; Shiers 1978; Altman 1982.

Chapter Six

1. See *Gay Community News* 5, no. 42 (1978):1; and 5, no. 44 (1978):1.

2. Castells argues that this development was mistakenly called "gentrification," a process where external capital "upgrades" a poor neighborhood, thereby displacing the local inhabitants for a profit to investors. Gay people, however, generally built their communities with little capital and through their own labor for their own use. See also "Gay Ghetto" in Levine 1979.

3. See Shilts 1982, 107; Weiss 1984, 77; see also the Academy Award–winning documentary *The Times of Harvey Milk*.

4. On coping strategies to persecution, see Adam 1978, chaps. 3–4.

5. The first two issues are discussed above. On the question of workplace lesbianism, see the very interesting work of Beth Schneider (1984a and 1984b).

6. Burris 1983, 312–13; see also Zurcher and Kirkpatrick 1976, 260 on the social profile of crusaders against pornography.

7. See Ericson 1982, 91; Crawford 1980, 11–15; Young 1982, 128; Huntington and Kaplan 1982, 63; Himmelstein 1983.

8. On the capitalist state and the media, see Miliband 1973; Parenti 1978; Chomsky and Herman 1979.

9. Young 1982, 105, 132–34, 141; Liebman and Wuthnow 1983, 2; *Body Politic* 55 (1979):16.

10. Young 1982, 141; on the complicity of the oppressed in their own oppression, see Adam 1978.

11. See news accounts in *Body Politic* 45 (1978):9, 46 (1978):11; *Gay Community News* 6, no. 2 (1978):11; Thompson 1985, 29; the film *Witches and Faggots—Dykes and Poofters*. I am also grateful for comments by Robert French.

Chapter Seven

1. Girard 1981, 179–81, my translation. The Swedish RFSI once challenged the Swedish government to disavow the WHO classification by having gay people around the country stay home from work one day and call in saying they were "sick" with homosexuality.

2. For this section, see news reports in the *Body Politic*, *Gay Community News*, and Pedersen 1985. I am also grateful for conversations with Wenche Lowzow and Kim Friele and for a copy of the parliamentary debates leading to passage of the law.

3. My thanks to Edward Sebesta for sending me campaign leaflets.

4. See, for example, Joyce 1986; Lesk, Popert, and Taylor 1986; Monk 1986. On violence against gay men and lesbians, see Berrill (n.d.) and Harry 1982.

5. See "Supreme Court Dumps Gay Tide," *Body Politic* 54 (1979):9.

6. My thanks to Kim Friele for sending me a transcript of the court proceedings.

7. On left antigay ideologies, see Weeks 1975; Fernbach 1981, 61–69; Derbyshire 1980.

8. In West Hollywood, John Heilman and Steve Schulte went to city hall; in Sydney, Craig Johnston, Brian McGahen, and Bill Hunt.

9. See Happel 1985; Dubow 1982. Canadian cities with sexual orientation legislation are: Toronto (1973), Ottawa (1976), Windsor (1977), and Kitchener (1982).

10. In the early 1980s, bath raids were recorded in: 1980 in Auckland, New Zealand, where 8 men were seized, Los Angeles (16 men), and Minneapolis(100); 1981 in Toronto and Edmonton (62); 1982 in Tampa, Florida (73); 1983 in Milwaukee (11), Wallasky, U.K. (10), and Toronto (9); 1984 in Atlanta, Brussels, and Antwerp. Also in 1984, San Francisco authorities closed the baths ostensibly to control the spread of AIDS and Montreal police arrested 188 men on "indecency" charges in a bar raid.

11. Clark 1981; "RCMP Policy in Respect of Homosexual Conduct," *Body Politic* 116(1985):19, 21. On the structure of imagery about subordinated peoples entertained by their oppressors, see Adam 1978.

12. Manson 1985; Hauer 1984, 11; Krichler 1984. The International Gay Association met in Vienna in 1983 and in Helsinki in 1984 in solidarity with the local movements.

13. Baldursson 1985; Vassilas 1984; see *Body Politic* news accounts on Greece in issues 45, 60, 64, 72–74, 101, 105, and 109.

14. (My translation.) In 1980, FAGC hosted the second meeting of the International Gay Associaton.

15. "El Rumanio," *Forumo, Bulteno de la Ligo de Samseksemaj Geesperantistoj* 31 (1984):5, my translation; on general treatments of eastern Europe, see Hauer et al. 1984; Brockman 1977; on Cuba, see Young 1981; Ginsberg 1974, 26; Salas 1979, 154–64; Arguelles and Rich 1984; and the film *Improper Conduct.* Here I differ with Stephen Murray's claim that to contend that modern gay and lesbian worlds emerge out of the development of capitalist societies "requires" that they emerge *only* in capitalist societies. See Murray 1984, 55.

16. Kyper 1979; see *Nuevo Ambiente* and news reports in *Gay Community News* and *Body Politic.*

17. Clarke 1984; news reports in *Body Politic.*

18. Grupo de Acción Gay 1985; Forgione 1982; I am grateful to Carlos Luis for sending me a copy of *Sodoma.*

19. See Botero 1981; Herrick 1984; and news accounts in *Body Politic* and *Gay Community News.*

20. Burstyn 1984; on the "potentially reactionary" premises of the nationalist position, see Eisenstein 1983.

21. For an early statement of gay male misgivings, see John D'Emilio 1980.

22. See issues 84, 92, and 104 of *Body Politic*; Burstyn 1985.

23. Rubin 1982; Nestle 1981; Sue Golding's remark was made at the 1985 Sex and the State conference in Toronto attended by the author. See also Hollibaugh and Moraga 1983; English, Hollibaugh, and Rubin 1981; Rubin 1984a.

24. Manion 1985, 76; see also Heath 1984 for a thorough-going critique of sexual reductionism.

25. But see Blumstein and Schwartz 1983, a painstaking investigation of how married heterosexual, unmarried heterosexual, gay, and lesbian couples manage to solve the day-to-day dilemmas of living together.

26. On cross-cultural studies of pedophilia, see Adam 1985; Herdt 1984; Lévi-Strauss 1969, 446; Evans-Pritchard 1970; 'Abd Allah 1917.

27. For two very different views from within the movement, see Ginsberg's characterization of man/boy love as "an exchange of nature-bounties. Older people gain vigor, refreshment, vitality, energy, hopefulness and cheerfulness from the attentions of the young; and the younger people gain gossip, experiences, advice, aid, comfort, wisdom, knowledge and teachings from their relation with the old" (1974, 16), and Michael Alhonte's critique of the tendency of older men to use money to assert dominance in a relationship and to project their own ideas of "age-appropriate" behavior onto youth as "either the young, ingenuous protege or the streetwise, butch, jock punk." Some, he concludes, "find me old enough to screw but not old enough to talk to" (1981, 157–58).

28. O'Carroll 1980; see also issue 49 of *Homophonies* on the French Groupe de Recherche pour une Enfance Différente; Monk 1981.

29. See NAMBLA Bulletin; news accounts in *Body Politic* and *Gay Community News*; Tsang 1981; Rubin 1984b.

30. "On the Liberation of Children and Youth," *Minor Problems* 4 (1984):15.

31. "Education Is the Power Relation," *Minor Problems* 1 (1983):9.

32. See O'Carroll's disavowal of a gay identity (1980, 208); on lesbian treatments of intergenerational sex, Kelly 1979; articles by Gayle Rubin and Pat Califia in *The Age Taboo*.

33. *Body Politic* 96 (1983):21; *Gay Community News* 13, no. 3 (1985):2.

34. *Gay Community News* 9, no. 24 (1983):3.

35. The best coverage of the AIDS crisis is in the *New York Native*. See also the *Advocate, Gay Community News,* and publications of AIDS support groups.

Chapter Eight

1. *Body Politic* 90 (1983):20; 91 (1983):19.

2. *Body Politic* 107 (1984):18; *Homophonies* 50 (1984):8; *Gay Community News* 10, no. 6 (1982):2; 12, no. 23 (1984):1; 12, no. 30 (1985):2.

3. The Nicaraguan revolution itself occurred in a largely agrarian nation with no internal organized gay presence and so developed no clear policy on homosexuality, but appears to have avoided the persecutory policies practiced by Cuba. (Based on questions posed to Sandinista officials by the author in Managua and on reports in the gay press.)

References

'ABD ALLAH, MAHMUD MOHAMMAD. 1917. "Siwan Customs." *Harvard African Studies* 1:7.

ABBOTT, SIDNEY. 1978. "Lesbians and the Women's Movement." In *Our Right to Love,* edited by Ginny Vida. Englewood Cliffs, N.J.: Prentice-Hall.

ABBOTT, SIDNEY, and BARBARA LOVE. 1972. *Sappho Was a Right-On Woman.* New York: Stein & Day.

ABRAHAM, DAVID. 1981. *The Collapse of the Weimar Republic.* Princeton, N.J.: Princeton University Press.

ADAIR, NANCY, and CASEY ADAIR. 1978. *Word Is Out.* San Francisco: New Glide Publications.

ADAM, BARRY D.. 1978. *The Survival of Domination.* New York: Elsevier/Greenwood.

———. 1979. "A Social History of Gay Politics." In *Gay Men,* edited by Martin Levine. New York: Harper & Row.

———. 1980. "Sexual Outlaws." *Canadian Journal of Political and Social Theory* 4 (2):75.

———. 1982. "Where Gay People Come From." *Christopher Street* 64:50.

———. 1985a. "Age, Structure, and Sexuality." *Journal of Homosexuality* 11 (3–4):19.

———. 1985b. "Structural Foundations of the Gay World." *Comparative Studies in Society and History* 27 (4):658.

———. 1986. "The Construction of a Sociological 'Homosexual' in Canadian Textbooks." *Canadian Review of Sociology and Anthropology* 23 (3):399.

ALBERT, EDWARD. 1985. "Learning to Live with It . . . the Routinization of AIDS Coverage." Paper presented to the American Sociological Association, Washington, D.C.

ALHONTE, MICHAEL. 1981. "Confonting Ageism." In *The Age Taboo,* edited by Dan Tsang. Boston: Alyson.

ALTMAN, DENNIS. 1971. *Homosexual Oppression and Liberation.* New York: Outerbridge & Dienstfrey.

———. 1978. "The State, Repression and Sexuality." *Gay Left* 6 (Summer):4.

———. 1979. *Coming Out in the Seventies.* Sydney: Wild & Woolley.

———. 1980. "What Changed in the Seventies?" In *Homosexuality: Power & Politics,* edited by the Gay Left Collective. London: Allison & Busby.

———. 1982. *The Homosexualization of America.* New York: St. Martin's.

———. 1986. *AIDS in the Mind of America.* Garden City, N.Y.: Doubleday.

ARBOLEDA, MANUEL. 1980. "Gay Life in Lima." *Gay Sunshine* 42–43:30.

ARGUELLES, LOURDES, and B. RUBY RICH. 1984. "Homosexuality, Homophobia, and Revolution." *Signs* 9 (4):683.

ATKINSON, TI-GRACE. 1973. "Lesbianism and Feminism." In *Amazon Expedition,* edited by Phyllis Birkby et al. Washington, N.J.: Times Change Press.

AUSTEN, ROGER. 1977. *Playing the Game.* Indianapolis: Bobbs-Merrill.

BAKER, ANDREA. 1985. "AIDS and the News." Paper presented to the American Sociological Association, Washington, D.C.

BAKTIS, DR. *Die Sexualrevolution in Russland.* Berlin: Verlag der Syndikalist. Reprint. Osnabruck: Archiv Antiautoritäre Erziehung.

BALDURSSON, GUTHNI. 1985. "From Sexual Aberration to Sexual Inversion." In *IGA Pink Book 1985,* edited by the International Gay Association. Amsterdam: COC-magazijn.

BARBEDETTE, GILLES, and MICHEL CARASSOU. 1981. *Paris Gay 1925.* Paris: Presses de la Renaissance.

BARITZ, LEON. 1960. *The Servants of Power.* Middletown, Conn.: Wesleyan University Press.

BAUMGARDT, MANFRED. 1984a. "Berlin, ein Zentrum der entstehenden Sexualwissenschaft und die Vorläufer der Homosexuellen-Bewegung." In *Eldorado,* edited by the Berlin Museum. Berlin: Frölich & Kaufmann.

———. 1984b. "Das Institut für Sexualwissenschaft und die Homosexuellenbewegung in der Weimarer Republik." In *Eldorado,* edited by the Berlin Museum. Berlin: Frölich & Kaufmann.

———. 1984c. "Die Homosexuellen-Bewegung bis zum Ende des Ersten Weltkrieges."In *Eldorado,* edited by the Berlin Museum. Berlin: Frölich & Kaufmann.

BAYER, RONALD. 1981. *Homosexuality and American Psychiatry.* New York: Basic Books.

BEARCHELL, CHRIS. 1983. "Why I Am a Gay Liberationist." *Resources for Feminist Research* 12 (1):59.

BERRILL, KEVIN. N.d. "Anti-gay Violence." New York: National Gay Task Force.

BERSON, GINNY. 1978. "Women's Music." In *Our Right to Love,* edited by Ginny Vida. Englewood Cliffs, N.J.: Prentice-Hall.

BÉRUBÉ, ALLAN. 1981. "Lesbians and Gay GIs in World War II." *Advocate* (October 15):20.

———. 1983. "Marching to a Different Drummer." In *Powers of Desire,* edited by Ann Snitow, Christine Stansell, and Sharon Thompson. New York: Monthly Review Press.

BÉRUBÉ, ALLAN, and JOHN D'EMILIO. 1984. "The Military and Lesbians during the McCarthy Years." *Signs* 9 (4):759.

BINGHAM, CAROLINE. 1971. "Seventeenth-century Attitudes toward Deviant Sex." *Journal of Interdisciplinary History* 1 (3):448.

BLACHFORD, GREGG. 1981. "Male Dominance and the Gay World." In *The Making of the Modern Homosexual,* edited by Kenneth Plummer. Totowa, N.J.: Barnes & Noble.

BLACKBOURN, DAVID, and GEOFF ELEY. 1984. *The Peculiarities of German History.* Oxford: Oxford University Press.

BLACKWOOD, EVELYN. 1984. "Sexuality and Gender in Certain Native American Tribes." *Signs* 10 (1):27.

BLEUEL, HANS PETER. 1974. *Sex and Society in Nazi Germany.* Philadelphia: Lippincott.

BLUMSTEIN, PHILIP, and PEPPER SCHWARTZ. 1983. *American Couples.* New York: Morrow.

BOCK, GISELA. 1983. "Racism and Sexism in Nazi Germany." *Signs* 8 (3):400.

BOLES, JANET. 1979. *The Politics of the Equal Rights Amendment.* New York: Longman.

BONNET, MARIE-JO. 1981. *Un choix sans équivoque.* Paris: Editions Denoël.

BORY, JEAN-LOUIS, and GUY HOCQUENGHEM. 1977. *Comment nous appelez-vous déjà?* Paris: Calmann-Levy.

BOSWELL, JOHN. 1980. *Christianity, Social Tolerance and Homosexuality.* Chicago: University of Chicago Press.

BOTERO, EBEL. 1981. "Our Sisters and Brothers in Colombia." *Gay Community News* 8 (25):12.

BRADY, JAMES. 1983. "Arson, Urban Economy, and Organized Crime." *Social Problems* 31 (1):1.

BRANDT, ALLAN. 1985. *No Magic Bullet.* New York: Oxford University Press.

BRASSAÏ. 1976. *The Secret Paris of the 30's.* New York: Pantheon.

BRAY, ALAN. 1982. *Homosexuality in Renaissance England.* London: Gay Men's Press.

BREINES, WINI. 1979. Review essay. *Feminist Studies* 5 (3):496.

———. 1982. *Community and Organization in the New Left.* New York: Praeger.

BRICK, BARRETT. 1979. "Judaism in the Gay Community." In *Positively Gay,* edited by Betty Berzon and Robert Leighton. Millbrae, Calif.: Celestial Arts.

BRISTOW, EDWARD. 1977. *Vice and Vigilance.* Dublin: Gill & Macmillan.

BRITISH SOCIETY FOR THE STUDY OF SEX PSYCHOLOGY. 1975. "The Social Problem of Sexual Inversion." Abridged translation of "Was soll das Volk vom dritten Geschlecht wissen?" In *A Homosexual Emancipation Miscellany, c. 1835–1952.* New York: Arno.

BRITTAIN, VERA. 1968. *Radclyffe Hall, A Case of Obscenity?* London: Femina.

BROCKMANN, JÜRGEN. 1977. "Antihomosexualität in den sozialistischen Ländern Osteuropas." In *Seminar: Gesellschaft und Homosexualitat,* edited by Rüdiger Lautmann. Frankfurt: Suhrkamp.

BROWN, RITA MAE. 1972. "Take a Lesbian to Lunch." In *Out of the Closets,* edited by Karla Jay and Allen Young. New York: Douglas/Links.

BROWNE, F. W. STELLA. 1977. "The Sexual Variety and Variability among Women." In *A New World for Women,* edited by Sheila Rowbotham. London: Pluto.

BRYANT, ANITA. 1977. *The Anita Bryant Story.* Old Tappan, N.J.: Fleming H. Revell.

BULLOUGH, VERN. 1976. *Sexual Variance in Society and History.* New York: Wiley.

BUNCH, CHARLOTTE. 1976. "Learning from Lesbian Separatism." *Ms.* 5 (5):60.

BURNHAM, JAMES. 1973. "Early References to Homosexual Communities in American Medical Writings." *Medical Aspects of Human Sexuality* 7 (8):41.

BURRIS, VAL. 1983. "Who Opposed the ERA?" *Social Science Quarterly* 65 (2):312.

BURSTYN, VARDA. 1984. "Anatomy of a Moral Panic." *Fuse* 8 (1–2):32.

BURSTYN, VARDA, ed. 1985. *Women against Censorship.* Vancouver: Douglas & McIntyre.

CALLENDER, CHARLES, and LEE KOCHEMS. 1983. "The North American Berdache." *Current Anthropology* 24 (4):443.

CAMUS, RENAUD. 1981. *Tricks.* New York: St. Martin's.

CARDEN, MAREN. 1974. *The New Feminist Movement.* New York: Russell Sage Foundation.

CARPENTER, EDWARD. 1908. *The Intermediate Sex.* London: Allen & Unwin.

———. 1975. *Intermediate Types among Primitive Folk.* New York: Arno.

———. 1982. *Iolaus.* New York: Pagan Press.

CARRIER, JOSEPH. 1976. "Cultural Factors Affecting Urban Mexican Male Homosexual Behavior." *Archives of Sexual Behavior* 5 (2):111.

CASEY, LEO. 1981. "Toronto the Bad." *This Magazine* 15 (1):4.

CASSELL, JOAN. 1972. *A Group Called Women.* New York: David McKay.

CASTELLS, MANUEL. 1983. *The City and the Grassroots.* Berkeley: University of California Press.

CHESEBRO, JAMES, and KENNETH KLENK. 1981. "Gay Masculinity in the Gay Disco." In *Gayspeak,* edited by James Chesebro. New York: Pilgrim.

CHOMSKY, NOAM, and EDWARD HERMAN. 1979. *The Washington Connection and Third World Fascism.* Boston: South End.

CLARK, JIL. 1981. "New Defense Dept. Policy Will Let Gays Be Drafted." *Gay Community News* 8 (28):1.

CLARK, LORENNE. 1980. "Pornography's Challenge to Liberal Ideology." *Canadian Forum* 59 (697):10.

CLARKE, MOFFAT. 1984. "A New Product in the Streets." *Rites* 1 (4):12.

COCTEAU, JEAN. 1958. *The White Paper.* New York: Macauley.

COHEN, JEAN. 1985. "Strategy or Identity." *Social Research* 52 (4):663.

COLLIER, DON, and JOHN WARD. 1980. "Who Are the Radical Fairies?" *Gay Community News* 8 (18):8.

COLQUHOUN, MAUREEN. 1980. *A Woman in the House.* Shoreham-by-Sea, U.K.: Scan Books.

CONOVER, PAMELA, and VIRGINIA GRAY. 1983. *Feminism and the New Right.* New York: Praeger.

COTT, NANCY. 1978. "Passionlessness." *Signs* 4 (2):219.

COWARD, D. A.. 1980. "Attitudes to Homosexuality in Eighteenth-Century France." *Journal of European Studies* 10:236.

COWARD, ROSALIND. 1983. *Patriarchal Precedents.* London: Routledge & Kegan Paul.

CRAWFORD, ALAN. 1980. *Thunder on the Right.* New York: Pantheon.

CROMPTON, LOUIS. 1976. "Homosexuals and the Death Penalty in Colonial America." *Journal of Homosexuality.* 1 (3):277.

———. 1981. "The Myth of Lesbian Impunity." *Journal of Homosexuality* 6 (Winter):11.

D'EMILIO, JOHN. 1980. "Women against Pornography." *Christopher Street* 4 (9):19.

———. 1983. *Sexual Politics, Sexual Communities.* Chicago: University of Chicago Press.

DAHMER, HELMUT. 1978. "Sexual Economy Today." *Telos* 36 (Summer):111.

DALY, MARY. 1978. *Gyn/Ecology.* Boston: Beacon.

DANNECKER, MARTIN, and REIMUT REICHE. 1973. "Nur als Kranke toleriert." *Der Spiegel* 27 (11):50.

DERBYSHIRE, PHILIP. 1980. "Sects and Sexuality." In *Homosexuality: Power & Politics,* edited by the Gay Left Collective. London: Allison & Busby.

DOBKOWSKI, MICHAEL, and ISIDOR WALLIMANN. 1983. *Towards the Holocaust.* Westport, Conn.: Greenwood.

DONZELOT, JACQUES. 1979. *The Policing of Families.* New York: Pantheon.

DOVER, K. J. 1978. *Greek Homosexuality.* New York: Vintage.

DUBOW, DAVID. 1982. "'Security Risks' and Circular Logic in the UK." *Body Politic* 87:21.

DUGGAN, LISA, NAN HUNTER, and CAROLE VANCE. 1985. "False Promises." In *Women against Censorship,* edited by Varda Burstyn. Vancouver: Douglas & McIntyre.

DWORKIN, ANDREA. 1978. "Why So-called Radical Men Love and Need Pornography." *Gay Community News* 6 (22):10.

EARLY, TRACY. 1977. "The Struggle in the Denominations." *Christianity and Crisis* 37 (9–10):110.

ECHOLS, ALICE. 1983. "The New Feminism of Yin and Yang." In *Powers of Desire,* edited by Ann Snitow, Christine Stansell, and Sharon Thompson. New York: Monthly Review Press.

————. 1984. "The Taming of the Id." In *Pleasure and Danger,* edited by Carole Vance. Boston: Routledge & Kegan Paul.

EHRENREICH, BARBARA, ELIZABETH HESS, and GLORIA JACOBS. 1982. "A Report on the Sex Crisis." *Ms.* 10 (9):88.

EISENSTEIN, HESTER. 1983. *Contemporary Feminist Thought.* Boston: G. K. Hall.

ELLIS, HAVELOCK. 1942. *Studies in the Psychology of Sex.* New York: Random House.

ELSHTAIN, JEAN BETHKE. 1982–83. "Homosexual Politics." *Salmagundi* 58–59:252.

ENGLISH, DEIRDRE, AMBER HOLLIBAUGH, and GAYLE RUBIN. 1981. "Talking Sex." *Socialist Review* 58 (July–August):43.

ERICSON, EDWARD. 1982. *American Freedom and the Radical Rights.* New York: Frederick Ungar.

EVANS, RICHARD. 1976. *The Feminist Movement in Germany, 1894–1933.* London: Sage.

EVANS, SARA. 1979. *Personal Politics.* New York: Knopf.

EVANS-PRITCHARD, E. E. 1970. "Sexual Inversion among the Azande." *American Anthropologist* 72 (6):1430.

EWEN, STUART, and ELIZABETH EWEN. 1982. *Channels of Desire.* New York: McGraw-Hill.

FADERMAN, LILLIAN. 1981. *Surpassing the Love of Men.* New York: Morrow.

————. 1983. *Scotch Verdict.* New York: Morrow.

FADERMAN, LILLIAN, and BRIGITTE ERIKSSON. 1980. *Lesbian-Feminism in Turn-of-the-Century Germany.* Weatherby Lake, Mo.: Naiad Press.

FERGUSON, ANN. 1981. "Patriarchy, Sexual Identity, and the Sexual Revolution." *Signs* 7 (1):11.

FERNBACH, DAVID. 1981. *The Spiral Path.* Boston: Alyson.

FIEDLER, LESLIE. 1954. *An End to Innocence.* Boston: Beacon.

FITZGERALD, FRANCES. 1981a. "A Disciplined, Charging Army." *New Yorker* 57 (May 18):59.

————. 1981b. "The Triumphs of the New Right." *New York Review of Books* 28 (November 19):25.

FLANDRIN, JEAN LOUIS. 1979. *Families in Former Times.* New York: Cambridge University Press.

FLEMING, THOMAS. 1983. "Criminalizing a Marginal Community." In *Deviant Designations,* edited by Thomas Fleming and L. A. Visano. Toronto: Butterworths.

FLORIDA LEGISLATIVE INVESTIGATION COMMITTEE. 1975. "Homosexuality and Citizenship in Florida." In *Government versus Homosexuals.* New York: Arno.

FLUVIÀ, ARMAND DE. 1978. "El movimiento homosexual en el estado español." In *El Homosexual ante la Sociedad Enferma,* edited by José Ramón Enriquez. Barcelona: Tusquets.

FOREMAN, ANN. 1977. *Femininity as Alienation.* London: Pluto.
FORGIONE, STEVE. 1982. "Living in Exile." *Gay Community News* 9 (30):7.
FOUCAULT, MICHEL. 1979. *Discipline and Punish.* New York: Vintage.
———. 1980. *Power/Knowledge.* New York: Pantheon.
———. 1982–83. "Sexual Choice, Sexual Act." *Salmagundi* 58–59:10.
———. 1984a. *Le souci de soi.* Paris: Gallimard.
———. 1984b. *L'usage des plaisirs.* Paris: Gallimard.
FREEMAN, JO. 1975. *Politics of Women's Liberation.* New York: Longman.
FRIEDAN, BETTY. 1963. *The Feminine Mystique.* New York: Norton.
FRONT HOMOSEXUEL D'ACTION RÉVOLUTIONNAIRE. 1971. *Rapport contre la normalité.* Paris: Editions Champ Libre.
GALLO, MAX. 1972. *The Night of Long Knives.* New York: Harper & Row.
GALLOWAY, BRUCE. ed.. 1983. *Prejudice and Pride.* London: Routledge & Kegan Paul.
GARCÍA GAUDILLA, NATY. 1981. *Libération des femmes.* Paris: Presses universitaires de France.
GAVIN, STEVE. 1971. "Consciousness Raising Exposes the Orwellian Lies of Sexist Amerika." *Come Out!* 2 (7b):19.
GAY REVOLUTION PARTY WOMEN'S CAUCUS. 1972. "Realesbians and Politicalesbians." In *Out of the Closets,* edited by Karla Jay and Allen Young. New York: Douglas/Links.
GAY WRITERS' GROUP. 1983. *It Could Happen to You.* Boston: Alyson.
GEARHART, SALLY, and WILLIAM JOHNSON. 1974. *Loving Women/Loving Men.* San Francisco: Glide Publications.
GERASSI, JOHN. 1966. *The Boys of Boise.* New York: Macmillan.
GERTH, H. H., and C. WRIGHT MILLS, eds. 1958. *From Max Weber.* New York: Oxford University Press.
GEYER, MICHAEL. 1984. "The State in National Socialist Germany." In *State-making and Social Movements,* edited by Charles Bright and Susan Harding. Ann Arbor: University of Michigan Press.
GIDE, ANDRÉ. 1937. *Return from the USSR.* New York: Knopf.
———. 1950. *Corydon.* New York: Farrar, Straus & Giroux.
GILBERT, ARTHUR. 1975. "Doctor, Patient, and Onanist Diseases in the Nineteenth Century." *Journal of the History of Medicine and Allied Sciences* 32 (1):55.
———. 1977. "Sexual Deviance and Disaster during the Napoleonic Wars." *Albion* 9 (Spring):98.
GINSBERG, ALLEN. 1974. *Gay Sunshine Interview with Allen Young.* Bolinas, Calif.: Grey Fox.
GIRARD, JACQUES. 1981. *Le mouvement homosexuel en France, 1945–1980.* Paris: Editions Syros.
GITTINGS, BARBARA, and KAY TOBIN. 1978. "Lesbians and the Gay Movement." In *Our Right to Love,* edited by Ginny Vida. Englewood Cliffs, N.J.:

Prentice-Hall.

GOLDSMITH, LARRY. 1981. "David Scondras." *Gay Community News* 9 (14):3.
———. 1983. "On the Hill and Out of the Closet." *Gay Community News* 11 (6):3.

GOLDSTEIN, ROBERT. 1978. *Political Repression in Modern America.* Cambridge, Mass.: Schenkman.

GORDON, LINDA, and ALLEN HUNTER. 1977–78. "Sex, Family and the New Right." *Radical America* 11 (6)–12 (1):14.

GOT, AMBROISE. 1923. "Le vice organisé en Allemagne." *Mercure de France* 161: 655.

GOULDNER, ALVIN. 1980. "Stalinism." In *Political Power and Social Theory.* Vol. 1, edited by Maurice Zeitlin. Greenwich, Conn.: JAI.

GRAMSCI, ANTONIO. 1971. *The Prison Notebooks of Antonio Gramsci.* New York: International.

GRIER, BARBARA, and COLETTA REID, eds. 1976. *The Lavender Herring.* Baltimore: Diana Press.

GRIFFITH, ROBERT. 1974. "American Politics and the Origins of 'McCarthyism.'" In *The Specter,* edited by Robert Griffith and Athan Theoharis. New York: New Viewpoints.

GRIFFITH, ROBERT, and ATHAN THEOHARIS, eds. 1974. *The Specter.* New York: New Viewpoints.

GRUBB, PAGE, and THEO VAN DER MEER. 1979. "Gayness in a Small Country." *Body Politic* 53:23.

GRUPO DE ACCIÓN GAY. 1985. "Liberación sin Aqualane." *Sodoma* 2:25.

GUNNISON, FOSTER. 1969. "The Homophile Movement in America." In *The Same Sex,* edited by Ralph Weltge. Philadelphia: Pilgrim.

GUSFIELD, JOSEPH. 1963. *Symbolic Crusade.* Urbana: University of Illinois Press.

HAHN, PIERRE. 1979. *Nos ancêtres les pervers.* Paris: Olivier Orban.

HAMILTON, RICHARD. 1982. *Who Voted for Hitler?* Princeton, N.J.: Princeton University Press.

HANNON, GERALD. 1976. "Anatomy of a Sex Scandal." *Body Politic* 24:10.
———. 1980. "Taking It to the Streets." *Body Politic* 71:9.
———. 1982. "Men Loving Boys Loving Men." In *Flaunting It!,* edited by Ed Jackson and Stan Persky. Vancouver: New Star.

HAPPEL, HANS-EBERHARD. 1985. "Kiessling und kein Ende." *Rosa Flieder.* (April–May):10.

HARDY, ROBIN. 1980. "Our Memories, Ourselves." *Body Politic* 61:23.

HARRISON, RACHEL, and FRANK MORT. 1980. "Patriarchal Aspects of Nineteenth-Century State Formation." In *Capitalism, State Formation and Marxist Theory,* edited by Philip Corrigan. London: Quartet.

HARRY, JOSEPH. 1976–77. "On the Validity of Typologies of Gay Males." *Journal of Homosexuality* 2 (2):150.

———. 1982. "Derivative Deviance." *Criminology* 19 (4):546.
HARRY, JOSEPH, and WILLIAM DEVALL. 1978. *The Social Organization of Gay Males.* New York: Praeger.
HAUER, GUDRUN, et al. 1984. *Rosa Liebe unterm roten Stern.* Hamburg: Frühlings Erwachen.
HEATH, STEPHEN. 1984. *The Sexual Fix.* New York: Schocken.
HEGER, HEINZ. 1980. *The Men with the Pink Triangle.* Boston: Alyson.
HEMMINGS, SUSAN. 1980. "Horrific Practices." In *Homosexuality, Power & Politics,* edited by the Gay Left Collective. London: Allison & Busby.
HENLEY, NANCY, and FRED PINCUS. 1978. "Interrelationship of Sexist, Racist, and Antihomosexual Attitudes." *Psychological Reports* 42:83.
HERDT, GILBERT. 1984. *Ritualized Homosexuality in Melanesia.* Berkeley: University of California Press.
HERON, ALASTAIR, ed. 1966. *Towards a Quaker View of Sex.* London: Friends Home Service Committee.
HERRICK, THADDEUS. 1984. "A View of Venezuelan Homosexuality." *Habari-Daftari* 4:26.
HERZEN, W. 1977. "Antithetical Sexual Sentiment and Section 175 of the Imperial Penal law, 1898." In *Bernstein on Homosexuality,* translated by Angela Clifford. Belfast, Northern Ireland: Athol Books.
HERZER, MANFRED. 1985. "Nazis, Psychiatrists, and Gays." *Cabirion* 12 (Spring-Summer):1.
HIMMELSTEIN, JEROME. 1983. "The New Right." In *The New Christian Right,* edited by Robert Liebman and Robert Wuthnow. New York: Aldine.
HIRSCHFELD, MAGNUS. 1975a. "Berlins drittes Geschlecht." In *Documents of the Homosexual Rights Movement in Germany, 1836–1927.* New York: Arno.
———. 1975b. "Sappho und Sokrates." In *Documents of the Homosexual Rights Movement in Germany, 1836–1927.* New York: Arno.
HOCQUENGHEM, GUY. 1978. *Homosexual Desire.* London: Allison & Busby.
———. 1979. *Race d'Ep!.* Paris: Editions Libres/Hallier.
HODGES, ANDREW. 1984. *Alan Turing.* New York: Simon & Schuster.
HOESS, RUDOLF. 1959. *Commandant of Auschwitz.* London: Pan Books.
HOHMANN, JOACHIM. 1982. *Keine Zeit für gute Freunde.* Berlin: Foerster Verlag.
HOLE, JUDITH, and ELLEN LEVINE. 1971. *Rebirth of Feminism.* New York: Quadrangle Books.
HOLLERAN, ANDREW. 1979. "Dear Anna K." *Christopher Street.* 3 (9):11.
HOLLIBAUGH, AMBER. 1978. "Sexuality and the State." *Socialist Review* 45 (May–June):55.
HOLLIBAUGH, AMBER, and CHERRIE MORAGA. 1983. "What We're Rollin around in Bed With." In *Powers of Desire,* edited by Ann Snitow, Christine Stansell, and Sharon Thompson. New York: Monthly Review Press.
HORKHEIMER, MAX. 1972. *Critical Theory.* New York: Seabury.

HUDDLESTON, SISLEY. 1928. *Paris Salons, Cafés, Studios.* New York: Lippincott.

HUGHES, PATRICIA. 1985. "Pornography." *Canadian Journal of Political and Social Theory* 9 (1–2):96.

HUGHEY, MICHAEL. 1982. "The New Conservatism." *Social Research* 49 (3):791.

HULL, ISABEL. 1982. *The Entourage of Kaiser Wilhelm II, 1888–1918.* Cambridge: Cambridge University Press.

HUMPHREYS, LAUD. 1972a. "New Styles of Homosexual Manliness." In *The Homosexual Dialectic,* edited by Joseph McCaffrey. Englewood Cliffs, N.J.: Prentice-Hall.

———. 1972b. *Out of the Closets.* Englewood Cliffs, N.J.: Prentice-Hall.

HUNTER, JAMES. 1983. *American Evangelicalism.* New Brunswick, N.J.: Rutgers University Press.

HUNTINGTON, DEBORAH, and RUTH KAPLAN. 1982. "Whose Gold Is behind the Altar?" In *World Capitalist Crisis and the Rise of the Right,* edited by Marlene Dixon, Susanne Jonas, and Tony Platt. San Francisco: Synthesis.

HYDE, H. MONTGOMERY. 1948. *The Trials of Oscar Wilde.* London: William Hodge.

HYDE, LOUIS, ed. 1978. *Rat & the Devil.* Hamden, Conn.: Archon.

IRONS, PETER. 1974. "American Business and the Origins of McCarthyism." In *The Specter,* edited by Robert Griffith and Athan Theoharis. New York: New Viewpoints.

ISHERWOOD, CHRISTOPHER. 1976. *Christopher and His Kind, 1929–1939.* New York: Farrar, Straus & Giroux.

JACKSON, ED. 1980–81. "Close, but Not Enough." *Body Politic* 69:9.

———. 1981. "Curbs on Bias." *Body Politic* 74:11.

JACKSON, ED, and STAN PERSKY, eds. 1982. *Flaunting It!.* Vancouver: New Star.

JAY, KARLA. 1983. "Life in the Underworld." *Resources for Feminist Research* 12 (1):18.

JAY, KARLA, and ALLEN YOUNG, eds. 1972. *Out of the Closets.* New York: Douglas/Links.

JOHNSON, BILL. 1979. "Prostestantism and Gay Freedom." In *Positively Gay,* edited by Betty Berzon and Robert Leighton. Millbrae, Calif.: Celestial Arts.

JOHNSTON, CRAIG. 1984. "The Gay Movements." *Social Alternatives* 4:18.

JOHNSTON, JILL. 1973. *Lesbian Nation.* New York: Simon & Schuster.

———. 1975. "Are Lesbians 'Gay'?" *Ms.* 3 (12):85.

JONG, BEN DE. 1985. "An Intolerable Kind of Moral Degeneration." In *IGA Pink Book 1985,* edited by the International Gay Association. Amsterdam: COC-magazijn.

JOYCE, ROB. 1986. "An Isolated Incident." *Body Politic* 123:19.

KAMENY, FRANKLIN. 1969. "Gay Is Good." In *The Same Sex,* edited by Ralph Weltge. Philadelphia: Pilgrim.

KARLINSKY, SIMON. 1979. "Death and Resurrection of Mikhail Kuzmin." *Slavic Review* 38:92.

KATZ, JONATHAN. 1976. *Gay American History.* New York: Crowell.

―――. 1983. *The Gay/Lesbian Almanac.* New York: Morrow.

KELLEY, KEN. 1978. "Anita Bryant." *Playboy* 25 (5):76.

KELLY, BETH. 1979. "On 'Woman/Girl Love'—or, Lesbians *Do* 'Do It.'". *Gay Community News* 6 (31):5.

KENNEDY, HUBERT. 1978a. "'Before all Europe I protest.'" *Body Politic* 42:24.

―――. 1978b. "Gay Liberation 1864." *Body Politic* 41:23.

―――. 1981. "The 'Third Sex' Theory of Karl Heinrich Ulrichs." *Journal of Homosexuality* 6 (Winter):106.

KIKEL, RUDY. 1981. "Is Gay Good Enough?" *Gay Community News* 9 (6):12.

KIRK, MARSHALL, and ERASTES PILL. 1985. "Waging Peace."*Christopher Street* 95:33.

KLEIS, PER. 1980. "Homosexual Retrospect." *Pan International* (Spring):4.

KLIMMER, RUDOLF. 1969. "Die Situation in der DDR." In *Weder Krankheit noch Verbrechen,* edited by Rolf Italiaander. Hamburg: Gala Verlag.

KOEDT, ANN. 1973. "Lesbianism and Feminism." In *Radical Feminism,* edited by Anne Koedt, Ellen Levine, and Anita Rapone. New York: Quadrangle Books.

KOGON, EUGEN. 1976. *The Theory and Practice of Hell.* New York: Octagon.

KOKULA, ILSE [INA KUCKUC, pseud.]. 1975. *Der Kampf gegen Unterdruckung.* Munich: Verlag Frauenoffensive.

―――. 1983. *Formen lesbischer Subkultur.* Berlin: Verlag rosa Winkel.

―――. 1984. "Lesbisch leben von Weimar bis zur Nachkriegszeit." In *Eldorado,* edited by the Berlin Museum. Berlin: Frölich & Kaufmann.

KRICHLER, KURT. 1984. "Le beau Danube rose." *Homophonies* 42:12.

KYPER, JOHN. 1979. "Organizing in Mexico." *Gay Community News* 7 (8):10.

LACEY, E. A. 1979. "Latin America." *Gay Sunshine* 40–41:22.

LACHMAN, LINDA. 1978. "Electoral Politics." In *Our Right to Love,* edited by Ginny Vida. Englewood Cliffs, N.J.: Prentice-Hall.

LARVENTZ, DON. 1985. "Sue Harris." *Body Politic* 111:9.

LAURITSEN, JOHN, and DAVID THORSTAD. 1974. *The Early Homosexual Rights Movement (1864–1935).* New York: Times Change Press.

LAUTMANN, RÜDIGER. 1980–81. "The Pink Triangle." *Journal of Homosexuality* 6 (1–2):146.

LAUTMANN, RÜDIGER, WINIFRIED GRIKSCHAT, and EGBERT SCHMIDT. 1977. "Der rosa Winkel in den nationalsozialistischen Konzentrationslagern." In *Seminar: Gesellschaft und Homosexualität,* edited by Rüdiger Lautmann. Frankfurt: Suhrkamp.

LEE, JOHN. 1978. *Getting Sex.* Toronto: General Publishing.

LENGERKE, CHRISTIANNE VON. 1984. "'Homosexuelle Frauen.'" In *Eldorado*, edited by the Berlin Museum. Berlin: Frölich & Kaufmann.

LENZ, REIMAR. 1979. *The Wholesale Murder of Homosexuals in the Third Reich*. Los Angeles: Urania Manuscripts.

LESK, ANDREW, KEN POPERT, and RIC TAYLOR. 1986. "Boys Will Be Boys." *Body Politic* 122:13.

LÉVI-STRAUSS, CLAUDE. 1969. *The Elementary Structures of Kinship*. Boston: Beacon.

LEVINE, MARTIN. 1985. "The New Moral Crusade." Paper presented to the Society for the Study of Social Problems, Washington, D.C.

LEVINE, MARTIN, ed. 1979. *Gay Men*. New York: Harper & Row.

LEVY, ROBERT. 1971. "The Community Function of Tahitian Male Transvestitism." *Anthropological Quarterly* 44 (1):12.

LIEBMAN, ROBERT. 1983. "Mobilizing the Moral Majority." In *The New Christian Right*, edited by Robert Liebman and Robert Wuthnow. New York: Aldine.

LIEBMAN, ROBERT, and ROBERT WUTHNOW. 1983. *The New Christian Right*. New York: Aldine.

LIENESCH, MICHAEL. 1982. "Right-Wing Religion." *Political Science Quarterly* 97 (3):413.

LIPSITZ, GEORGE. 1983–84. "The Drum Major Instinct." *Telos* 58:101.

LUKER, KRISTIN. 1984. *Abortion and the Politics of Motherhood*. Berkeley: University of California Press.

MCADAM, DOUG. 1982. *Political Process and the Development of Black Insurgency, 1930–1970*. Chicago: University of Chicago Press.

MCCASKELL, TIM. 1976. "We Will Conquer a Space Filled with Light." *Body Politic* 27:8.

———. 1979. "Rage." *Body Politic* 54:21.

———. 1980. "Reich Replay." *Body Politic* 68:20.

MACDONALD, A. P., et al. 1973. "Attitudes toward Homosexuality." *Journal of Consulting and Clinical Psychology* 40 (1):161.

MANCHESTER, WILLIAM. 1968. *The Arms of Krupp, 1587–1968*. Boston: Little, Brown.

MANION, EILEEN. 1985. "We Objects Object." *Canadian Journal of Political and Social Theory* 9 (1–2):69.

MANN, KLAUS. 1948. *André Gide and the Crisis of Modern Thought*. London: Dennis Dobson.

MANSON, ULF. 1985. "The Censorship Law of 1971." In *IGA Pink Book 1985*, edited by the International Gay Association. Amsterdam: COC-magazijn.

MARCUSE, HERBERT. 1955. *Eros and Civilization*. New York: Vintage.

———. 1961. *Soviet Marxism*. New York: Vintage.

MAROEY, ROBERT VAN. 1969. "Freundschaftsbundnisse in Belgien." In *Weder Krankheit noch Verbrechen*, edited by Rolf Italiaander. Hamburg: Gala Verlag.

MAROTTA, TOBY. 1981. *The Politics of Homosexuality.* Boston: Houghton Mifflin.

MARSHALL, JOHN. 1980. "The Politics of Tea and Sympathy." In *Homosexuality: Power and Politics,* edited by the Gay Left Collective. London: Allison & Busby.

———. 1981. "Pansies, Perverts and Macho Men." In *The Making of the Modern Homosexual,* edited by Kenneth Plummer. Totowa, N.J.: Barnes & Noble.

MARTIN, DEL, and PHYLLIS LYON. 1972. *Lesbian/Woman.* San Francisco: Glide Publications.

MARTIN, ROBERT. 1979. *The Homosexual Tradition in American Poetry.* Austin: University of Texas Press.

MARTIN, ROBERT A. 1983. "Student Homophile League." *Gay Books Bulletin* 9:30.

MAYNE, XAVIER. 1975. *The Intersexes.* New York: Arno.

MEDVEDEV, ROY. 1977. "New Pages from the Political Biography of Stalin." In *Stalinism,* edited by Robert Tucker. New York: Norton.

MERRILL, MICHAEL. 1977–78. "Life after Dade." *Body Politic* 39:11.

MILES, ANGELA. 1981. "The Integrative Feminine Principle in North America Feminist Radicalism." *Women's Studies International Quarterly* 4 (4):485.

MILIBAND, RALPH. 1973. *The State in Capitalist Society.* London: Quartet.

MILLETT, KATE. 1969. *Sexual Politics.* New York: Avon.

MIRABET I MULLOL, ANTONI. 1985. *Homosexualidad Hoy.* Barcelona: Editorial Herder.

MITZEL, JOHN. 1980. *The Boston Sex Scandal.* Boston: Glad Day Books.

MONK, JIM. 1981. "The Subject that Refuses to Go Away." *Body Politic* (November):31.

———. 1986. "License to Kill Gays." *Body Politic* 125:16.

MONTER, E. WILLIAM. 1981. "Sodomy and Heresy in Early Modern Switzerland." *Journal of Homosexuality* 6 (Winter):41.

MOORE, BARRINGTON. 1966. *The Social Origins of Dictatorship and Democracy.* Boston: Beacon.

MOSSE, GEORGE. 1982. "Nationalism and Respectability." *Journal of Contemporary History* 77:221.

MUELLER, CAROL. 1983. "In Search of a Constituency for the 'New Religious Right.'" *Public Opinion Quarterly* 47:213.

MURRAY, STEPHEN. 1984. *Social Theory, Homosexual Realities.* New York: Gai Saber.

MURRAY, STEPHEN, and KENNETH PAYNE. 1985. "The Remedicalization of Homophobia." Paper presented to the Society for the Study of Social Problems, Washington, D.C.

MYRON, NANCY, and CHARLOTTE BUNCH, eds. 1975. *Lesbianism and the Women's Movement.* Baltimore: Diana Press.

NANDA, SERENA. 1986. "The Hijras of India." *Journal of Homosexuality* 11 (3–4):35.

NESTLE, JOAN. 1981. "Butch/Fem and Sexual Courage." *Body Politic* 76:31.

NEUMAN, R. P. 1975. "Masturbation, Madness, and the Modern Concepts of Childhood and Adolescence." *Journal of Social History* 8 (Spring):1.

NEWTON, HUEY. 1972. "A Letter to the Revolutionary Brothers and Sisters about the Women's Liberation and Gay Liberation." In *The Homosexual Dialectic,* edited by Joseph McCaffrey. Englewood Cliffs, N.J.: Prentice-Hall.

NIXON, JOAN, and GINNY BERSON. 1978. "Women's Music." In *Our Right to Love,* edited by Ginny Vida. Englewood cliffs, N.J.: Prentice-Hall.

NOLL, DOLORES. 1978. "Professional and Union Caucuses." In *Our Right to Love,* edited by Ginny Vida. Englewood Cliffs, N.J.: Prentice-Hall.

NORTON, RICTOR, and LOUIE CREW. 1974. "The Homophobic Imagination." *College English* 36 (3):247.

OAKS, ROBERT. 1978. "'Things fearful to name.'" *Journal of Social History* 12 (2):268.

O'CARROLL, TOM. 1980. *Paedophilia.* London: Peter Owen.

OFFERMANN, BERND. 1984. "Bogar, lesbiska, tillsammans." *Rosa Flieder* 37:12.

PARENTI, MICHAEL. 1978. *Power and the Powerless.* New York: St. Martin's.

PARSONS, GAIL. 1977. "Equal Treatment for All." *Journal of the History of Medicine and Allied Sciences* 32 (1):55.

PATRICK, ROBERT. 1979. "Seriously Now, Robert Patrick." *Gay Community News* 6 (50):8.

PATTON, CINDY. 1985. *Sex and Germs.* Boston: South End.

PEARCE, FRANK. 1973. "How to Be Immoral and Ill, Pathetic and Dangerous, All at the Same Time." In *The Manufacture of the News,* edited by Stanley Cohen and Jock Young. London: Constable.

PEDERSEN, LIS. 1985. "The Anti-discrimination Law." In *IGA Pink Book 1985,* edited by the International Gay Association. Amsterdam: COC-magazijn.

PERRY, TROY. 1973. *The Lord Is My Shepherd and He Knows I'm Gay.* New York: Bantam.

PETERSSON, STIG-AKE. 1985. "Parliamentary Commission Studies Homosexuality." In *IGA Pink Book 1985,* edited by the International Gay Association. Amsterdam: COC-magazijn.

PIEPER, MECKI. 1984. "Die Frauenbewegung und ihre Bedeutung für lesbische Frauen (1850–1920)." In *Eldorado,* edited by the Berlin Museum. Berlin: Frölich & Kaufman.

PONSE, BARBARA. 1978. *Identities in the Lesbian World.* Westport, Conn.: Greenwood.

POSTER, MARK. 1978. *Critical Theory of the Family.* New York: Seabury.

PRAUNHEIM, ROSA VON. 1980. *Army of Lovers.* London: Gay Men's Press.

PRONK, MARIA. 1985. "Homosexuality and International Law." In *IGA Pink Book 1985,* edited by the International Gay Association. Amsterdam: COC-magazijn.

PROUST, MARCEL. 1963. "By Way of Sainte-Beuve." In *Eros*, edited by Alistair Sutherland and Patrick Anderson. New York: Citadel.

RADICALESBIANS. 1971. "The Woman-identified Woman." In *Liberation Now!*, edited by Deborah Babcox and Madeline Belkine. New York: Dell.

RAMSAY, S. W., P. M. HERINGA, and I. BOORSMA. 1974. "A Case Study: Homosexuality in the Netherlands." In *Understanding Homosexuality*, edited by J. A. Loraine. New York: Elsevier.

RANKIN, JIM. 1970. "Nacho Upside Down." *Gay Sunshine* 1 (2):4.

RAPP, RAYNA. 1978. "Family and Class in Contemporary America." *Science and Society* 42 (Fall):286.

READE, BRIAN. 1970. *Sexual Heretics*. New York: Coward-McCann.

RECHY, JOHN. 1977. *The Sexual Outlaw*. New York: Dell.

REY, MICHEL. 1982. "Police et sodomie à Paris au XVIIIe siecle." *Revue d'Histoire Moderne et Contemporaire* 29:116.

———. 1985. "Parisian Homosexuals Create a Lifestyle, 1700–1750." *Eighteenth Century Life* 9 (3):179.

RHODES, S. A. 1940. "The Influence of Walt Whitman on André Gide." *Romanic Review* 31 (2):156.

RICH, ADRIENNE. 1983. "Compulsory Heterosexuality and Lesbian Existence." In *Powers of Desire*, edited by Ann Snitow, Christine Stansell, and Sharon Thompson. New York: Monthly Review Press.

RICH, B. RUBY. 1981. "Maedchen in Uniform." *Radical America* 15 (6):16.

RIMBAUD, ARTHUR, and PAUL VERLAINE. 1979. *A Lover's Cock and Other Gay Poems*. San Francisco: Gay Sunshine Press.

RIVERS, J. E. 1983. *Proust and the Art of Love*. New York: Columbia University Press.

ROBERTSON, MARIE. 1982. "We Need Our Own Banner." In *Flaunting It!*, edited by Ed Jackson and Stan Persky. Vancouver: New Star.

RODGERSON, GILLIAN. 1984. "'Ordination is Not a Human Right.'" *Body Politic* 107:7.

ROGIER, JAN. 1969. "75 Jahre Emanzipation in den Niederlanden." In *Weder Krankheit noch Verbrechen*, edited by Rolf Italiaander. Hamburg: Gala Verlag.

ROWBOTHAM, SHEILA, and JEFFREY WEEKS. 1977. *Socialism and the New Life*. London: Pluto.

RUBIN, GAYLE. 1982. "The Leather Menace." *Body Politic* 82:34.

———. 1984a. "Anti-porn Laws and Women's Liberation." *Gay Community News* 12 (23):8.

———. 1984b. "Thinking Sex." In *Pleasure and Danger*, edited by Carole Vance. Boston: Routledge & Kegan Paul.

RUEHL, SONJA. 1982. "Inverts and Experts." In *Feminism, Culture and Politics*, edited by Rosalind Brunt and Caroline Rowan. London: Lawrence & Wishart.

RUGGIERO, GUIDO. 1985. *The Boundaries of Eros.* New York: Oxford University Press.

RUSCHE, HERBERT. 1984a. "Erklärung zum Überfall von Neonazis auf einer Veranstaltung des VRG." *Rosa Flieder* (April-May):35.

———. 1984b. "Meinungsbild zum Sexualstrafrecht." *Rosa Flieder* 38 (December-January):27.

RUSSO, VITO. 1981. *The Celluloid Closet.* New York: Harper & Row.

SAHLI, NANCY. 1979. "Smashing." *Chrysalis* 8 (Summer):22.

ST. JOAN, JACKIE. 1978. "A Survey of Lesbian Publications." In *Our Right to Love,* edited by Ginny Vida. Englewood Cliffs, N.J.: Prentice-Hall.

SALAS, LUIS. 1979. *Social Control and Deviance in Cuba.* New York: Praeger.

SAWATSKY, JOHN. 1980. *Men in the Shadows.* Toronto: Doubleday.

SCHILLING, HEINZ-DIETER. 1983. *Schwule und Faschismus.* Berlin: Elefanten.

SCHMIDT, PAUL. 1979. "Visions of Violence." In *Homosexualities and French Literature,* edited by George Stambolian and Elaine Marks. Ithaca: Cornell University Press.

SCHNEIDER, BETH. 1984a. "The Office Affair." *Sociological Perspectives* 27 (4):443.

———. 1984b. "Peril and Promise." In *Women-Identified Women,* edited by Trudy Darty and Sandee Potter. Palo Alto, Calif.: Mayfield.

SEVERIN, N. K. 1983. "Anatomy of a Gay Conservative." *Christopher Street* 72:29.

SHIERS, JOHN. 1978. "Two Steps Forward, One Step Back." In *Homosexuality: Power & Politics,* edited by the Gay Left Collective. London: Allison & Busby.

SHILTS, RANDY. 1982. *The Mayor of Castro Street.* New York: St. Martin's.

SIMMONS, CHRISTINA. 1979. "Companionate Marriage and the Lesbian Threat." *Frontiers* 4 (Fall):54.

SIMPSON, JOHN. 1983. "Moral Issues and Status Politics." In *The New Christian Right,* edited by Robert Liebman and Robert Wuthnow. New York: Aldine.

SIMPSON, RUTH. 1977. *From the Closets to the Courts.* New York: Viking.

SKOCPOL, THEDA. 1979. *States and Social Revolutions.* New York: Cambridge University Press.

———. 1984. *Vision and Method in Historical Sociology.* New York: Cambridge University Press.

SMART, BARRY. 1985. *Foucault, Marxism and Critique.* London: Routledge & Kegan Paul.

SMITH, F. B. 1976. "Labouchere's Amendment to the Criminal Law Amendment Bill." *Historical Studies* 17:67.

SMITH-ROSENBERG, CARROLL. 1975. "The Female World of Love and Ritual." *Signs* 1 (1):1.

SNITOW, ANN. 1985. "Retrenchment versus Transformation." In *Women against Censorship,* edited by Varda Burstyn. Vancouver: Douglas & McIntyre.

SNITOW, ANN, CHRISTINE STANSELL, and SHARON THOMPSON. 1983. *Powers of Desire.* New York: Monthly Review Press.

SOFER, YEHUDA. 1985. "Gays Caught between Progressiveness and the Ideology of a State Religion." In *IGA Pink Book 1984,* edited by the International Gay Association. Amsterdam: COC-magazijn.

SOHN-RETHEL, ALFRED. 1978. *Economy and Class Structure of German Fascism.* London: CSE Books.

SONTAG, SUSAN. 1978. *Illness as Metaphor.* New York: Farrar, Straus & Giroux.

SPENDER, CHARLES, ed. 1974. *The World of Serge Diaghilev.* London: Paul Elek.

STACEY, JUDITH. 1983. "The New Conservative Feminism." *Feminist Studies* 9 (3):559.

STEAKLEY, JAMES. 1975. *The Homosexual Emancipation Movement in Germany.* New York: Arno.

———. 1983. "Iconography of a Scandal." *Studies in Visual Communications* 9 (2):22.

STEIN, GERTRUDE. 1940. *Paris France.* New York: Charles Scribner's Sons.

STIMPSON, CATHARINE. 1982–83. "The Beat Generation and the Trials of Homosexual Liberation." *Salmagundi* 58–59:373.

STONE, LAWRENCE. 1977. *The Family, Sex and Marriage.* New York: Harper & Row.

STRAVER, CEES. 1973. "Les homosexuels aux Pays-Bas." In *Les minorités homosexuelles,* edited by Steven de Batselier and H. Laurence Ross. Gembloux, Belgium: Editions Duculot.

STÜMKE, HANS-GEORGE, and RUDI FINKLER. 1981. *Rosa Winkel, Rosa Listen.* Hamburg: Rowohlt.

SWICEGOOD, TOM. 1974. *Our God Too.* New York: Pyramid.

SYLVESTRE, PAUL FRANÇOIS. 1976. *Propos pour une libération (homo)sexuelle.* Montreal: Editions de l'Aurore.

———. 1979. *Les homosexuels s'organisent.* Ottawa: Editions Homeureux.

———. 1983. *Bougrerie en Nouvelle-France.* Hull, Quebec: Editions Asticou.

SYMONDS, JOHN ADDINGTON. 1896. *A Problem in Modern Ethics.* New York: Benjamin Blom.

TAYLOR, CLARK. 1982. "Folk Taxonomy and Justice in Dade County, Florida, 1954." *Anthropological Research Group on Homosexuality Newsletter.* 4 (1–2):9.

TAYLOR, WILLIAM, and CHRISTOPHER LASCH. 1963. "Two 'Kindred Spirits.'" *New England Quarterly* 36 (1):23.

TEAL, DONN. 1971. *The Gay Militants.* New York: Stein & Day.

THEIS, WOLFGANG. 1984. "Anders als die Andern." In *Eldorado,* edited by the

Berlin Museum. Berlin: Frölich & Kaufmann.

THOMPSON, DENISE. 1985. *Flaws in the Social Fabric.* Sydney: George Allen & Unwin.

THOMPSON, E. P. 1980. *The Making of the English Working Class.* Harmondsworth, U.K.: Penguin.

TIELMAN, ROB. 1979. *The Persecution of Homosexuals in the Netherlands during the Second World War.* Los Angeles: Urania Manuscripts.

————. 1982. *Homoseksualiteit in Nederland.* Amsterdam: Boom, Meppel.

TOURAINE, ALAIN. 1981. *The Voice and the Eye.* New York: Cambridge University Press.

TRACEY, MICHAEL, and DAVID MORRISON. 1979. *Whitehouse.* London: Macmillan.

TRANSLATION GROUP. 1984. *Gays in Indonesia.* Fitzroy, Australia: Sybylla Press.

TROW, MARTIN. 1958. "Small Businessmen, Political Intolerance, and Support for McCarthy." *American Journal of Sociology* 68 (3):270.

TRUMBACH, RANDOLPH. 1977. "London's Sodomites." *Journal of Social History* 11 (1):9.

TSANG, DAN, ed. 1981. *The Age Taboo.* Boston: Alyson.

TSUZUKI, CHUSHICHI. 1980. *Edward Carpenter, 1844–1929.* New York: Cambridge University Press.

TYTELL, JOHN. 1976. *Naked Angels.* New York: McGraw-Hill.

ULRICHS, KARL. 1975. "Vier Briefe." In *Documents of the Homosexual Rights Movement in Germany, 1836–1927.* New York: Arno.

U.S. SENATE, COMMITTEE ON EXPENDITURES IN THE EXECUTIVE DEPARTMENTS, SUBCOMMITTEE ON INVESTIGATIONS. 1975. "Employment of Homosexuals and Other Sexual Perverts in Government." In *Government versus Homosexuals.* New York: Arno.

U.S. SENATE, COMMITTEE ON NAVAL AFFAIRS. 1975. "Alleged Immoral Conditions at Newport (R.I.) Naval Training Station." In *Government versus Homosexuals.* New York: Arno.

VANCE, CAROLE. 1984. *Pleasure and Danger.* Boston: Routledge & Kegan Paul.

VAN DER MEER, THEO. 1985. "Legislation against Sodomy and the Creation of an Identity." Paper presented to the Sex and the State Conference, Toronto.

VASSILAS, YANNI. 1984. "Greek Gay Life under Socialists." *Gay Community News* 11 (32):15.

VIRGIL. 1984. "Un mouvement élitiste." *Homophonies* 48:12.

VISMAR, ERHARD. 1977. "Perversion und Verfolgung unter dem deutschen Faschismus." In *Seminar: Gesellschaft und Homosexualität,* edited by Rüdiger Lautmann. Frankfurt: Suhrkamp.

WALKOWITZ, JUDITH. 1980. "The Politics of Prostitution." *Signs* 6 (1):130.

——. 1983. "Male Vice and Female Virtue." In *Powers of Desire*, edited by Ann Snitow, Christine Stansell, and Sharon Thompson. New York: Monthly Review Press.

WALTER, AUBREY. 1980. *Come Together.* London: Gay Men's Press.

WARD, MICHAEL, and MARK FREEMAN. 1979. "Defending Gay Rights." *Radical America* 13 (4):11.

WARNER, TOM. 1976. "Saskatcon." *Body Politic* 30:11.

WEEKS, JEFFREY. 1975. "Where Engels Feared to Tread." *Gay Left* 1:3.

——. 1977. *Coming Out.* London: Quartet.

——. 1981. *Sex, Politics, and Society.* London: Longman.

WEINBERG, MARTIN, and ALAN BELL, eds. 1972. *Homosexuality: An Annotated Bibliography.* New York: Oxford University Press.

WEISS, MIKE. 1984. *Double Play.* Reading, Mass.: Addison-Wesley.

WERRES, JOHANNES. 1973. "Les homosexuels en Allemagne." In *Les minorités homosexuelles,* edited by Steven de Batselier and H Laurence Ross. Gembloux, Belgium: Editions Duculot.

WHITE, EDMUND. 1980. "The Political Vocabulary of Homosexuality." In *The State of the Language,* edited by Leonard Michaels and Christopher Ricks. Berkeley: University of California Press.

WHITMAN, WALT. 1955. *Leaves of Grass.* New York: New American Library.

WICKES, GEORGE. 1975. "A Natalie Barney Garland." *Paris Review* 61:91.

——. 1976. *The Amazon of Letters.* New York: Putnam's.

WILDE, OSCAR. 1973. "The Soul of Man under Socialism." In *Complete Works of Oscar Wilde.* London: Collins.

WILDEBLOOD, PETER. 1955. *Against the Law.* London: Widenfeld & Nicolson.

WILLIAMS, COLIN, and MARTIN WEINBERG. 1971. *Homosexuals and the Military.* New York: Harper & Row.

WILLIAMS, WALTER. 1986. "Persistence and Change in the Berdache Tradition among Contemporary Dakota Indians." *Journal of Homosexuality* 11 (3–4):191.

WILLIS, ELLEN. 1981. "Betty Friedan's 'Second Stage.'" *Nation* (November 14):494.

——. 1983. "Feminism, Moralism, and Pornography." In *Powers of Desire,* edited by Ann Snitow, Christine Stansell, and Sharon Thompson. New York: Monthly Review Press.

WILSON, DOUG, et al. 1984. "Police Entrapment." *Rites* 1 (6):9.

WILSON, JAMES. 1974. *Charmed Circle.* New York: Praeger.

WITTMAN, CARL. 1972. "Refugees from Amerika." In *The Homosexual Dialectic,* edited by Joseph McCaffrey. Englewood Cliffs, N.J.: Prentice-Hall.

WITZEL, KLAUS DIETER. 1985. "The Ebbinghaus Case." In *IGA Pink Book 1985,* edited by the International Gay Association. Amsterdam: COC-magazijn.

WOLFENDEN, SIR JOHN, et al. 1962. *Report of the Committee on Homosexual Offenses and Prostitution.* London: Her Majesty's Stationery Office.

WUTHNOW, ROBERT. 1983. "The Political Rebirth of American Evangelicals." In *The New Christian Right*, edited by Robert Liebman and Robert Wuthnow. New York: Aldine.

YOUNG, ALLEN. 1973. "Gay Gringo in Brazil." In *The Gay Liberation Book*. San Francisco: Ramparts.

————. 1981. *Gays under the Cuban Revolution*. San Francisco: Grey Fox.

YOUNG, PERRY. 1982. *God's Bullies*. New York: Holt, Rinehart & Winston.

ZURCHER, LOUIS, and R. GEORGE KIRKPATRICK. 1976. *Citizens for Decency*. Austin: University of Texas Press.

Selected Bibliography

ABBOTT, SIDNEY, and BARBARA LOVE. *Sappho Was a Right-On Woman.* New York: Stein & Day, 1972. Chronicles the heady days from 1969 to 1972 as new definitions of lesbianism emerged from the turmoil of feminist and gay liberationist activism. The book is close to the events and itself shows the transitions in the ways lesbians were thinking about and organizing themselves.

ALTMAN, DENNIS. *Homosexual Oppression and Liberation.* New York: Outerbridge & Dienstfrey, 1971. Written by an Australian participant in New York's gay liberation struggles of 1969–70, this book is widely regarded as the classic statement on liberation philosophy. Altman's 1982 *Homosexualization of America* reflects on the flourishing gay culture of the decade following the Stonewall Rebellion.

D'EMILIO, JOHN. *Sexual Politics, Sexual Communities.* Chicago: University of Chicago Press, 1983. The most complete account of the homophile movement of the 1950s and 1960s in the United States, contextualized in a social history of the era.

Eldorado, edited by the Berlin Museum. Berlin: Frölich & Kaufmann, 1984. A lavishly illustrated collection on the "history, daily life, and culture" of homosexual women and men in Germany in the century preceding 1950. Based on a 1984 exhibition at the Berlin Museum, it offers a rich and meticulously researched portrait of the early gay movement and its environs. In German.

FADERMAN, LILLIAN. *Surpassing the Love of Men.* New York: Morrow, 1981. A panoramic history of the four-century evolution from "romantic friendship" to lesbian feminism based on literary sources. The lesbian movement per se occupies only the last chapter, but deeply informs the conceptual framework of the whole book.

FADERMAN, LILLIAN, and BRIGITTE ERIKSSON. *Lesbian-Feminism in Turn-of-the-Century Germany.* Weatherby Lake, Mo.: Naiad Press, 1980. A collection of the significant literary and political documents on lesbianism from 1895 to 1921 in Germany, including Anna Rüling's 1904 address to the Scientific-Humanitarian Committee. In English.

GALLOWAY, BRUCE, ed. *Prejudice and Pride*. London: Routledge & Kegan Paul, 1983. An excellent overview of the concerns of the modern gay movement. Drawing from the files of the British Campaign for Homosexual Equality, the contributors sketch a comprehensive portrait of living gay and lesbian in a homophobic society.

GAY LEFT COLLECTIVE. *Homosexuality: Power & Politics*. London: Allison & Busby, 1978. Compiled by the editorial collective of the 1970s journal *Gay Left*, this book presents one of the best theoretical treatments of the place of gay and lesbian movements in advanced capitalist society.

GIRARD, JACQUES. *Le mouvement homosexuel en France, 1945–1980*. Paris: Editions Syros, 1981. The definitive history of the gay movement in France from the founding of Arcadie after the war to the liberationist outbursts of the 1970s. In French.

GRIER, BARBARA, and COLETTA REID, eds. *The Lavender Herring*. Baltimore: Diana Press, 1976. Selections from the *Ladder*, the first enduring lesbian journal in the United States, which show the move from homophile to feminist consciousness through the 1960s.

HUMPHREYS, LAUD. *Out of the Closets*. Englewood Cliffs, N.J.: Prentice-Hall, 1972. An entertaining sociological account of the early days of gay liberation (1969–72) in the United States; a book that has stood the test of time.

IGA Pink Book 1985, edited by the International Gay Association. Amsterdam: COC-magazijn, 1985. A collection of essays sponsored by the International Gay Association on gay and lesbian life and organization in Cuba, the German Democratic Republic, Iceland, Israel, the Soviet Union, Austria, the Federal Republic of Germany, Finland, Norway, and Sweden. More "pink books" are to follow.

JACKSON, ED, and STAN PERSKY, eds. *Flaunting It!*. Vancouver: New Star, 1982. An anthology drawn from Canada's leading gay journal, the *Body Politic*, from 1972 to 1982. The book addresses a wide range of themes and includes a chronology of movement events.

KOKULA, ILSE. *Der Kampf gegen Unterdruckung*. Munich: Verlag Frauenoffensive, 1975. Treats the development of an autonomous lesbian movement in Berlin in the early 1970s. In German.

LAURITSEN, JOHN, and DAVID THORSTAD. *The Early Homosexual Rights Movement (1864–1935)*. New York: Times Change Press, 1974. The first book to reveal the story of the early German gay movement to modern gay liberationists. Contains one of the very few references to gay people under Stalinism.

MAROTTA, TOBY. *The Politics of Homosexuality*. Boston: Houghton Mifflin, 1981. Focused on the New York gay and lesbian militants of the Stonewall Rebellion and its aftermath, the book is much more distant from the events it describes than are Abbott and Love, Altman, and Humphreys, resulting in a more integrated and somewhat more conservative narrative of the events.

MARTIN, DEL, and PHYLLIS LYON. *Lesbian/Woman.* San Francisco: Glide Publications, 1972. Written by cofounders of the Daughters of Bilitis, *Lesbian/Woman* offers a glimpse of the homophile 1950s and of the authors' own changes during the radicalism of the 1960s.

MIRABET I MULLOL, ANTONI. *Homosexualidad Hoy.* Barcelona: Editorial Herder, 1985. The most important reference in Spanish on homosexuality, this book provides an encyclopedic overview of changing theories, as well as a précis of the emergence of a gay movement in post-Franco Spain, especially in Barcelona. In Spanish and Catalan.

STEAKLEY, JAMES. *The Homosexual Emancipation Movement in Germany.* New York: Arno, 1975. This slim volume remains the most important text in English on the prewar German gay movement.

STÜMKE, HANS-GEORG, and RUDI FINKLER. *Rosa Winkel, Rosa Listen.* Hamburg: Rowohlt, 1981. The most comprehensive treatment of the gay movement in Germany, this book carefully documents the early period, the destruction of gay people and their movement in the Holocaust, and the persecution of the 1950s and 1960s in the Federal Republic of Germany. In German.

SYLVESTRE, PAUL FRANÇOIS. *Les homosexuels s'organisent.* Ottawa: Editions Homeureux, 1979. The only sustained (if dated) chronicle of the growth of the gay movement in Canada. In French.

TEAL, DONN. *The Gay Militants.* New York: Stein & Day, 1971. The first documentary history of the Stonewall Rebellion, *The Gay Militants* remains a gold mine of original sources that conveys the flavor of the period like no other.

TIELMAN, ROB. *Homoseksualiteit in Nederland.* Amsterdam: Boom, Meppel, 1982. The major gay history of the Netherlands, including the development of the COC, by a former president. In Dutch.

VIDA, GINNY, ed. *Our Right to Love.* Englewood Cliffs, N.J.: Prentice-Hall, 1978. This comprehensive anthology sponsored by the National Gay Task Force covers a wide range of lesbian topics from relationships to activism and from health to culture.

WEEKS, JEFFREY. *Coming Out.* London: Quartet, 1977. The leading gay history of Great Britain. *Coming Out* has been followed in an "unintended trilogy" by *Sex, Politics and Society* and *Sexuality and Its Discontents,* which treat the social and theoretical histories of sexuality and its observers.

Index

Acquired Immune Deficiency Syndrome
(AIDS), 113, 128, 149, 156–61, 165,
171, 172
Adhesive comrades, 13, 78, 99
Aesthetic-decadent movement, 28
Albert, Edward, 157
Alhonte, Michael, 172
Altman, Dennis, 78, 99
Amsterdam, 8, 60, 66, 92, 155
Anders als die Andern, 23
Anderson, Margaret, 42
Anderson, Mary, 9
Anthony, Francis, 11
Antidiscrimination laws. *See* Sexual
orientation protection, Domestic
partners legislation
Arcadie, 61, 66, 138
Argentina, 89, 142–43
Asians, 106, 141–42
Atkinson, Ti-Grace, 91, 93, 95
Australia, 82, 85–86, 119–20, 123, 124,
130, 131, 136, 152, 154–55, 157, 162,
169
Austria, 138
Axgil, Axel, 60, 61

Babets, Don, 162
Bacon, Sir Francis, 4
Baktis, Dr., 46
Barbadette, Gilles, 26
Barnes, Djuna, 29
Barney, Natalie, 25, 28–30, 39
Baudelaire, Charles, 28, 167

Bearchell, Chris, 95, 96
Beardsley, Aubrey, 29
Beaudry, André, 66
Beauvoir, Simone de, 77
Bebel, August, 19
Belgium, 12, 87, 132, 156, 169, 171
Berkeley, California, 79, 162
Berlin, 12, 17, 19, 21, 22, 24, 25, 47,
65, 91, 92, 116, 139–41
Bérubé, Allan, 62
Beyria, Gustave-Léon, 31
Black people, 27, 40, 57, 68–70, 72, 73,
79, 104–6, 110, 112, 113, 133, 136,
141, 165
Blömer, Gerd, 133–34
Boise, Idaho, 59
Boston, 39, 69, 82, 90, 130, 154, 165
Brand, Adolf, 18, 20, 22, 49
Brandt, Allan, 159
Briggs, John, 105, 106
Britt, Harry, 130
Brooks, Romaine, 39
Brown, Rita Mae, 76, 90, 95, 96
Brown, William, 8
Browne, Stella, 37, 38
Bryant, Anita, 102–4, 106, 109, 119
Bunch, Charlotte, 93
Burnside, John, 96
Business lobby. *See* Capitalism

Califia, Pat, 172
Camus, Renaud, 169

Canada, 59, 73, 82, 84–86, 92, 104,
    118–20, 123, 126, 128, 131–37, 141,
    148, 152, 154, 155, 160, 171
Capitalism, 3, 6, 8, 10–11, 23, 34, 36,
    37, 41, 43, 45, 54, 65, 88, 99, 100,
    110–12, 115, 117, 150, 163, 167, 171;
    Business lobby, 51, 56, 71, 104–6,
    108, 114–15, 130, 158
Carassou, Michel, 26
Carpenter, Edward, 32, 35–37, 41, 78,
    148
Castelhaven, Earl of, 4
Castells, Manuel, 105, 170
Censorship, 23, 33, 39, 43–44, 47, 49,
    50, 70, 87, 138, 139, 144, 145, 148,
    160, 163
Chicago Society for Human Rights, 3,
    42–43
Chicago, 40, 43, 69, 73, 76, 78, 79, 81,
    134
Christian Democrats, 65, 86, 124, 131,
    135; *See also* Conservatism
Clark, Lorenne, 153
Cocteau, Jean, 25, 31, 32, 66
Cohn-Bendit, Daniel, 77
Colette, 28
Colombia, 143
Colquhoun, Maureen, 129
Communism, 46, 47, 49, 52, 54, 57, 58,
    60, 62, 70, 93, 114, 124, 127, 128,
    139–41, 163, 168, 171
Conservatism, 18, 19, 21, 23, 29, 32,
    49, 51, 57–58, 65, 66, 84, 117–20,
    122, 124, 125, 128, 129, 147, 148; *See
    also* Christian Democrats, New Right,
    Republican Party
Coward, D.A., 8
Coward, Rosalind, 150
Crowley, Aleister, 29
Cuba, 104, 136, 139, 158, 173
COC (Cultuur-en-Ontspannings
    Centrum), 60, 65, 87, 169

D'Emilio, John, 58, 62, 63, 69
Daly, Mary, 94, 145
Daughters of Bilitis, 61, 64, 69, 71–72,
    85, 89, 91, 169

Decriminalization of homosexuality, 25,
    70, 82, 84–86, 122, 125, 128, 131–33,
    138, 140
Democratic Party (U.S.A.), 104, 128,
    129, 147; *See also* Liberalism
Denmark, 60, 86, 152, 155
Detroit, 40, 69, 73, 169
Devall, William, 100
Diaghilev, Sergei, 27
Disabled, 134
Dognon, André du, 27
Dolan, Terry, 114, 116
Domestic partners legislation, 123, 128,
    162
Douglas, Lord Alfred, 35
Dover, K.J., 1
Dworkin, Andrea, 146, 147

Ebbinghaus, Alexander, 153
Eigene, 18, 20, 23, 167
Ellis, Havelock, 12, 32, 37, 41
England. *See* United Kingdom
Equal Rights Amendment (U.S.A.), 102,
    103, 108, 109, 113, 128, 147
Eulenburg scandal, 21–22, 131, 167
Evangelicalism, 20, 103, 104, 106, 108,
    109, 111–14, 116, 117, 119, 124, 135,
    137, 140; *See also* Protestantism

Faderman, Lillian, 4, 5, 28, 38
Falwell, Jerry, 103, 113, 157
Family, 3–4, 6, 8–9, 11, 34, 37, 78, 98,
    105, 108–11, 139, 151, 153, 162, 167
Farabundo Marti National Liberation
    Front (FMLN), 165
Feinstein, Diane, 162
Feminism, 8, 12, 20–21, 25, 51, 73, 76,
    77, 79, 102, 105, 106, 109, 129, 130,
    138, 144, 151, 153; Cultural or
    nationalist feminism, 91, 93–95, 97,
    143–50, 172; *See also* Lesbian
    feminism; Women's movement
Feudalism, 2–6, 11, 45
Fiedler, Leslie, 57
Fierstein, Harvey, 170
Finkler, Rudi, 167
Finland, 138

FitzGerald, Frances, 109
Forster, E.M., 30, 37
Foucault, Michel, 41, 165
France, 7, 25–32, 66–67, 87–88, 103, 123, 124, 127, 131, 134, 136–38, 152, 158, 162, 164, 172
Francone, Vincenzo, 135, 140
Freeman, Jo, 61
French Revolution, 5, 10, 11, 13, 14, 26, 28, 49
French, Robert, 170
Friedan, Betty, 90, 148
Friedländer, Benedict, 20
Friele, Kim, 124, 169–71

Gainesville, Florida, 59, 73
Gay liberation, 73–89, 92, 93, 95, 96, 99, 100, 109
Gay movement, early German, 17–26, 31, 40–42, 46, 49; prewar U.S., 42; in the 1980s, 121–60; *See* Gay liberation, Homophile movement, Lesbian feminism, Lesbian movement, New Right
Gay relationships, 8, 13–14, 54, 98, 100, 169, 172; *See also* Adhesive comrades, Domestic partners legislation, Love, Romantic friendship
Gay world, 6–12, 15, 23, 24, 27, 29, 30, 59, 69, 99, 100, 140, 171
Gearhart, Sally, 145
George, Stefan, 20, 50
Gerber, Henry, 42, 43
Germany: Empire, 14, 17–22; Weimar Republic, 22–26, 31–32, 77; Third Reich, 49–55; Democratic Republic, 52, 140–141; Federal Republic, 65–66, 86, 92, 103, 129, 131–133, 140, 148, 153–155, 168
Gide, André, 30–31, 47
Ginsberg, Allen, 68, 78, 99, 149, 169, 172
Girard, Jacques, 66, 169
Gittings, Barbara, 71, 95, 96
Golding, Sue, 150
Goldman, Emma, 41, 43
Goodman, Paul, 77

Goodstein, David, 105
Gordon, Linda, 110
Got, Ambroise, 24
Gouldner, Alvin, 47
Gramsci, Antonio, 41
Great Britian. *See* United Kingdom
Greece, ancient, 2, 13, 20, 28, 31, 35, 36, 153; modern, 138
Grier, Barbara, 91

Hall, Radclyffe, 29, 37, 39, 44, 117, 145, 148
Halle, Felix, 50
Hardwick, Michael, 125–26
Harry, Joseph, 98, 100
Hay, Henry, 62, 96, 168
Heger, Heinz, 53, 54
Herzen, W., 12
Hiller, Kurt, 23, 25, 50, 66
Himmler, Heinrich, 51, 52, 54
Hirschfeld, Magnus, 17–20, 22–24, 31, 37, 41, 48–50
Hislop, George, 84, 119
Hispanics, 79
Hitler, Adolf, 52
Hocquenghem, Guy, 45, 134, 149
Hodann, Max, 50
Hohmann, Joachim, 65
Hole, Judith, 73
Holleran, Andrew, 100
Homophile movement, 60–68, 70, 71, 73–74, 78, 79, 86, 90
Homosexual: persons, 1–2, 15, 108; subculture, *See* Gay world, Lesbian world
Homosexuality: anthropological research on, 1–2; 19th C. theories of, 12–16, 18, 30, early 20th C. theories of, 36
Höss, Rudolf, 54
Housman, Laurence, 37
Houston, 125, 133
Hughes, Patricia, 146
Humphreys, Laud, 99, 116
Hunter, Allen, 110

Iceland, 138
Indonesia, 141

Institute for Sex Research, 23, 25, 50, 65
International Gay and Lesbian Association, 122, 131, 165, 171
Iran, 135
Ireland, 131, 135, 138
Isherwood, Christopher, 47, 50, 168
Israel, 134–36
Italy, 87, 127–29, 134, 135, 138

Jackson, Jesse, 112, 129
James I, 4
Jansen, Wilhelm, 20
Jean, David, 162
Jews, 5, 10, 24, 45, 48, 49, 51–53, 103, 108, 135, 136, 165
Johnston, Jill, 89, 91, 94, 95

Kameny, Franklin, 68, 70, 71, 81
Katz, Jonathan, 9, 40
Kertbeny, K. M., 14
Kikel, Rudy, 98
Kinsey Report, 63
Kogon, Eugen, 54
Krause, E., 20
Kreis, Der, 50, 66, 169
Krupp, Alfred, 22
Kuzmin, Mikhail, 48

Labor movement, 105, 106, 130–31, 138
Labour Party, 74, 85, 124, 128–130; *See also* Social Democrats
Laporte, Rita, 91
Laurence, Leo, 79
Lauritsen, John, 48, 167
Lautmann, Rüdiger, 52, 53
Lee, John A., 149
Lees, Edith, 38, 42
Lesbian feminism, 89–97, 100; lesbian separatism, 93–94, 96
Lesbian identity, 10, 28, 38–39, 42, 89, 94, 95; political lesbians, 93–95
Lesbian movement: early German, 21, 25; homophile, 62, 64; in the 1980s, 121–161; *See also* Daughters of Bilitis, Lesbian feminism, New Right.
Lesbian world, 6, 9, 12, 24–25, 27, 29, 59, 61, 92, 94, 99, 140, 171

Lestrade, Gaston, 31
Levine, Ellen, 73
Liberalism, 10, 18, 19, 26, 29, 31, 51, 57, 83–85, 102, 111, 124, 127, 128, 145
Lipsitz, George, 112
Llangollen, Ladies of, 5
London, 7, 12, 37, 50, 82, 83, 91, 92, 128, 148, 165
Los Angeles, 61, 62, 69, 76, 79, 81, 82, 92, 158, 171
Louys, Pierre, 28, 64
Love, romantic, 4, 9, 16
Lowzow, Wenche, 124, 129, 169, 170
Luis, Carlos, 171
Lyon, Phyllis, 64

MacKinnon, Catherine, 147
Man-boy relationships, 78, 116, 119, 133, 144, 151–56, 172
Manion, Eileen, 146, 151
Marcuse, Herbert, 48, 77
Martin, Del, 64, 81, 90
Marx, Karl, 12, 26
Masculinity, 36–37, 41, 57–58, 96–99, 115, 139, 169
Mattachine, 61–64, 68–72, 75, 79, 168
Matthiesen, F. O., 39, 168
McCarthyism, 56–60, 62, 64, 70, 104, 108, 115
McKay, Claude, 40
Media treatment, 40, 48, 58, 60, 62, 69, 78–80, 87, 91, 102, 104, 113–15, 133, 138, 156–57, 163–64, 168, 170
Medicine, role of: 15–16, 19, 29–31, 33, 34, 36, 39, 40, 54, 60, 67, 71, 81, 82, 125
Mellors, Bob, 83
Melville, Herman, 14, 47
Merrill, George, 35
Mexico, 89, 137, 142, 165
Miami, 59, 102–105
Miles, Angela, 145
Militarism, 22, 58, 76, 108, 115, 132, 158, 164
Milk, Harvey, 102, 105–7, 114, 130, 170
Millett, Kate, 91, 155

Molly house, 7–9
Montreal, 84, 118, 171
Murray, Stephen, 171

Napoleonic Code, 10, 14, 31
National Gay and Lesbian TaskForce, 82, 125, 160
National Organization for Women, 90, 91, 144
Nazism, 17, 49–55, 60, 61, 65, 103, 106, 111, 116, 123, 141, 154, 168
Netherlands, 8, 17, 22, 53, 60, 61, 65, 76, 86–87, 136, 152, 155, 162, 163
New Democratic Party (Canada), 84, 119, 128; *See also* Social Democrats
New Left, 68–74, 76, 77, 80, 83, 118
New Right, 102–17, 122, 125, 131, 147, 150–53
New York, 9, 12, 39–41, 43, 44, 58, 62, 69, 71, 72, 74–76, 79–83, 89–92, 133–36, 150, 158–60, 162, 165
New Zealand, 85, 86, 131, 148, 171
Newton, Nuey, 79
Nobel, Elaine, 130
Norway, 61, 86, 123, 124, 126–27

O'Carroll, Tom, 154, 172
Oberg, Erich, 17
Owles, Jim, 80

Paez, Fred, 133
Parenting, 123, 162
Paris, 8, 10, 11, 26–28, 30, 32, 39, 47, 50, 61, 66, 74, 76, 92, 127, 133, 135, 136, 165
Patrick, Robert, 100
Pedophilia. *See* Man-boy relationships
Perry, Troy, 136
Peru, 143
Pezzana, Angelo, 129
Philadelphia, 40, 72, 145, 169
Poll, Christabell, 85
Ponse, Barbara, 94
Pornography, 143–49, 152, 170
Pougy, Liane de, 28
Praunheim, Rosa von, 86

Protestantism, 49, 51, 59, 61, 111, 112, 124, 136, 137, 147; *See also* Evangelicalism
Proust, Marcel, 29–30
Psychiatry, 26, 65, 67, 76, 81–83, 103, 107; *See also* Medicine
Purity campaigns, 33, 38, 51, 146

Quebec, 86, 118, 123, 126, 156, 165

Radical faeries, 96
Rechy, John, 149
Reich, Wilhelm, 46
Republican Party (U.S.A.), 57, 58, 104, 116, 125, 147, 157; *See also* Conservatism
Rimbaud, Arthur, 14
Robertson, Marie, 92
Robertson, Pat, 113
Robinson, Marty, 80
Röhm, Ernst, 49, 52
Roman Catholicism, 26, 28, 31, 53, 56, 61, 67, 103, 108, 118, 124, 126, 131, 135–37
Romantic friendship: among women, 4–5, 9–10, 28, 34, 38, 40, 42, 44; among men, 35–37; *See also* Adhesive comrades, Gay relationships
Rubin, Gayle, 150, 172
Ruggiero, Guido, 7
Rüling, Anna, 21
Rusche, Herbert, 129
Russia. *See* Soviet Union

Sado-masochism, 78, 144, 148–50, 152
Sagarin, Edward, 63, 71
Sahli, Nancy, 38
San Francisco, 40, 61, 63, 64, 69, 70, 72, 78, 79, 81, 82, 90, 104–7, 128, 130, 135, 141, 150, 158–60, 162, 165, 171
Sappho, 2, 28
Sarria, José, 70
Sartre, Jean-Paul, 87
Schlafly, Phyllis, 109
Schorer, Jacob, 17

Schuyf, Judith, 169
Scientific-Humanitarian Committee, 17–24, 41, 65, 66, 116, 134
Scondras, David, 130
Seattle, 73, 104, 106
Sebesta, Edward, 170
Sexual orientation protection, 82, 102, 104, 122–28, 131, 135, 162; *See also* Domestic partners legislation
Shelley, Martha, 96
Sherman, Martin, 168
Silverstolpe, Fredrik, 167
Simpson, Ruth, 90
Smith, Chris, 130
Snitow, Ann, 95
Social Democrats, 12, 19, 20, 22–24, 49, 86, 127, 129, 131, 165
Socialism, 19, 22, 23, 32, 34, 35, 47–49, 51, 76, 78, 93, 124, 127, 133, 145
Sodomy, 4, 5, 7, 8, 10
Sontag, Susan, 157
South Africa, 141
Soviet Union, 27, 46–48, 56, 57, 140, 141
Spain, 127, 133, 137–39, 165
Spear, Allan, 129
Spohr, Max, 17, 19
Squarcialupi, Vera, 124
Stalinism, 46–48
Stansell, Christine, 95
Steakley, James, 24, 167, 168
Stein, Gertrude, 27, 30, 38
Stevenson, Edward, 39
Stirner, Max, 20
Stöcker, Helene, 20, 50
Stone, Lawrence, 3
Stonewall Rebellion, 75–76, 79
Stravinsky, Igor, 27
Studds, Gerry, 129–30
Stümke, Hans-Georg, 167
Sunthorst, De Arent Van, 169
Sweden, 17, 60, 86, 138, 152, 162, 170
Switzerland, 50–51, 66, 134, 154, 169
Sydney, 12, 85, 92, 119, 130, 133, 157, 171
Symonds, John Addington, 13, 16, 29, 31

Terrigno, Valerie, 130
Thiele, Adolf, 119

Third-sex theory, 15–16, 21, 30, 31, 35
Thompson, Sharon, 95
Thorne, Alison, 155
Thorsell, Eric, 17
Thorstad, David, 48, 167
Tielman, Rob, 169
Tinney, James, 136
Tobin, Kay, 95, 96
Toronto, 73, 84, 118–20, 132, 147, 148, 171, 172
Transvestism, among women, 5, 9, 27; among men, 27, 40, 98–99; movement, 79, 84, 96; *See also* Radical faeries
Trudeau, Pierre, 84
Turing, Alan, 59

Ulrichs, Karl, 14–16, 18–20, 29, 31, 35
United Kingdom, 4, 11, 13, 32–39, 59, 67, 74, 83–84, 86, 90, 117, 127–32, 136, 141, 148, 152, 154, 155
United States, *pre-1945*, 4, 9, 11, 13, 39–44, 50; *1945–1969*, 56–64, 68–78; *1970–1986*, 78–82, 86, 89–101, 123, 125, 126, 128–37, 141, 152, 156–160, 162, 163, 165; *See also* New Right
Uranian, 18, 19, 21, 36
Urnings, 11, 15

Vance, Carole, 146
Vancouver, 84, 126, 130, 131
Venezuela, 143
Venice, 7
Verlaine, Paul, 14, 30
Vivien, Renée, 28, 29

Walkowitz, Judith, 33
Wallace, Henry, 57, 168
Walter, Aubrey, 83
Ware, John, 85
Washington, 39, 70, 72, 73, 91, 125, 136, 141
Weber, Max, 121
Weeks, Jeffrey, 7, 32, 132, 167
Well of Loneliness. *See* Hall, Radclyffe
West Hollywood, California, 130, 158, 162, 171
White, Dan, 106–7
Whitehouse, Mary, 117, 120

Whitman, Walt, 13–14, 16, 29, 30, 35, 36, 42, 78

Wilde, Oscar, 27, 29, 31–35, 37, 42

Wildeblood, Peter, 59, 60

Willis, Ellen, 146

Wilson, Doug, 132

Wisconsin: 123–24, 162, 171

Wittig, Monique, 150

Wittman, Carl, 75, 78, 104

Women's movement, 18, 20, 25, 33, 36–38, 49–51, 73, 89, 90, 92–94, 144, 150, 153; *See* Equal Rights Amendment, Feminism, Lesbian movement

World League for Sexual Reform, 24

Yugoslavia, 141

Zahnd, Alfred, 31

Ziegler, Alexander, 154

Ziemers, Jürgen, 140